NTC's
GUIDE
to
GRAMMAR
TERMS

ABOUT THE AUTHOR

Richard A. Spears, Ph.D., is a specialist in lexicography, English language structure, phonetics, language standardization and codification, and English as a second language.

NTC's GUIDE to GRAMMAR TERMS

Richard A. Spears

Consulting Editor
Steven Racek Kleinedler

NTC Publishing Group
a division of NTC/CONTEMPORARY PUBLISHING GROUP
Lincolnwood, Illinois USA

Library of Congress Cataloging-in-Publication Data
Spears, Richard A.
   [NTC's dictionary of grammar terminology]
   NTC's guide to grammar terms : with complete examples of correct
usage / Richard A. Spears : consulting editor, Steven Racek Kleinedler.
     p. cm.
   Originally published as: NTC's dictionary of grammar terminology.
1991.
   Includes index.
   ISBN 0-8442-5749-4 (p)
   1. English language—Grammar—Terminology. 2. English language—
Terms and phrases. I. Kleinedler, Steven Racek. II. Title.
PE1097.S64 1997   96-51180
425'.01'4—dc21   CIP

ISBN: 0-8442-5749-4

Published by NTC Publishing Group,
a division of NTC/Contemporary Publishing Group, Inc.,
4255 West Touhy Avenue,
Lincolnwood (Chicago), Illinois 60646-1975 U.S.A.
Manufactured in the United States of America.

  9 VP 0 9 8 7 6 5 4 3 2

Contents

To the User

This dictionary brings together the many terms used in traditional grammar and language arts with those terms from linguistics that are commonly accepted in pedagogical grammar. The 900 entries include the common standard terms used in traditional English grammar studies during this century and many of the less common ones still lurking in older textbooks and scholarly discussions of grammar. Each term is clearly defined and is followed by example sentences that illustrate how the structure or point of grammar is applied. The entries have been selected for the needs of students and teachers alike and to demonstrate the many varieties of English grammar terms.

The grammars that have been used in schools in this century often treat the relationship between grammar terms and their definitions as if they were fixed and dependable parts of the human intellectual experience. They are not. The entries in this dictionary demonstrate that there is considerable synonymy, inconsistency, and contradiction in grammar terms in general. This dictionary is not an attempt to reform grammar terminology, however. The abundance of terms and the inexact and ambiguous definitions in grammar terminology is a result, to a great extent, of attempts at such reform. The purpose of this dictionary is to provide a road map through the terminological maze of traditional grammar.

Modern *formal grammar* studies, most of which are carried out in advanced degree programs at large universities, are not centered on terminology. These studies focus on the structures and processes themselves, and they use formalistic devices to represent structures and processes rather than a lexicon of specific terms. New terms for use in commenting on or explaining the formalistic devices are often created on an *ad hoc* basis and altered at will, often without notice, by various practitioners. Terms from these studies are, for the most part, beyond the scope of this dictionary. The exception to this is in the area of *case grammar*, where some of the terms of modern theory and traditional terminology intersect. Many of these terms are covered in this dictionary. Even though this dictionary focuses on traditional terms, it will be useful to students who are studying formal theory because it explains the basic structures that are the focus of many of these theories.

As a school subject, grammar probably deserves much of its reputation as a source of anguish and confusion, some of which comes from trying to attach specific terms to structures and processes that are poorly understood by both teachers and students. While this dictionary defines each of the terms listed, it must be remembered that the important link is between the term and some structure or process in the English language, not between the term and its definition. If one is willing to cut through the terminological problems presented by two centuries of accumulated terminology, the subject is simpler, interesting, and stimulating.

Using the Dictionary

One who is seriously interested in grammar or terminology in general should browse through, or even read, this dictionary. In doing so, one will get an overview of the nature of grammar terminology and the problems resulting from (1) borrowing terms from Latin and Greek grammar, (2) attempting to provide names for just about every phenomenon, and (3) the proliferation of terms created by periodic attempts at reform through the creation of additional, "improved" terms.

In this dictionary, users will find an abundance of terms with many synonyms. See, for instance, *adverb of extent, adverb of degree, adverb of amount*. There are also names for things that probably do not require names. See *internal accusative*, for instance. There are terms created at different times and with different purposes for the same structural or semantic function, such as *absolute phrase, absolute construction, absolute element, free construction*. There are many instances of optional ellipsis, such as *adjectival* and *adjectival noun*, which may seem like two separate terms rather than just one. There are some instances of "reversible" synonyms, such as *adjective numeral* and *numeral adjective*. There are also the occasional misnomers, such as *plural verb*. In addition, English grammar terminology includes numerous *moods* that purport to show the speaker's attitude or intentions, some *aspects* that are really *moods*, and a rich collection of approximately 20 terms for subtle semantic variations of the *genitive*.

Each entry has at least two examples, usually more, illustrating the grammar concept referred to by each term. The elements in the examples that illustrate the term are shown in bold print. These examples are the ultimate key to understanding the concepts to which the terms refer. The structures in bold print in the examples are what students need to understand and need to be able to identify. This dictionary is ideal for teachers and students who may be accustomed to terminology different from that used in their current classroom textbook.

The dictionary uses cross-referencing to lead users to the primary entries for each "cluster" of synonyms. Additional cross-referencing leads users to similar or related topics. Each simple term that appears frequently as a part of a compound term is accompanied by a list of the compound terms that contain the simple term. For instance, at *verb*, there is a list of 69 other entries, such as *action (of the verb)*, *active verb*, *atelic verb*, *auxiliary verb*, *causative verb*, *complete verb*, *complex transitive verb*, *compound verb*, etc., that contain the term *verb*.

At the back of this book, there is an index of prepositions, pronouns, verbal auxiliaries, conjunctions, and other function words showing in which entries these words are mentioned or given a name. This index is a valuable device for the English language, where so much grammar and syntax is indicated by function words rather than by word endings or other inflection. The index is also extremely useful for the mainstreamed nonnative learner of English who is faced with learning the most complex kinds of English—in English—through the use of a terminological system that is probably unfamiliar and less than clear.

This dictionary had its birth in the college classroom. The initial gathering and defining of approximately 300 of the terms were done by students enrolled in *Traditional English Grammar* at Northwestern University. A second group of students in another year edited and refined the work of the first group. Their research, editing, criticisms, and suggestions were very helpful in determining the final form of the book. My thanks to Lisa Katz, Courtenay Carmody, Celia Duroe, Linda Kristensen, Anne Marie McNamee, Anne Welsh, Mary Ellen Spore, Daniel B. Holmquist, Anita North, Holly Salo, Amie Balatico,

Julie Courts, Cynthia Jacobson, Mithchel Hsieh, Katharine Schrichte, Christopher Webb, Christa Van Zant, Lori Kettner, Shelley Ward, Wendy Gibson, Kaori Yagashita, Katherine Frerichs. The basic core of terms was then added to, with the consulting editor, Steven Kleinedler, doing much of the research. I am grateful to Professor Robert Gundlach for his comments and suggestions on the pedagogical aspects of the dictionary and to Adele McGann, whose knowledge of the subject matter and meticulous editing added much to the dictionary.

Guide to the Use of the Dictionary

1. Entries are alphabetized according to an absolute alphabetical order that ignores all punctuation, spaces, and hyphens.

2. Entry heads appear in **boldface type**. When words or expressions that are not entries in this dictionary are cited, they appear in *italics*.

3. An entry head may have one or more alternate forms. The alternatives are printed in **boldface type** and are preceded by "AND."

4. Definitions are in roman type. Alternate or closely related definitions are separated by semicolons.

5. A definition may be followed by comments in parentheses. These comments give additional information about the entry head.

6. Sometimes a definition is preceded by a brief qualifying phrase in square brackets that restricts the definition or provides words that make the definition syntactically correct. For an example, see *connote*.

7. Many terms have more than one major sense or meaning. These meanings are numbered with boldface numerals.

8. An entry head enclosed in square brackets, e.g., **[compound]**, leads to other entry heads that contain the word in brackets. Entry heads in square brackets do not have definitions.

9. In some entries, comments direct the user to other entries for additional information through the use of the terms "compare to," "see," or "see also." The expressions mentioned are in *slanted type*.

10. In some instances, a term that is an entry in the dictionary is used to define another word. Such expressions are in *slanted type*.

11. In an entry phrase, parentheses can be used to collapse two or three semantically related phrases into one. For instance, **copulative (conjunction)** stands for both **copulative** and **copulative conjunction**.

Terms and Symbols

☐   marks the beginning of an example.

AND   indicates that one or more alternative entry forms follow.

Compare to   means to consult the entry indicated and look for similarities to the entry head containing the "compare to" instruction

See   Go to the entry indicated.

See also   Find additional information at the entry indicated.

A

abessive (case)   a *grammatical case* denoting *without*. (From the Latin word *abesse*, "to be absent." There is no true *abessive case* in English, and the meaning associated with the *abessive case* is conveyed by the *preposition without*. See a brief description of the role of *case* in English at *case* and *case grammar*. The examples show the way English expresses the *semantic* relationship *conveyed* by this *case*.)   □   *I prefer mine **without mustard**, please.*   □   *Bread **without butter** is dry, but more healthful.*   ⊓   *What good is a desk **without a drawer?***

ablative absolute   [in Latin] a *construction* involving the *ablative case*, that comes before a *complete sentence* and provides information basic or relevant to the understanding of the *complete sentence*. (The term is sometimes applied to English *phrases* that perform the same *semantic* function, even though English has no *ablative case*. In English, this *construction* is called the *nominative absolute*. An *ablative absolute* in English states a reason that explains the *clause* that follows. Without using the *ablative absolute*, the examples might have begun: "Because things had been put right.../ Because Adam and Eve had fallen.../ Since the project was finished...." See also *absolute phrase, nominative absolute*. In the examples, the *constituents* in bold print approximate the meaning of the *ablative absolute* in English.)   □   ***Things having been put right**, the mayor shook hands all round and departed.*   □   ***Adam and Eve having fallen**, all was lost.*   □   ***Having finished the project**, Bob and Sue celebrated.*   □   ***Having slept***

through the previous class, Bill was totally unprepared to answer the professor's question.

ablative (case) a *grammatical case* found in some Indo-European languages denoting separation, direction away from, manner, or agency. (There is no true *ablative case* in English, but the meanings associated with the *ablative case* are *conveyed* by *prepositions* such as *from* and *out of*. See the previous entry. See a brief description of the role of *case* in English at *case* and *case grammar.* The examples show the way English expresses the *semantic* relationship *conveyed* by this *case*.) □ *I have just flown in from Frankfort.* □ *John is tired out from all this flying.* □ *He stood there and screamed out of sheer terror.*

absolute pertaining to a *constituent* that is *grammatically independent* from the rest of the *utterance;* pertaining to an otherwise *dependent constituent* used independently. (See *absolute adjective, absolute degree, absolute genitive, absolute nominative, absolute possessive.*)

absolute adjective See *adjectival (noun).*

absolute construction See *absolute phrase.*

absolute degree See *superlative degree.*

absolute element See *absolute phrase.*

absolute genitive See *independent possessive (pronoun).*

absolute nominative See *nominative absolute.*

absolute phrase AND **absolute construction, absolute element, free construction** a *word* or *phrase* that is *grammatically independent* of the rest of the *sentence* of which it is a part, and is not joined to the rest of the *sentence* by a *relative pronoun* or a *conjunction.* (It *modifies* or restricts the entire *sentence* or *clause* to which it is attached. The examples show *absolute phrases* in bold print. It should be noted that some people object to this use of *hopefully*.) □ ***That said,** we left.* □ ***To tell the truth,** I just love grammar!* □ ***Hopefully,** everyone will be there on time.* □ ***Regrettably,** the king was stricken with the flu on the very day of my visit.*

absolute possessive See *independent possessive (pronoun).*

abstract noun a *subclass* of *nouns* that stand for concepts or ideas that are not observable or measurable, excluding real or imaginary objects, persons, or substances. (The examples show *abstract nouns* in bold print.) □ ***Justice** is blind.* □ *His **argument** was difficult to understand.* □ *We understood him only with **difficulty.*** □ ***Courage** is a fine virtue.* □ *We were trained to conceal our **fear** behind a pleasant, smiling face.*

accidence the *inflections* on *words;* the *prefixes* and *suffixes* used as the *inflections* that indicate *grammatical relationships* and *grammatical categories.* (The term is not of great importance in English because English has few *inflections.* The examples show a sampling of the English *affixes* that can be considered to be *accidence.*) □ *He walked to school every day.* □ *These roses smell so good.* □ *This is the tenth time I've called you!* □ *The dogs barked all night long* □ *I'm really fed up with all this!* □ *They had to cannibalize parts from the old tanks to keep the new ones running.*

accusative (case) a *grammatical case* marking the *direct object* of a *transitive verb.* (In languages that have an *accusative case,* this *case* is usually indicated by a *suffix* placed on the *direct object* of a *transitive verb* or the *object of a preposition.* Semantically, it expresses the goal of an action or motion. English has no *suffix* or any other marking for *accusative nouns,* but it does have *objects* of *transitive verbs* and *prepositions.* It can also serve to mark the "*object*" of an *adjective.* The term *object(ive) case* should cover *accusative case, dative case,* and the *objects of prepositions.* The distinction between *accusative case* and *dative case* is recognized even in English, but sometimes *accusative case* is used generically for all *object(ive) cases.* See a brief description of the role of *case* in

English at *case* and *case grammar.* The examples show the closest thing to *accusative case* in English, the *objective pronouns* used as direct objects.) □ *Give me **the book.*** □ ***Whom** do you seek?* □ *Bob saw **Jane** and **me.*** □ *Please put your **feet** under your **chair** and keep **them** there.*

action noun   See *gerund.*

action (of the verb) AND **action (of a verb)**   the actual doing, being, or happening of a *verb;* what the *verb conveys.* (Not a fixed *grammatical* term, but an expression often used in trying to explain the meaning of a *verb.* See *metalanguage.*)

action verb   a *verb* expressing the idea of doing something rather than the idea of being in a state. (Compare to *linking verb.* The examples show *action verbs* in bold print.) □ *The cook **beat** the egg with a whip.* □ *We **drank** up all the orange juice.* □ *What have you **done?*** □ *The crows **flew** back into the woods.*

active verb   a *verb* indicating an action rather than a state. (Compare to *stative verb.* The examples show *active verbs* in bold print.) □ *He **ran** from here to the post office.* □ *She plans to **drive** her car, so you can leave yours at home.* □ *We are going to **build** the greatest building in the city.* □ *Jane **wove** this on her own loom.*

active voice   refers to a state of the *verb* where the *agent* of a *sentence* is described as performing the *action of the verb,* usually preceding the *verb* and the rest of the *predicate.* (Most definitions indicate that both *transitive verbs* and *intransitive verbs* can be in the *active voice.* See also *passive voice,* which can affect only *transitive verbs.* The examples show *verbs* in the *active voice* in bold print.) □ *Andy **cooked** a fine dinner.* □ *That criminal **robbed** the bank!* □ *The horses **ran** from us.* □ *Please **give** me your attention!*

actor   essentially a *subject, author,* or *agent* of a *verb.* (Some writers distinguish between *actor* and *agent* and others treat them as synonymous. See also the comments at *agent.* The examples show *actors* in bold print.) □ ***Tom** baked the cake.* □ ***Bob's uncle** brought *in the morning paper, grumbling all the way out and back.* □ *The piles and piles of heavy, wet hay had to be moved, an armload at a time, by **the farmer and his son**.* □ *How can you expect **me** to lift all those heavy boxes?*

additive clause   See *nonrestrictive clause.*

adessive (case)   a *grammatical case* denoting "location at or in a place." (From the Latin word *adesse*, "to be present, to be at a place." There is no true *adessive case* in English, and the meaning associated with the *adessive case* is *conveyed* by various *adverbs of place.* See a brief description of the role of *case* in English at *case* and *case grammar.* The examples show the way English expresses the *semantic* relationship *conveyed* by the *adessive case.*) □ *The calendar is **on the wall**.* □ *We left all the papers you asked for untouched, **on the desk**.* □ *Here they are, right where they belong, **at the entrance to the tunnel**.*

adherent adjective   See *attributive adjective.*

adjectival   **1.** the *adjective* form of the word *adjective,* as in *adjectival noun.* **2.** See *adjectival (noun).*

adjectivally   the *adverb* form of *adjective.*

adjectival (noun) AND **absolute adjective, flat adjective**   an *adjective* functioning as a *nominal.* (The examples show *adjectival nouns* in bold print.) □ *The **poor** will be with us always.* □ *Do you want a **red** or a **blue**?* □ *Give me the **chocolate**.* □ *Of course, we expect the **wealthy** to pay more taxes!*

adjective   a member of a group of *words* that are used to *modify,* supplement, add to, or restrict the meaning of *nouns* or *nominals.* (*Adjective* can be considered a *function class,* that is, other *structures* may function as *adjectives.* They typically occur before *nouns* or in the *predicate* referring to *nominals* in the *subject.* There are both original *adjectives* and derived *adjectives,* and this leads to a confusing definition. See *comparative (degree)* and *su-*

perlative (degree). See these related terms: *absolute adjective, adherent adjective, adjectival, adjectivally, adjectival (noun), adjective clause, adjective complement, adjective numeral, adjective phrase, appositive adjective, attributive adjective, comparison of adjectives, compound adjective, definitive (adjective), demonstrative (adjective), descriptive adjective, flat adjective, gerundial adjective, gradable adjective, indefinite adjective, intensifying adjective, limiting adjective, numeral adjective, possessive adjective, predicate adjective, pronominal adjective, proper adjective, verbal adjective.* The examples show *adjectives* that are not derived from some other *part of speech.*) □ *The **red** barn burned down.* □ *Those boys started a **big** fight.* □ *Give us the **biggest** one.* □ *The fire is terribly **hot**.* □ *The car was **enormous**.*

adjective clause a *dependent* clause that *modifies* a *noun* or *pronoun*, usually following the *constituent* it *modifies*, and *introduced* by a *relative pronoun.* (The examples show *adjective clauses* in bold print.) □ *Will someone **who can cook** please go to the kitchen immediately!* □ *I usually buy the first suit **that I see**.* □ *I just have to have the sundae **that has all the whipped cream on top of it**.* □ *I should not have bought the first suit **that I tried on**.*

adjective complement a *word* or *phrase* that adds to the meaning of or amplifies an *adjective.* (See also the discussion at *complement.* The examples show *adjective complements* in bold print.) □ *I am glad **that he vacuumed the rug**.* □ *We were only too happy **to oblige**.* □ *The old man was tired **from climbing all the stairs**.* □ *The face of the shy young man simply turned red **from embarrassment**.*

adjective numeral AND **numeral adjective** an indication of *number* modifying a *nominal.* (This includes both *cardinal numerals* and *ordinal numerals.* The examples show *adjective numerals* in bold print.) □ ***Four** cows came home.* □ ***Three** little pigs went to market.* □ ***Seven** boys walked right down the middle of the road.* □ *She made only **one** comment about the things she had observed.*

adjective phrase 1. a *prepositional phrase* that *modifies* a *nominal.* (See *phrase, prepositional phrase.* Compare to *adjective clause.*

The examples show *adjective phrases* in bold print.) ☐ *My car is the one **without hubcaps**.* ☐ *Please buy me a pound **of shrimp**.* ☐ *My Uncle George brought us peaches **from Georgia**, where he lives.* ☐ *The little boy **with long blond hair** sat quietly for only a moment.* **2.** a *phrase* consisting of an *adjective* and its *modifiers*. (The first sense is more common in *traditional grammar* terminology. The examples show *adjective phrases* in bold print.) ☐ *The **very old and obese** woman stuffed rolls into her mouth as fast as she could.* ☐ *Come and give me a kiss, you **dear, sweet little** thing!* ☐ *You can just keep **those great big nasty** hands to yourself!* ☐ *She tried to leave us with **seven warm teeny-tiny baby** rabbits to care for.*

adjunct   a *constituent* of a *grammatical construction* of less importance than the rest of the *construction*, typically an *adverbial modifier* that shows time, place, frequency, or manner. (The notion of "less importance" is also expressed as "nonessential." There are no agreed-upon dimensions of "importance" or "essentialness," but the *head* of a *construction* would not typically be an *adjunct*. See *adverbial adjunct, noun adjunct*. The traditional concept of relative "importance" cannot be applied rigorously. The information conveyed by an *adjunct* may be the only information intended to be conveyed. Presumably, *adjuncts* can be omitted without damaging the *grammaticality* of the *sentence*. If the *sentence* "He left immediately" is an answer to the question "How soon after the accident did he leave?" the *adjunct immediately* is the most important part of the *sentence*, not the least—even though, as an *adjunct*, it can be omitted. Compare to *disjunct*. The examples show *adjuncts* in bold print.) ☐ *She spent the rest of her days quietly **in prison**.* ☐ *We were told that we must do it **quite often**, but, in reality, we seldom did it when we were not required to do it.* ☐ *They were not able to meet us **at noon**.* ☐ *Bill flew the plane **as well as could be expected**.*

adnominal   a *word* or *phrase* that occurs within a *noun phrase* and modifies its *head*. (*Adnominals* include *adjectives, noun adjuncts*, and *prepositional phrases*. The examples show *adnominals* in bold print.) ☐ *I would prefer a **red** car if you have one.* ☐ ***Older** people might not agree with your assessment.* ☐ *You will find that **wood** furni-*

ture is terribly expensive these days. □ ***Cotton*** *cloth is usually very soft and is preferred for cleaning eyeglasses.* □ *The cows **in the pasture** stood solemnly in the rain.* □ *A good friend **of ours** keeps chickens and pigs.*

adverb a *word* or *phrase* that *modifies* a *verb, adjective, sentence,* or another *adverb.* (Many *adverbs* are formed from *adjectives* by adding an *-ly suffix* to the *adjective.* See these related terms: *adverbial, adverbial accusative, adverbial adjunct, adverb(ial) clause, adverbial genitive, adverbial noun, adverbial objective, adverb(ial) phrase, adverb of amount, adverb of degree, adverb of direction, adverb of extent, adverb of frequency, adverb of manner, adverb of place, adverb of recurrence, adverb of sequence, adverb of time, adverb particle, adverb phrase, adverb substitute, comparison of adverbs, conjunctive (adverb), descriptive adverb, double adverb, flat adverb, gradable adverb, interrogative (adverb), linking adverb, locative adverb, negative adverb, prepositional adverb, preverb adverb, relative adverb, sentence adverb, sentential adverb, temporal adverb, time adverb.* The examples show various *adverbs* in bold print.) □ *She drove the car **slowly.*** □ *She drove the car **very slowly.*** □ *She drove the **painfully** slow car.* □ *She **then** sped away.* □ ***Suddenly,** she was gone.*

adverbial **1.** having to do with an *adverb.* (See *adverbial adjunct, adverbial genitive.*) **2.** a *structure* functioning as an *adverb.* (See *adverb, adverb(ial) clause, adverb(ial) phrase* for definitions. The examples show *adverbials* in bold print.) □ *She tended the **painfully** swollen leg.* □ *She **then** took a nap.* □ ***Just before the dog starts barking,** put it outside.* □ *I will buy your books, **unless you want to keep them.*** □ ***Although she was a good swimmer,** she nearly drowned.* **3.** one of three different *adverbial modifiers.* (See *adjunct, conjunct,* and *disjunct.*)

adverbial accusative AND **adverbial objective** a *noun* that is neither part of a *prepositional phrase* nor in a *genitive structure,* but seems to function as an *adverb.* (In terms of *word order, the adverbial accusative* occupies the position of a *direct object.* The examples show *adverbial accusatives* in bold print.) □ *I really wanted to stay **home** all day.* □ *We walked for hours on end and wept* *when we thought of the long **way** we had yet to go.* □ *Don't spend too much **time** trying to fix it.*

adverbial adjunct an *adverbial* that is a *constituent* of a *grammatical construction* and that is of less importance than the rest of the construction. (See comments at *adjunct*. See also *noun adjunct*. The examples show *adverbial adjuncts* in bold print.) □ *She departed **in great haste**.* □ *Given the chance, many of them would flee **to Hungary**.* □ *We sat and chatted **the whole afternoon**.* □ ***Cleverly**, he disguised his anger with a loud laugh.*

adverb(ial) clause a *dependent clause* that functions as an *adverb*, modifying a verb, adjective, or another *adverb*. (An *adverbial clause* is introduced by a *subordinating conjunction*. The examples show *adverbial clauses* in bold print.) □ ***Just before the pain starts**, take these tablets.* □ *Put your money **where your mouth is**.* □ ***Although he is alone**, he is never lonely.* □ *I will buy your ticket, **unless you want to use it**.*

adverbial genitive a *noun* that can be construed to be in the *genitive case*, functioning as an *adverb*. (A designation applying to a few English *forms* that can be equated historically with the *genitive case* in Old English, such as with the *words* underlying modern *nowadays*. The *-s* that may appear on *adverbs* such as *upwards, downwards, [long] ways,* etc., is considered to be a *genitive construction* with an apostrophe before the *-s*. The "genitive-ness" of the *construction* is of historical interest only. The examples show *adverbial genitives* in bold print.) □ *We traveled a **long ways** before resting.* □ *The industrial averages moved **upwards** most of the week.* □ *I prefer to work **nights**.* □ *I work very hard every day of the week and really cut loose **weekends**.* □ *Peoria is a long **ways** off.*

adverbial noun a *noun* that functions as an *adverb*. (This category includes *adverbial accusative* and *adverbial genitive*. The examples show *adverbial nouns* in bold print.) □ *Peoria is a long **way** off.* □ *Ship it **Federal Express**.* □ *Gathering all their possessions, they fled **east**.* □ *Yes, we're open **nights**.*

adverbial objective See *adverbial accusative*.

adverb(ial) phrase　**1.** a *prepositional phrase* that *modifies* a *verb,* *adjective,* or another *adverb.* (The examples show *adverbial phrases* in bold print.) □ *Tom will meet us **over there**.* □ *Our plan was successful **beyond my wildest dreams**.* □ *The entire wagon train went **around the bend** and shrank out of sight.* **2.** a *phrase* consisting of an *adverb* and its *modifiers.* (The examples show *adverbial phrases* in bold print.) □ *We left **very quickly** and did not look back **even once**.* □ *She flicked the fly from the end of her nose **incredibly gracefully**.* □ *You apologize **too much**, you know.* □ *The little beast, whatever it was, crept in **quite foxlike** and explored all around.*

adverb of amount　See *adverb of extent.*

adverb of degree　See *adverb of extent.*

adverb of direction　the separable *particle* in certain of the *phrasal verbs.* (These *adverbs* indicate direction when there is no *direct object* of the *verb.* The same *adverbs* can be classified as *prepositions* when followed by an *object.* That is, it is difficult to determine whether the *object* is just the *object of a preposition* or the *object* of a *compound verb.* In a sense, the *adverb of direction* is also the *"preposition"* in a *prepositional verb.* See *phrasal verb, prepositional verb.* The expression is most useful when reserved for the *adverbial* elements of *compound verbs* that actually show direction—such as "pick something up"—rather than those *adverbial* elements that do not show direction, such as "call someone up." The examples show *adverbs of direction* in bold print.) □ *You are too close. Please move **back**.* □ *Pick **up** this stuff and put it away.* □ *Bob ran **up** the stairs.* □ *Just stand **by**. I'll be with you in a minute.*

adverb of extent AND **adverb of degree, adverb of amount**　a *word* or *phrase* functioning as an *adverb* indicating extent, *degree,* or amount. (Traditionally defined as an *adverb* that answers the question "How much?" Many *adverbs of extent* are derived from *adjectives* by adding an *-ly* suffix to the *adjective.* The examples show *adverbs of extent* in bold print.) □ *We have a **tremendously** large debt to pay off.* □ *There is still **very** much to be done.* □ *Oh, I* *feel so **awfully** bad.* □ *Edna was able to accomplish everything **extraordinarily** quickly.*

adverb of frequency   a *semantic subclass* of *words* or *phrases* functioning as an *adverb* indicating how often. (Typically: *always, never, ever, often, hardly, sometimes, frequently, occasionally, usually, scarcely ever, seldom, rarely, hardly ever, seldom if ever.* The examples show *adverbs of frequency* in bold print.) □ *She **hardly** goes there nowadays.* □ *We **usually** keep a lot of those on hand.* □ ***Occasionally,** it rains so hard that the basement floods.* □ *Oh, I would **never** do anything like that.*

adverb of manner   a *word* or *phrase* functioning as an *adverb* indicating in what manner something is or has been done. (Traditionally defined as an *adverb* that answers the question "How?" Many *adverbs of manner* are derived from *adjectives* by adding an *-ly* suffix to the *adjective.* An *adverb of manner* does not follow forms of the *verb be.* The examples show *adverbs of manner* in bold print.) □ *He did the job **well**.* □ *She finished the test **quickly**.* □ *They entered into the battle **without fear**.* □ *They all found the address **easily**.*

adverb of place   See *locative adverb*.

adverb of recurrence   a *semantic subclass* of *words* or *phrases* functioning as an *adverb* indicating how many times something is repeated. (Typically: *again, once, twice, one time, two times, three times,* etc. The examples show *adverbs of recurrence* in bold print.) □ *I've found my way there at least **a hundred times**!* □ *She looked for him in the lobby **twice**.* □ *I counted the books **once**, and then I counted them **again**.* □ *I have only enough gas to go back and forth **two times**.*

adverb of sequence   a *semantic subclass* of *words* or *phrases* functioning as an *adverb* indicating the position of an action in a chain of events. (Typically: *at last, now, then, first, second, third, next, soon,* etc. The examples show *adverbs of sequence* in bold print.) □ ***Now,** we can get some sleep.* □ *What are you going to do **next**?* □ ***First,** we will learn how to paddle a canoe.* □ ***Soon,** everyone will be here.*

adverb of time AND **temporal adverb, time adverb**   a *word* or *phrase* functioning as an *adverb* indicating when—at what time or by what time—something was or will be done. (The examples show *adverbs of time* in bold print.)   □ *They will all be there **tomorrow**.*   □ *We hope to be there **on time**.*   □ *Bob and Sue set out on their trip to California **at about noon**.*   □ ***Shortly after dawn**, a short, stocky, and very determined Wallace J. Ott strode up to the door of the sheriff's office.*

adverb particle AND **prepositional adverb**   the second element of a *phrasal verb;* a *form* identifiable as a *preposition* that *modifies* a verb. (See also *phrasal verb, prepositional verb,* and *phrasal prepositional verb.* The examples show *adverb particles* in bold print.)   □ *I will call her **up** as soon as possible.*   □ *Fred should have brought them **out**.*   □ *The pitcher struck the batter **out** in no time at all.*   □ *Don't throw all that stuff **around** like that!*

adverb phrase   See *adverb(ial) phrase.*

adverb substitute   a *word* or *phrase* that can stand for an *adverb* in a previous *utterance.* (These are limited to *then, there, thus, so, this way,* and *that way.* The examples show *adverb substitutes* in bold print.)   □ *This one goes in the corner. Please put it **there**.*   □ *We'll meet at noon. See you **then**.*   □ *I asked you to walk more quickly. Please do **so**.*   □ *This must be done with a little twist of the wrist. Now, you try to do it **that way**.*

adversative conjunction   See *disjunctive (conjunction).*

affected object   an *object* of a *verb* that undergoes the *action of the verb* and is affected by it, but is not produced by the *action of the verb.* (Compare to *effected object.* See also *result(ative) case.* The examples show *affected objects* in bold print.)   □ *Leon baked **potatoes** in preparation for the picnic.*   □ *You are simply going to take some time off and paint **the house**.*   □ *The professor carefully graded the students' **essays**.*   □ *Bob cleaned **the floor, the tub, and the mirror** before collapsing.*

affirmative (aspect) AND **positive (aspect)**   the general positive meaning of a *verb* that asserts a proposition. (The opposite of *negative aspect.* There is no special *aspect* marking in this *construc-*

tion. Unlike other *aspects,* this one does not include a time element. The examples show *verbs* in the *affirmative aspect* in bold print.) ☐ *You are simply grand.* ☐ *I will be there on time.* ☐ *They should have been able to complete it by Wednesday.* ☐ *He keeps bees.*

affix a meaningful *particle* or *morpheme* that is attached to another *word.* (There are three types of *affix,* namely, *prefix, infix,* and *suffix.* See each entry for further explanations and specific examples. The examples show various common types of *affixes* in bold print.) ☐ *The record player dropped to the floor.* ☐ *Please do not be unhappy.* ☐ *Do not be so bloody inde-doggone-pendent.* ☐ *Bill is rather stout for an ex-marine.*

affixation **1.** the process of affixing something onto something else. **2.** the use of *affixes* to show *grammatical categories* such as *person, number, tense, case, aspect, gender,* etc. (Typically used in contrast with other means of indicating *grammatical categories,* such as *word order.* The examples show in bold print different types of *affixation* in English.) ☐ *She runs a deli on North Main Street.* ☐ *Jane spent a year as head keeper at the zoo* ☐ *Usually, the word* red *serves as a premodifier.* ☐ *This one is much longer than that one.*

agent the animate *author* or doer of the *action of a verb,* as opposed to the *object* that "suffers" or undergoes the *action of the verb;* an *actor.* (The *subject* of a *transitive verb* is the *agent. Agents* are typically *animate nouns* that cause the happening described by the *verb.* The *agent* of a *passive transitive verb* is found in the *by phrase,* and the *object* appears in the normal *subject* position. The *agent* "sends" the action, and an *object* "receives" it. Some would distinguish *actor* from *agent* in that an *agent* must bring about an effect directly. Within this distinction, in the *sentence* "Tom baked the cake," Tom is clearly an *actor,* but since Tom is not the source of the heat that actually did the baking of the cake, Tom may not be the *agent.* The examples show *agents* in bold print.) ☐ *The teacher gave Jane her test paper back.* ☐ *Willy was given back his test paper by the teacher.* ☐ *The flying glass injured one* *of the older men.* □ *Close the door, or the **wind** will blow everything off your desk.*

agentive pertaining to an *agent;* the *adjectival* form of *agent.*

agentive (case) a *grammatical case* that characterizes the *substantive* that serves as the *agent* of a *verb.* (A *grammatical case* denoting the *subject,* doer, or *actor.* Ultimately from the Latin word *agere,* "to act." There is no *formal* indication of the *agentive case* in English, except in the *personal pronouns.* Otherwise, this "case" is indicated by *word order.* See comments at *case* and *case grammar.* The examples show *nominals* in the *agentive case* in bold print.) □ ***He** gave Bob a good beating.* □ *Willy was given back his suit by **the dry cleaner.*** □ ***The vicious dog** bit my father.* □ ***The silent wolves** bore down on our horses.*

agentive object the apparent *object* of a *verb* that, in fact, initiates or performs the *action of the verb* itself. (The apparent *subject* of the *verb* causes, controls, or facilitates the *agentive object* to perform the action. Typically: *run, walk, jump, fly, gallop,* and a few other *verbs.* The examples show *agentive objects* in bold print.) □ *Bill flew **the airplane** from Cleveland to Detroit.* □ *Would you please go walk **the dog**?* □ *The rider jumped **the horse** over the barrier.* □ *Do you think it is windy enough to fly **a kite**?*

agentive suffix the *-er suffix* indicating the *author* of an action. (A few other Latin *forms* are used in English: *-or, -ress, -rix,* etc. The examples show *agentive suffixes* in bold print.) □ *The **brewer** finished brewing the beer and left for the day.* □ *The rules need to be read aloud today. Who will be the **reader**?* □ *My wife was appointed execu**trix** of her mother's estate.* □ *Do you really think that I am my brother's **keeper**?*

agreement See *(grammatical) agreement.*

allative (case) a *grammatical case* denoting movement to or toward a place. (Ultimately from the Latin word *afferre,* "to carry to." There is no true *allative case* in English, and the meaning associated with the *allative case* is *conveyed* by *prepositions* such as *to* or *toward*. See a brief description of the role of *case* in English at *case* and *case grammar*. The examples show the way English expresses the *semantic* relationship *conveyed* by this *case*.) ☐ *Slowly, we moved ourselves* **toward the door** *to freedom.* ☐ *Jane walked all the way* **to town.** ☐ *The bird flew* **toward the open window** *and escaped.*

allomorph   one of the set of *phonological* realizations that represent a *morpheme;* a *morpheme* variant. (The *word crawled* represents two *allomorphs* of two different *morphemes,* or units of meaning. The *allomorph* of the *morpheme* that is spelled "crawl" is /krɔl/, and the *allomorph* of the *past tense morpheme* that is spelled "ed" is /d/. In the examples, each *sentence* is represented in standard spelling followed by a *phonetic* representation of the *allomorphs* contained in the spelled variety. The mark "|" in the examples represents the boundaries between the *allomorphs*.) ☐ *We spend too much money on trifles.* |wi|spɛnd|tu|mətʃ|mənɪ|ɔn|traɪfl|z|. ☐ *The houseboat loomed forbodingly against the reddening sky.* |ðə|haʊs| bot|lum|d|forbod|ɪŋ|lɪ|əgents|ðə|rɛd|n̩|ɪŋ|skaɪ|. ☐ *They all wept without ceasing for ages.* |ðɛ|ɔl|wɛp|t|wɪθ|aʊt|sis|ɪŋ|for|edʒ|əz|.

anaphora   the use of a *word* or a *phrase* whose *referent* occurs earlier in the *sentence* or previously in the *discourse*. (In the examples, the first element in bold print is the *referent* of the *anaphora*, and the second element in bold print is the *anaphoric* element, in these examples, the *anaphoric pronoun*.) ☐ *I want to visit the* **zoo,** *but Bill doesn't want to go* **there.** ☐ **Stacy's** *purple dress fit* **her** *well.* ☐ *The memory of* **Jeff's** *smile warmed all those who knew* **him.** ☐ *First, take* **two beaten eggs** *and put* **them** *into the mixing bowl.*

anaphoric   having to do with *anaphora;* having to do with an instance of *anaphora*.

anaphoric pronoun   a *pronoun* whose *referent* occurs earlier in the *sentence* or previously in the *discourse*. (The *anaphoric pronoun* is shown in bold print.) ☐ *I want to visit the zoo, but Bill doesn't want to go* **there.** ☐ *Stacy's purple dress fit* **her** *well.* ☐ *The memory of Jeff's smile warmed all those who knew* **him.** ☐ *First, take two beaten eggs and put* **them** *into the mixing bowl.*

animate noun   a *semantic subclass* of *nouns* embracing living creatures. (Compare to *inanimate noun*. These *nouns* refer to things that are able to cause things to happen. There are instances where nonliving entities, such as the wind, behave as *animate nouns*. The examples show *animate nouns* in bold print.) □ *The **cat** killed the **beetle**.* □ ***Pigs** eat a lot.* □ *My **uncle** shot a charging **moose**.* □ *The playful **monkey** threw all his food at the **spectators**.* □ *The **wind** blew over our mailbox.*

antecedent   **1.** the *word, phrase,* or *clause* to which a *pronoun* refers; the *nominal* to which a *pronoun* refers. (In the examples, both the *pronoun* and its *antecedent* are in bold print.) □ ***John** was in the garden when **his** phone rang.* □ *Only **Sally** knows where **she** put **her** shears.* □ *Where are the **shears**, and who knows where to find **them**?* □ *I bought **ten new red cups**, and I forgot where I put **them**.* □ ***It will probably rain tomorrow**, and **that** will make everyone sad.* **2.** in *anaphora*, the actual entity to which reference is made. (In the examples, the first element in bold print is the *antecedent* of the subsequent *anaphoric* element in bold print.) □ *I want to visit the **zoo**, but Bill doesn't want to go **there**.* □ ***Stacy**'s purple dress fit **her** well.* □ *The memory of **Jeff**'s smile warmed all those who knew **him**.* □ *First, take **two beaten eggs** and put **them** into the mixing bowl.*

anticipatory subject   the *form it* used to displace the real [or original] *subject* of a *sentence*. (Compare to *expletive*, in which the *it* or *they* has no *antecedent* in the *sentence*. In the examples, the second *sentence* shows an *anticipatory subject*. See also *cleft sentence, postponed subject*. The *anticipatory subject* is shown in bold print.) □ *Running a railroad can be troublesome. / **It** can be troublesome running a railroad.* □ *Having a day off from work is nice. / **It** is nice having a day off from work.* □ *The benevolent minister was the one who paid the call. / **It** was the benevolent minister who paid the call.* □ *The small creature huddling in the corner suddenly rushed at the intruder. / **It** was the small creature huddling in the corner that suddenly rushed at the intruder.*

aorist   a *simple past tense* in Greek, indicating that the *action of the verb* took place at some unspecified time in the past and may or may not have continued beyond some point in the past. (The term is used occasionally for *past tense* or *perfect tense* in English. The examples show *verbs* in the *aorist* in bold print.) □ *The moose* **died** *slowly and painfully.* □ *We* **have done** *that already.* □ *He* **fled,** *leaving all his possessions behind.* □ *The authorities* **counted** *on your forgetting to sign the form.*

apodictive mood a *verbal construction* that expresses the speaker's conviction that a certain state must exist when there is insufficient evidence to allow a statement of fact to be made. (The *construction* is built around *must be* or other *words* expressing *must be.* The term is not widely used. The examples show the *constituents* that exhibit the *apodictive mood*.) □ *The roast* **must be done by now.** □ *He* **must be finished with his speech.** *It is nearly noon.* □ *Here, have a drink of water. You* **must be parched!** □ *The waffle iron* **must be exactly where you put it** *the last time you used it.*

apparent subject See *grammatical subject.*

apposition the relationship between an *appositive* and the *nominal* or *noun phrase* it enhances. (Usually in the *phrase in apposition to something.* See *appositive* for examples of *nominals* in *apposition.*)

appositive a *nominal* that follows another *nominal*, identifying, explaining, clarifying, or enhancing it. (The two *noun phrases* refer to the same entity or situation. An *appositive* is essentially equivalent to the element with which it is in *apposition.* An *appositive* is positioned after the *word* or *phrase* it enhances. See *emphatic appositive, appositive adjective, appositive phrase.* The examples show various *forms* of the *appositive* in bold print.) □ *My brother,* **Bill,** *lives in Evanston.* □ *Walter,* **a boy in my class,** *sails every weekend.* □ *Fred,* **my uncle who lives in Georgia,** *stopped smoking a year ago.* □ *Eating chocolate,* **a pastime I adore,** *is very bad for me.* □ *Taxidermy,* **a very profitable hobby of mine for nearly thirty years,** *is a messy and smelly business.*

appositive adjective an *adjective* that stands after the *nominal* it modifies. (Compare to *attributive adjective.* Often such *construc-*

tions are poetic, literary, or stilted. Some are borrowed from Latin or French. Others, such as the *idiom for the time being,* are special uses of the *present participle.* The examples show *appositive adjectives* in bold print.) □ *The owl haughtily surveyed the little princess with hair **black** and lips **red.*** □ *Our garden, bursting with roses **scarlet,** flourished until early September.* □ *Of course, we don't possess proof **positive,** but you must admit, our case is a strong one.* □ *The symphony, **dissonant and jarring,** was mercifully short.* □ *I did not choose to come here and join a battle **royal** with my colleagues.* □ *Her fever was horribly high for four days **running.*** □ *I shall leave it just as it is, for the time **being.***

appositive phrase an *appositive* taking the *form* of a *phrase* rather than a single *word.* (The examples show *appositive phrases* in bold print.) □ *Walter, **a boy in my neighborhood,** cuts the grass.* □ *Fred, **my oldest uncle,** stopped smoking a year ago.* □ *Eating chocolate, **a pastime I adore,** is very bad for me.* □ *Keeping pigeons, **my hobby for years,** is inexpensive and fun.*

arbitrary gender **1.** the use of the *masculine gender* to refer to *antecedents* when their biological sex is unknown or irrelevant. (See comments at *feminine (gender)* and *masculine (gender).* Some people claim that the use of the *masculine gender* always indicates male sex and should not be used where biological sex is unknown or irrelevant. Currently, there is considerable substitution of *they, them, their,* and *theirs* [all *pronouns* having *common gender*] for *he, him,* and *his*—despite the *number* violation—to make it impossible to construe the use of the *masculine gender* as exclusively male. The examples show *pronouns* expressing *arbitrary gender* in bold print.) □ *Take this into the post office and ask the clerk if **he** will weigh it for you.* □ *If someone wants a fresh cup of coffee, **he**'ll have to go to the kitchen for it.* □ *Each person should hang up **his** coat and hat immediately.* □ *Whoever spills **his** milk will have to clean it up.* **2.** the use of the *feminine gender* to refer to certain countries, ships, automobiles, the earth, nature, etc. (The examples show *pronouns* expressing *arbitrary gender* in bold print.) □ ***She** drives like a dream, doesn't **she?*** □ *The passengers will disembark soon after **she** drops anchor.* □ *When nature works **her** magic in the spring, I'll plant nasturtiums.* □ *France takes care of **her** poor as well as any other country.*

argument the part of a *proposition* that is named or discussed. (As opposed to the *predication*, which asserts something about the *argument*. The examples show the *arguments* in bold print.) □ ***My stereo*** *is brand-new and works like a charm.* □ ***Four young girls*** *are entering the room.* □ ***Paris*** *is the capital of France.* □ ***The path ahead*** *is fraught with peril.*

article a small *word* that precedes most kinds of *nouns*, indicating the degree of specificity. (In English, this category is traditionally limited to *a, an,* and *the*. *Articles* are a type of *determiner*. See *definite article* and *indefinite article*. The examples show *articles* in bold print.) □ ***A*** *large balloon went up over **the** crowd.* □ *Give me **a** break!* □ *Give me **the** eggs!* □ *Jane made such **an** effort to be on time that she forgot her papers.*

aspect a category of a *verb* relating to the way the *verb* is viewed or experienced relative to time. (*Aspect* indicates whether the *action of the verb* is beginning, ended, in progress, instantaneous, or repeated. Exceptions to this definition are the *affirmative (aspect)* and the *negative (aspect)*, which seem to be misnomers or are using the *word aspect* in a purely descriptive sense. The terminology on this point can be confusing, with both *tense* and *aspect* being used for the same phenomena by various writers. Each of the different types of *aspect* occurs in a *verb phrase* with a *verb* bearing some sort of *tense* indication. Sometimes the term used to describe an *aspect* is called a *tense*, sometimes an *aspect*, and sometimes either one. There are many historical and current types of *aspect* in English, involving a number of overlapping terms. See the various entries that include *aspect* at *affirmative (aspect), continuous (aspect), durative (aspect), effective aspect, future continuous (aspect), future perfect aspect, future perfect continuous (aspect), future perfect progressive (aspect), future progressive (aspect), habitual aspect, imperfect(ive) (aspect), ingressive aspect, iterative aspect, negative aspect, past continuous (aspect), past perfect aspect, past perfect continuous (aspect), past perfect progressive (aspect), past progressive (aspect), perfect(ive) aspect, point-action aspect, positive (aspect), present continuous (aspect), present perfect aspect, present perfect continuous (aspect),* *present perfect progressive (aspect), present progressive (aspect), progressive (aspect), terminate aspect.*)

aspectual   having to do with *aspect.*

atelic verb   a *verb* whose *action* has no clear terminal point or "expiration." (For instance, *go, run, play, fall, rise, continue, grow, expand,* etc. Compare to *telic verb.* The examples show *atelic verbs* in bold print.)   ☐ *The tree is* **growing** *very slowly.*   ☐ *I felt as if I were* **falling**.   ☐ *How long will this* **continue**?   ☐ *I can't* **go** *on much farther.*

attributive adjective AND **adherent adjective**   an *adjective* that comes before the *noun* it affects. (Compare to *predicate adjective. Attributive adjectives* are said to *premodify* the *nouns* they precede. This refers to the position of an *adjective.* Some *adjectives* must come before the *nouns* they *modify,* some must come after, and some come either before or after. An *adjective* that appears before the *noun* it *modifies* is identified as an *attributive adjective* regardless of whether it can also come after the *noun* it *modifies.* The examples show *attributive adjectives* in bold print.)   ☐ *A* **black** *cat darted across our path.*   ☐ *The* **old rickety red** *barn stood near the edge of the pasture.*   ☐ *The* **unfair** *judgment was still upheld by the court in the second trial.*   ☐ *I have had enough of these* **watered-down** *statements of fact.*

author   the doer of the *action of the verb.* (One of a number of possible synonyms for *agent* or *actor* used in *grammatical* explanations. Carries the sense of *cause,* which is lacking in the term *subject.* See *agent* and *subject.* See also *agentive suffix.* The examples show *authors* in bold print.)   ☐ **Fred** *did everything he could to save the life of the wounded deer.*   ☐ *Will* **Jane** *remember to put the eggs in the refrigerator?*   ☐ **Our favorite chef** *prepared all the food for the banquet.*   ☐ **It** *bit me!*

auxiliary   a *formal* indicator of *grammatical* information that is a separate *word* or *particle* rather than an *inflection,* which, together with the *verb,* constitutes a *verb phrase;* a *verbal auxiliary.* (See also *auxiliary verb, emphatic auxiliary, modal (auxiliary),* *passive auxiliary, perfect auxiliary, progressive auxiliary, verbal auxiliary.* The examples show a number of different *auxiliaries* in bold print.) □ *They **had** done it already.* □ ***Do** be a good fellow and call her **up.*** □ *You know you **ought to have** gone to her at once.* □ *I **will not** ever do it again!*

auxiliary verb AND **helping verb** a type of *verbal auxiliary* that supplements the *main verb* of the *predicate* and that can occur as a free-standing *verb*. (This includes various *forms* of the *verbs be, have,* and *do* used to show differences in *tense* and *aspect. Helping verb* is most commonly used in pedagogy. See comments at *verbal auxiliary.* The examples show various *auxiliary verbs* in bold print.) □ *None of us **had** thought to close the gate behind us.* □ *If we **had** gone home when we were supposed to, none of this would **have** happened.* □ *Yes, Cheryl **does** remind me of your cousin.* □ *I **will** do it if you think I **should.*** □ *She **ought to have** been more careful.* □ *I **have** been to town to buy a turkey.* □ *We **are** having turkey again tonight.*

B

bare infinitive AND **flat infinitive, flat verb**   in English, the *infinitive* without the *to particle;* the *head* of an *infinitive phrase.* (This is the *form* of the *verb* most often used with *modal auxiliaries.* The examples show *bare infinitives* in bold print.) ☐ *I simply must* **take** *more care of my books.* ☐ *You can* **do** *it, I know you can.* ☐ *You really should* **leave.** ☐ *Would you please go* **find** *a wrench that will* **fit** *this bolt?*

bare predicate   See *simple predicate.*

base (form)   **1.** a simple *word* or *morpheme* to which *affixes* can be added. (The examples show various *base forms* in bold print.) ☐ *We have five* **cats.** ☐ *Look! They are* **falling** *now!* ☐ *The* **jugglers** *traveled with many* **circuses.** ☐ **Finders keepers.** **2.** a *form* of a *word* or *morpheme* from which any alternate *forms* or *allomorphs* can be derived rationally and efficiently. (A concept borrowed from *linguistics,* especially *phonology* and *morphology.* Given the *forms* [kæf] and [kæv] as in *calf* and *calves,* respectively, one of the *phonetic* representations [kæf] or [kæv] is chosen as the *base form* and the other *form* is said to be derived from it through a regular rule-governed process. The theory and methodology are not essential to the understanding of *grammar,* but in some modern *grammar* writings, the term has appeared occasionally. See also *root* and *stem.*)

benedictive mood   a *mood* of a *sentence* or *clause* that *conveys* the speaker's wishing for something good to happen. (Compare to *de-*

siderative mood. Each example *sentence* is in the *benedictive mood*.) ☐ *Oh, please let everything turn out all right.* ☐ *May you prosper and bear many children.* ☐ *Let the sun shine in on us all!* ☐ *May all good things come your way.*

benefactive case   the characteristic of a *nominal* representing a person or other living creature that benefits from the *action of the verb*. (From *case grammar*. Typically, these *nominals* are *indirect objects* or are in *prepositional phrases* where *for* is the *preposition*. See a brief description of the role of *case* in English at *case* and *case grammar*. The examples show the way English expresses the *semantic* relationship *conveyed* by this *case*.) ☐ *Believe me, I did it for you and you alone.* ☐ *He gave Susan three or four of the larger ones.* ☐ *Please bring me some of the freshest ones you have for my dessert.* ☐ *Andy told Jane to close her eyes, and then he gave her his frog*

bound allomorph   See the following entry.

bound form AND **bound allomorph**   [in *morphology*] a *morpheme* (represented by an *allomorph*) that cannot stand alone in a *well-formed utterance*; a *morpheme* (or *allomorph*) that requires the presence of some other *morpheme* (or *allomorph*). (The *form* is always dependent on the presence of some other *form* or some specific *class of forms* All *prefixes*, *infixes*, and *suffixes* are *bound forms*. Most *forms* that are considered *inflections* fall into this category. See also *compound*. Compare to *free form*. The examples show a wide variety of *bound forms*.) ☐ *Fred was completely disgusted with Bill.* ☐ *She walked quickly home.* ☐ *Please do not despair about the broken vase.* ☐ *We are still waiting for you to return the pieces of the broken vase.* ☐ *I cannot even conceive of such a thing!* ☐ *It is probably best not to think of me as a mender of wounded hearts.*

C

cardinal number AND **cardinal numeral**   a number that indicates quantity rather than *order*. (Compare to *ordinal number*. The examples show *cardinal numbers* spelled out in bold print.)   ☐ ***Four*** *geese flew over our house this morning.*   ☐ *We saw* ***six*** *of them yesterday.*   ☐ *The auditorium seats* ***two hundred.***   ☐ ***Seventy*** *is more than* ***two*** *times the size of the first group.*

cardinal numeral   See the previous entry.

case   **1.** a type of marking of a *noun*, usually by *suffixation,* that shows the *grammatical relationship* of the *marked noun* with the elements in its *clause*. (Latin has a number of *noun cases;* Finnish has over a dozen. English has many of the *case* relationships that are found in other languages, but marks only the *genitive case* and six *accusative case pronouns* with *inflection*. See also *common case*.) **2.** the underlying *semantic* relationships that are indicated by *grammatical* or *syntactic markers* as described in sense 1. (Clearly, according to the definition in the first sense, English has very little in the way of *formal case*. According to the definition in sense 2, *case* is relevant to the description of English *semantics,* however. English uses *word order* and proximity to indicate most *nominal* relationships. Nonetheless, there are special *pronoun forms* in English that reflect *case* markings from an earlier time: *him, his, her, hers, our, ours, me, mine, us, whom, whose, theirs, them.* These *forms* and the *-'s* marker of the *possessive* are remnants of *case* but are not part of a *noun case* system. When some *gram-*

marians speak of *case* in English, they are referring to *semantic* relationships that are not marked by special *forms* in English. Usually reference is made to the fact that these relationships are indicated by *prepositions* in English. The term **case phrase,** once used for *prepositional phrase*, reflects the fact that *prepositions* serve the role of *case inflections* in English. *Prepositional phrases* do correspond to Old English and Latin cases, but it is necessary to know which relationships exist in English and which of the *prepositions* are used to indicate them. A type of theoretical *formal grammar* called *case grammar* is based on representing the *case* relationships in a *deep structure*. The *cases* used in *case grammar* are entered in this dictionary as well as other *cases* used in other languages such as Finnish, which is especially rich in *noun case*. See *abessive (case), ablative (case), accusative (case), adessive (case), agentive (case), allative (case), benefactive case, case grammar, case phrase, comitative (case), common case, dative (case), essive (case), experiencer case, factitive case, genitive (case), illative (case), inessive (case), instructive (case), instrumental (case), locative (case), nominative (case), object(ive) case, oblique case, possessive case, result(ative) case, subject(ive) case.* The examples show the *genitive case* and some of the *pronouns* that exhibit *objective case*.) ☐ *Tim's wallet was stolen.* ☐ *Those books are hers, not mine.* ☐ *For whom is this intended?* ☐ *Whose is this?* ☐ *Whose hat is on my desk?* ☐ *Please do it for me.* **3.** the state of a spelling letter, either upper *case* or lower *case*. (Not related to senses 1 and 2.)

case grammar   a type of theoretical *formal grammar* in which the *nouns* in a *sentence* are related to the *verb* through various *case* relationships. (In English, these *cases* are represented in the *deep structure*, but do not appear as *inflected case forms* in the *surface structure* except in the *genitive case* and a few *pronouns*. *Case grammar* in English reveals important *syntactic* and *semantic* relationships. See Cook, 1989, in the bibliography for more information. The two example *sentences* demonstrate the way *case grammar* and *traditional grammar* provide different views of English *sentences*. In both example *sentences*, in terms of *case grammar*, *George* is in the *benefactive case*, even though, in terms of *traditional grammar, George* is an *indirect object* in the first *sentence* and the *subject* in the second.) □ *The judges awarded George a gold medal for bravery.* □ *George received a gold medal for bravery from the judges.*

case phrase See under *case.*

cataphora the introduction of a *word* or *phrase* early in a *sentence* or series of *sentences* that will be referred to later on in the *sentence* or series of *sentences;* the uttering of a *pronoun* in a *sentence* or series of *sentences* before its *antecedent.* (Compare to *anaphora.* See also *anticipatory subject.* In the examples, both the *pronoun* and its *antecedent* are shown in bold print. Note that the *antecedent* follows the *pronoun.*) □ *As Harley gazed into **her** eyes,* ***Nancy** responded with a disarming smile.* □ *As the falcon clutched **it**, suddenly **the snake** struck at the bird's breast.* □ *From the moment I saw **it** on sale, I knew **the expensive stereo system** was to be mine.* □ *Although **she** had known **him** for years, **Jane** looked at **John** as if he were a perfect stranger.*

cataphoric sentence the use of a *sentence* or *clause* to anticipate or *introduce* a more specific or more detailed *sentence.* (See *cataphora.* In the examples, the *cataphoric sentences* are in bold print.) □ ***I've got a secret!*** *I saw Mommy kissing Santa Claus!* □ ***I'll tell you what I'm going to do.*** *I'll give you another hundred dollars for your old car, if you'll buy a new one with wire wheels.* □ ***You know what?*** *You're a wonderful person!* □ ***Now, here's the layout.*** *You go around back and ring the bell, and I'll knock on the front door, while Max crawls in the basement window.*

causal clause a *subordinate clause* stating the cause for the action of the *main clause.* (These are *introduced* by *since, inasmuch as, because,* etc. The examples show *causal clauses* in bold print.) □ ***Because I ate too much,*** *I gained a little weight.* □ ***Since the clocks all stopped when the power went out,*** *we overslept and missed breakfast.* □ ***Inasmuch as Aunt Jane wove this herself,*** *it ought to be kept in the family.* □ ***Since you are the oldest,*** *you get first choice.*

causative verb a *transitive verb* that includes the notion of making something happen. (A *causative verb* always has an *agent. Boil* is an *intransitive verb* in the *sentence* "The water is boiling." *Make* is a *transitive verb* and a *causative verb* in "The child made the water boil." The synonymous version of this is "The child boiled the water," which contains a *transitive verb* that is a *causative verb*. See also *inchoative verb*. The examples show *causative verbs* in bold print.) ☐ *John* **baked** *the cake.* ☐ *Tom* **rolled** *the huge ball of snow up the hill.* ☐ *Jane* **drowned** *the kitten by accident.* ☐ *Bob* **felled** *a large tree.*

class See *(noun) class*. (See also *closed class, form class, function class, grammatical subclass, open class, semantic subclass, subclass, word class*.)

classifying genitive See *genitive of attribute*.

clause any group of *words* that has a *subject* and a *verb*. (Many uses of *clause* refer to a *clause* that functions as a specific *part of speech* or other specific *grammatical structure* within another *sentence*. Some grammarians use *phrase* to include *clause*. Others use *clause* as if it had the definition found at *phrase*. Terms for various types of *clauses* are *additive clause, adjective clause, adverb(ial) clause, causal clause, clause of concession, clause of condition, clause of degree, clause of manner, clause of place, clause of purpose, clause of result, clause of time, collateral clause, comment clause, comparative clause, complement(ary) clause, concessive clause, conditional clause, coordinate clause, defining relative clause, dependent clause, descriptive clause, determinative clause, essential clause, head clause, independent clause, infinitive clause, main clause, nominal clause, nondefining relative clause, nonessential clause, nonrestrictive clause, noun clause, parenthetical clause, principal clause, relative clause, restrictive clause, restrictive (relative) clause, subordinate clause, subordinate clause fragment, superordinate clause, verbless clause, wh-clause*.)

clause of concession See *concessive clause*.

clause of condition See *conditional clause*.

clause of degree a *subordinate clause* indicating a particular amount or degree of a quality or property. (These are *introduced* by *as* or *than*. The examples show *clauses of degree* in bold print.)

□ *I am younger **than I look**.* □ *You are just **as young as you feel**.*
□ *This one is redder **than that one is**.* □ *I am not as agile **as I used to be**.*

clause of manner a *subordinate clause* indicating the way something was done, has happened, or appears to have happened. (These are *introduced* by *as, as if,* or *as though* in *edited English* and the same list plus *like* in *colloquial English*. The examples show *clauses of manner* in bold print. The last example is a *starred form* in this set because it is not *edited English*.) □ *It was done as easily **as it could be**.* □ *He did it just **as he was told**.* □ *It was the kind of cat that looked **as if it had just eaten a canary**.* □ *I felt **as though I had been through a washing machine**.* □ **He gobbled down his lasagna **like he hadn't eaten for days**.*

clause of place a *subordinate clause* indicating location. (These are *introduced* by *where* or *wherever*. The examples show *clauses of place* in bold print.) □ *You can go **wherever you want**!* □ *I don't know **where Jane left it**.* □ *Put it **wherever you will be able to find it the next time you need it**.* □ *I simply can't imagine **where all the other members are tonight**.*

clause of purpose a *subordinate clause* indicating the reason for doing something or the reason for something happening. (These are *introduced* by *in order that, in order to, so that,* or *that*. The examples show *clauses of purpose* in bold print.) □ ***In order to unite into a better group***, we adopted a more democratic government. □ *We work **that we may prosper**.* □ *He drew up a chair, **so that he could sit close to us**.* □ ***So that no one would be left out***, we invited almost everyone in town.

clause of result a *subordinate clause* indicating the result of the assertion made in the *main clause*. (These are *introduced* by *so, that,* or *so that*. The examples show *clauses of result* in bold print.) □ *She was so tired **that she went right to sleep**.* □ *They plant the seeds **so that they can harvest the grain**.* □ *The truck was carrying such a great load **that it almost fell over**.* □ *She always speaks loudly **so that she can be heard**.* □ *She always speaks loudly **so she can be heard**.*

clause of time   a *subordinate clause* indicating the point or period of time of the *action of the verb* in the *main clause*. (These are *introduced* by *as, when, whenever,* and *while.* The examples show *clauses of time* in bold print.) ☐ *The hen clucked loudly* **whenever she laid an egg.** ☐ *John arrived* **as we departed.** ☐ *Bob played the cello* **while everything on the barbecue burned to a cinder.** ☐ **When the clock struck twelve,** *the lovely coach turned into a pumpkin.*

cleft infinitive   See *split infinitive.*

cleft sentence   a *sentence* that has been divided into two *clauses* for the purpose of emphasizing an element of meaning. (The first of the *clauses* generally starts with *it,* followed by some *form* of the verb *be.* Compare to *pseudo-cleft sentence,* which uses a wh-*clause.* In the examples, it is the first *clause* that contains the element that is to be emphasized.) ☐ *It was the detective who wrested the ace of spades from the thug.* ☐ *It was the thug from whom the detective wrested the ace of spades.* ☐ *It was the ace of spades that the detective wrested from the thug.* ☐ *It was Jane who showed up late this time.*

closed class AND **closed set**   any one of several *word* types that can contain a finite number of members. (As opposed to an *open class* or an *open set* that has an infinite or indefinite number of members. *Prepositions, determiners,* and *modal auxiliaries* belong to *closed classes,* while *nouns, verbs,* and *adjectives* are found in *open classes.*)

closed set   See the previous entry.

cognate object AND **internal accusative**   the *object* of a *transitive verb* that appears to be a *nominal* form of the *verb* itself. (The examples show *cognate objects* in bold print.) ☐ *They built a fine* **building** *on the site of the old train station.* ☐ *Randy fought the good* **fight.** ☐ *Jane lit the* **light** *so everyone could see.* ☐ *Tom sighed a great* **sigh.** ☐ *At nearly midnight, the old man breathed his last* **breath.**

cognitive meaning   See *denotation.*

cohortative mood AND **hortative**   a *mood* that *conveys* a sense of urging or instruction on the part of the speaker. (This is essentially a *semantic* evaluation of the *sentence* rather than a specific *con-*

struction. The examples are *sentences* in the *cohortative mood.*)
☐ *Please do come if you can.* ☐ *You will be happier if you do it this way.* ☐ *Let's do it my way for once.* ☐ *You really should try a little harder.*

collateral clause See *subordinate clause.*

collective noun a *noun* that stands for the members of a group considered as a unit. (Although it is known that *collective nouns* refer to a number of things or people, *singular agreement* with *verbs* is the rule in American English. The examples show *collective nouns* in bold print.) ☐ *The army needs new uniforms.* ☐ *My school class has only twenty students in it.* ☐ *The company is going to hire two hundred employees.* ☐ *The jury has just come back into the courtroom.*

collective pronoun a *pronoun* that stands for a group or mass of entities rather than individual entities. (These are *all, both, few, many, more, most, other, several, some.* Compare to *indefinite pronoun, separative pronoun.* The examples show *collective pronouns* in bold print.) ☐ *Some remained, but most fled just after the first act.* ☐ *I noticed that several remained behind to chat with the speaker.* ☐ *Few were able to come.* ☐ *We gave some to both even though there was only enough for one.*

collocation 1. the probability that several *words* will occur in close proximity; the tendency for specific *words* to occur frequently in close proximity due to *grammatical* or *semantic* affinity. 2. a set of *words* that occur in close proximity frequently. (The examples show, in bold print, two or more *words* that can be considered a *collocation.*) ☐ *I think I will call up my cousin.* ☐ *Tom has to have two jobs to eke out a living.* ☐ *There is only some rancid butter in the cupboard.* ☐ *I have to attend a meeting in the next town.* ☐ *The surgical team has to perform an operation this morning.* 3. word order as compared with *inflection.* (This has to do with the use of location or adjacency of *words* or *constructions* to show *grammatical relationships.*)

colloquial English   English that is informal or spoken. (Some of the *constructions* and *forms* of *colloquial English* are incorrect in *edited English*.)

combining form   **1.** a *bound form* or *morpheme* that is used in combination with other *forms*. (These *forms* are often Latin or Greek borrowings. The term does not apply to *affixes*. The *combining form* is shown in bold print. The *o* between words in bold print is a linking vowel peculiar to formations of this type.) □ *If by **phon**ograph you mean record player, yes.* □ *They refused to study **as**tronomy.* □ *The scientist found a new way to measure **astral** brightness.* □ *I would hate to be afflicted with **siderodromophobia**.* **2.** one of the elements of a *compound (noun)*. (The examples show one of the *combining forms* in bold print.) □ *Do you have a **pocket**knife with you?* □ *Wallace is not what I would call blood**thirsty**.* □ *Have you ever been on a **house**boat?*

comitative (case)   a *grammatical case* denoting *with, accompanying*. (From the Latin word *comitatus*, "companion." There is no true *comitative case* in English, and the meaning associated with it is conveyed by the *preposition with*. Mention of this *case* is some times made in discussions of "accompaniment." See a brief description of the role of *case* in English at *case* and *case grammar*. The examples show the way English expresses the *semantic* relationship conveyed by this *case*.) □ *He always did it **with a flourish**.* □ *Jane just loves vanilla ice cream **with chocolate syrup**.* □ *Did you come **with anyone**, or are you alone?*

comma fault   See the following entry.

comma splice AND **comma fault**   the separating of the *independent clauses* of a *compound sentence* with a comma rather than the appropriate *conjunction*. (A *comma splice* results in a *run-on sentence*. The examples show *sentences* exhibiting *comma splices*. Since each is incorrect it is a *starred form*.) □ **Ingrid was from Sweden, she spoke with an accent.* □ **Fred was busy, he found time to take a bath.* □ **She cleaned behind the radiator, she put fresh flowers in the vases, she left her bill on the hall table.* □ **I am tired of all this, I am* *going to take a nap.* □ **I am afraid to fly in a small plane like that, I will anyway.*

comment clause   a *clause,* typically a *parenthetical clause* or *parenthetical expression,* that makes a comment or renders an opinion about another *clause* in the same *sentence.* (This *clause* may function as an *adjunct* or a *disjunct.* The examples show *comment clauses* in bold print.) □ *Tom would not,* **I venture to guess,** *approve of your actions.* □ **Knowing of your inexplicable fear of clowns,** *I decided to abandon our trip to the circus.* □ *Sadly,* **I must say,** *it is time to go home.* □ *This is,* **I realize,** *very difficult for you.*

common case   in English, the *case* of all *nouns* that are not in the *genitive case.* (English makes little use of *case,* but the terms *genitive case* for *nouns* and *pronouns* and *objective case* for *pronouns* are widely used. The term *common case* provides a *case* name for everything else. See the comments at *case* and *oblique case.* The items in bold print in the examples are in the *common case.*) □ *The* **police officer** *gave* **one** *to* **Tom.** □ *He put John's* **book** *on the* **mantle.** □ *This large* **animal** *here is called a* **moose.** □ *Keep your* **feet** *off the* **table.**

common gender AND **epicene gender**   **1.** a *form* of a *word* that can be applied to males or females. (See *gender.* Compare to *neuter gender* and *arbitrary gender.* The *third person plural pronoun* reflects *common gender.* The examples show *pronouns* exhibiting *common gender* in bold print.) □ *The men and women put* **their** *hats on the hooks.* □ *The* **cellist** *wore her favorite long black dress.* □ *The new* **cellist** *dropped his bow and made the conductor frown.* □ *All the* **children** *brought* **their** *lunches yesterday.* **2.** arbitrary *gender,* sense 1; the *forms* indicating *masculine gender, he, his,* and *him,* used when sex is not apparent or relevant. (The term *arbitrary gender* implies that the *forms* of the *masculine gender* are used arbitrarily for *referents* that may be *masculine, feminine,* or mixed groups of both sexes. This pair of terms implies that there is a unique set of *pronouns*—that just happen to be identical with the *forms* used for *masculine gender*—that stand for *referents* that may be *masculine, feminine,* or mixed groups of both sexes. Currently, there is considerable substitution of *they, them, their,* and *theirs* for *he, him,* and *his*—despite the *number* violation—to make it impossible to construe these *pronouns* as exclusively *masculine.* See comments at *masculine (gender)* and *feminine (gender).* The examples show *pronouns* in the *common gender* in bold print.) ☐ *Take this into the post office and ask the clerk if **he** will weigh it for you.* ☐ *If someone wants a fresh cup of coffee, **he** 'll have to go to the kitchen for it.* ☐ *Each person should hang up **his** coat and hat immediately.* ☐ *Whoever spills **his** milk will have to clean it up.*

common noun a *noun* that is a member of a general class; a *noun* that is not—by itself—the name of a unique person, place, or thing. (*Common nouns* are not capitalized except at the beginning of a *sentence.* Compare to *proper noun.* In the examples, the *common nouns* are in bold print.) ☐ *My **cousin** is the best **plumber** in the whole **town** of Springfield.* ☐ *Most of us try for many **years** with no **notion** of **success.*** ☐ *They are the **people** most likely to cause **trouble.*** ☐ *Four **rabbits** crouched in the **dawn,** munching **grass.***

comparative **1.** the second *degree* of the *comparison of adjectives* and the *comparison of adverbs.* (See *comparative clause, comparative (degree), comparative sentence, double comparative, redundant comparative.*) **2.** an *adjective* or *adverb* displaying the *comparative degree.* (The examples show *comparatives* in bold print.) ☐ *That dog is **smaller** than this dog.* ☐ *He drove **faster** than ever before.* ☐ *It depends on which of the two is **quicker.*** ☐ *The one that is **more expensive** attracts my attention every time.*

comparative clause a *subordinate clause* in a *comparative sentence* that includes the entity to which an entity in the rest of the *sentence* is compared. (These are *introduced* by *as, than, more than,* etc. The *verb(al) phrase* or parts of it in a *comparative clause* is often deleted, especially when it is *be, do,* or *have.* The *verb(al) phrase* that can be deleted is shown in square brackets in the examples.) ☐ *Fred is taller **than Bob [is tall].*** ☐ *We all have a lot more sense **than Jane [has sense].*** ☐ *Gordon cannot seem to bring himself to breathe **as he should [breathe].*** ☐ *You have a lot more **than we have.*** ☐ *Joe works **as much as Steve [works].***

comparative (degree) the second of three levels of relative intensity in *adjectives* and *adverbs; the forms* signifying more than the least, but less than the most of a particular quality. (Most single-syllable *adjectives* and *adverbs* form the *comparative degree* by adding the *suffix -er.* Others exhibit *periphrastic comparison* and are preceded by *more.* Still others are *irregular* in *form,* i.e., *good > better.* The specific *form* for each *irregular adjective* or *adverb* must be learned. See also *positive (degree)* and *superlative (degree).* The examples show only the *marker* of the *comparative* in bold print.) □ *That dog is **smaller** than this dog.* □ *He drove **faster** than ever before!* □ *This one is **more** bubbly than that one.*

comparative sentence a *sentence* containing a *comparative clause.* (Each example is a *comparative sentence.*) □ *Fred is taller than Bob.* □ *We all have a lot more sense than Jane does.* □ *Gordon cannot seem to bring himself to breathe as he should.* □ *You have a lot more than we have.* □ *Joe works as much as Steve.*

comparison of adjectives See comments at *comparison of adverbs.*

comparison of adverbs the procedure of indicating relative *degrees* of equality or inequality in a characteristic or quality expressed as an *adverb* or *adjective.* (*Degrees* of a given quality are expressed by the *positive degree, comparative degree,* or the *superlative degree,* the entry for each of which should be consulted. The *positive degree* and the *comparative degree* of a given quality with reference to two or more actions or entities are compared with *as* or *than.* The *superlative degree* in such comparisons is indicated with various *periphrastic* devices—such as *nominalization*—as shown in the examples.) □ *Tom is **as tall as** William.* □ *I can run **as fast as** the wind.* □ *Tom is **taller than** William.* □ *I can run **faster than** the wind.* □ *Tom is the **tallest** of all.* □ *I am the **fastest** runner.*

complement **1.** a *word, phrase,* or *clause* that, when following a *verb, completes* or enhances the meaning and *syntactic structure* of a *sentence.* (See *direct object, indirect object, predicate adjective,* and *predicate nominative.* See these *complement* entries: *adjective complement, complement(ary) clause, complementizer,* *compound complement, object(ive) complement, prepositional complement, subject(ive) complement.* Named for the notion that a *complement* "completes" the "thought" *introduced* by the *subject* and the *verb* or is an *adjunct* to this "thought." The *complement* is said to provide the component of meaning that would otherwise be left unsaid. The examples show various types of *complements*.) ☐ *The dog is **happy**.* ☐ *The dog is a **golden retriever**.* ☐ *The cat appears **confused**.* ☐ *I do not care for this type of **thing**.* ☐ *We are pleased **that you could come**.* ☐ *They appointed her **interim mayor**.* **2.** [for a *word*, *phrase*, or *clause*] to *complete* or enhance the meaning and the *syntactic structure* of some part of the *sentence* by providing additional information. (See the discussion of the previous sense.)

complement(ary) clause   a *clause* functioning as a *complement;* a *complement* that takes the *form* of a *dependent clause.* (This describes the *form* of the *complement*, not the function. See the discussion at *complement.* The examples show *complementary clauses* in bold print.) ☐ *The prelate wondered **how he should break the news to the congregation**.* ☐ *A panacea is **what we need to develop**.* ☐ *I need to know **why you did it**.* ☐ *Let's not fight about **how she ought to do it**.*

complementizer   a *function word* or other *form* that *introduces* a *complement.* (This includes the *relative pronouns* and the *infinitive marker to.* The examples show *complementizers* in bold print.) ☐ *I want **to** go.* ☐ *We are just so happy **that** you and Sue are back together.* ☐ *June needed **to** get back to the ship and get her camera.* ☐ *You know how important it is **that** everyone remain calm.*

complete   **1.** pertaining to a *grammatical structure* that has all its parts. (Not necessarily a *grammar* term, but part of *grammatical metalanguage*, nonetheless. In some of the definitions, an intuitive sense of *complete* on the part of the user of the *grammar* is essential. See, for instance, *complete sentence* and *complement.* As discussed at *understood*, there is an inherent conflict between the concepts of *understood* and *complete. Structures* termed *complements* are said to make *complete* an *utterance* that would otherwise be detectably "incomplete" without the *complement*. Of course, there are many *constituents* that can be removed from a *sentence*—rendering it incomplete—that are not said to be *complements* that *complete* a *sentence*. There are *structures*, such as *imperative sentences*, that are obviously "incomplete" in that they lack a major *grammatical* element that is said to be *understood*. See the use of the *word* in *grammar* terminology in the entries that follow. See also *(complete) predicate, complete sentence, complete subject, complete tense, complete verb, complex preposition, complex sentence, complex transitive verb.*) **2.** to cause an *utterance* to be *grammatically well-formed* by being present in the *utterance;* to contribute materially to the logical or *semantic* wholeness of a *sentence*. (The second part of the definition describes a state that is often difficult for a speaker of English to assess and may also be impossible for a foreign speaker to assess. The successful use of a *pedagogical grammar* often depends on this ability, however.)

(complete) predicate   the entire *predicate* of a *clause*, including the *verb(s), modifier(s), complement(s), object(s)*, and *auxiliaries*. (Usually referred to as *predicate*. Compare to *simple predicate*. The examples show *complete predicates* in bold print.)   ☐ *The children* **ran all the way home.**   ☐ *People* **seldom accomplish the things that they set out to do.**   ☐ *I* **will give you everything you ask for.**   ☐ *The large red fish and the smaller black one with the yellow tail* **died.**   ☐ *She* **sneezed.**

complete sentence   a *sentence* that has all its parts present and intact, as opposed to a *phrase, dependent clause, compound*, etc.; a series of *words* having a *subject* and a *predicate* except for an *exclamatory sentence;* a *grammatically well-formed utterance* that is the product of *edited English*. (This is more an evaluative and pedagogical term than a *grammar* term. Most *grammar* terms deal with *complete* and *grammatically well-formed constructions*. There is an implication that a natural and preexisting sense of logic is a dependable measure of completeness and incompleteness. The examples show *complete sentences*.)   ☐ *Birds can fly.*   ☐ *The old man leapt from his chair and danced a jig.*   ☐ *Keep your* *hands to yourself, or I'll slap them.* □ *The car pulled up to the door and drew to a stop.*

complete subject the entire *noun phrase* or *nominal* serving as the *syntactic subject* of a *sentence*, including all *determiners, modifiers,* and *complements.* (The *complete subject* may include many types of *grammatical structures.* Compare to *simple subject.* The *complete subjects* in the following examples are shown in bold print.) □ ***The latest, new, chart-busting, trend-setting album from Domino and the Derricks, this year's hottest young herd of hopefuls,*** *is setting sales records around the country.* □ ***Few of the keys on the aged typewriter*** *worked dependably, but **I** kept trying.* □ ***Bees, which tend to gather around clover,*** *can be annoying at this time of year.* □ ***I*** *spy.*

complete tense the *imperfect(ive) (aspect).* (See comments at *complete.*)

complete verb an *intransitive verb.* (If one thinks of a *transitive verb* as requiring an *object* to be *complete,* then an *intransitive verb,* because it requires nothing to *complete* it, can be called a *complete verb.* The term should be distinguished from *complete predicate.* See *intransitive verb* for further comments and examples.)

complex preposition a *preposition* made of two or more *prepositions.* (This is a very large set of items. Examples: *according to, as for, as to, because of, by means of, due to, from among, in accordance with, in back of, in front of, in respect to, inside of, in spite of, instead of, out of.* The examples show *complex prepositions* in bold print.) □ *I'm sorry. I have an appointment, and I can't get **out of** it.* □ *Put this one **in back of** that one.* □ ***In accordance with*** *our agreement, I will submit three copies of the report.* □ *Jane was obliged to choose **from among** a vast assemblage of eager applicants.*

complex sentence a *sentence* with only one *independent clause* and one or more *dependent clauses.* (In a *complex sentence,* the *independent clause* is called the *superordinate clause.* Each example is a *complex sentence.*) □ *I can do whatever I want after I get home.* □

As soon as I complete the plans, they will start to build. □ *I will go there whenever I am ready.* □ *After they restore the painting, they will rehang it.*

complex transitive verb   a *verb* that takes a *direct object* and an *object(ive) complement*. (See the comments at *object(ive) complement*. The examples show *complex transitive verbs* in bold print.) □ *They **appointed** Mrs. Wallace the coordinator of the committees.* □ *The entire body **elected** him high sheriff by acclamation.* □ *The peasants, in their clumsy way, **crowned** Ethelred king.* □ *He was **voted** the least likely to accomplish his goals.*

[compound]   See *compound adjective, compound complement, compound-complex sentence, compound-complex word, compound (noun), compound object, compound predicate, compound sentence, compound subject, compound tense, compound verb, compound word.*

compound adjective   a combination of two or more *words* functioning as a single *adjective;* an *adjective* composed of two *words* joined together. (The examples show *compound adjectives* in bold print.) □ *I don't know how I ever got mixed up with a **blue-eyed** devil like Bob!* □ *John lived out the rest of his days in a state of **guilt-ridden** anxiety.* □ *Now, in this case, we have some lovely examples of **hand-made** objects from the upper reaches of the Amazon River.* □ *The **poison-tipped** arrow found its mark, and soon the helpless bird lay at our feet.* □ *You are an **out-and-out** liar!*

compound complement   two or more *complements* connected by a *conjunction* or some other linking *constituent* or *construction*. (A number of different types of *complements* are shown here in bold print.) □ *They named Bob **secretary and treasurer of the company**.* □ *We were at once **pleased and delighted**.* □ *I will paint this vase **orange and blue**.* □ *I am glad **that he did it and that he was pleased with the results**.*

compound-complex sentence   a *compound* sentence with one or more *subordinate clauses*. (See also *complex sentence*. Each example is a *compound-complex sentence*.) □ *I know what you think* *about what I am doing, but have you thought what I may think of what you are doing?* □ *The snow stopped falling when the sun rose, but the temperature dropped below zero.* □ *The birds began to sing when the hawk had passed, and peace returned to the meadow.* □ *Sam went to the bank when the rain stopped, and Jane stayed at the cabin because she had many things to do.*

compound-complex word a *word* composed of a *compound word* and one or more *affixes*. (The boundaries of the *constituents* of the *compound-complex words* in the examples are indicated by "|.") □ *John is an |ex-|prize|fight|er|.* □ *They were not able to |re| broad|cast|* the event.

compound (noun) See *(noun) compound.*

compound object two or more *objects* linked by a *coordinating conjunction*. (In the examples, the *compound objects* are in bold print.) □ *Betty fried **bacon and eggs** for her breakfast.* □ *Jane doesn't like **blue** or **purple**.* □ *Please give me **some chicken** and **some shrimp**.* □ *I am really tired of **dirt and noise**.*

compound predicate AND **compound verb** two or more *verbs* or two or more *verb(al) phrases*, having the same *subject*, connected by a *coordinating conjunction*. (See also the separate entry for *compound verb*. The examples show *compound predicates* in bold print.) □ *Fred **reads books and writes letters** every Saturday morning.* □ *Sally **will have to be at work on time and will have to work harder**.* □ *The guests can **stand** or **sit**.* □ *John will **prepare the turkey and wash the vegetables**.*

compound sentence AND **coordinate sentence** a *sentence* consisting of two or more *independent clauses* and no *dependent clauses*. (Each of the examples is a *compound sentence*.) □ *Her father died, and she cried.* □ *I ran home, and I fell on the way.* □ *Tom drove down to the village, but Mary stayed behind.* □ *The rains fell, and the frogs sang all night long.*

compound subject a *subject* consisting of two or more *nominals*. (The examples show *compound subjects* in bold print.) □ ***Fred and Ted*** *sped home.* □ ***The old gray mare and the young stallion*** *watched each other warily.* □ ***Fred and the former coach of the foot-***

ball team shared a room at the convention. □ ***Margaret and her unpleasant younger daughter*** stood haughtily next to the exit. □ ***Cockles, mussels, rice, and fried squid*** sat on the table in white enameled basins.

compound tense a combination of both *tense* and *aspect* in the *verb(al) phrase*. (See *phrasal tense*. For instance, the first example shows a combining of the *past tense* and the *perfect*. The term *compound tense* is borrowed from Latin *grammar*. The examples show various *compound tenses* in bold print.) □ *He **had gone** there once before.* □ *We **could not have wished** for more.* □ *Jane **had been hoping** for something like this all along.* □ *They will want to **have been fishing** for hours by sunrise.*

compound verb **1.** a *verb form* made up of an *adjective* or a *preposition* plus a *verb*. (When an *adjective* comes before the *verb*, it is often joined to the *verb* by a hyphen. When a *preposition* precedes the *verb*, the entire *form* is usually written solidly, as one *word*. The examples show *compound verbs* in bold print.) □ *It will be impossible to **double-cross** my parents.* □ *This part will **overhang** this part by a little bit.* □ *The secretary tried to **undercut** the mayor and got fired for his trouble.* □ *She just **whipstitched** it together as a costume for the play.* **2.** See *compound predicate*.

compound word a *word* consisting of a combination of two or more *forms* that, in combination, behave *grammatically* as one *word*. (Not all *compound words* are *nouns*. See also *(noun) compound*. The examples show *compound words* in bold print.) □ *Ask the **gatekeeper** to let you in.* □ *Use a **wheelbarrow** to move the load.* □ *She is known as an **upright** individual.* □ *We were completely **undone** by the news.* □ *Who left the newspaper **outside** in the rain?* □ *The **houseboat** was quite comfortable for a family of four.* □ *My **brother-in-law** took me to the airport.* □ *It would be bad to **double-cross** her.* □ *This part will **overhang** the edge a little bit.* □ *The teacher tried to **undercut** the principal.*

concessive clause AND **clause of concession** a *subordinate clause* indicating concession on the part of the speaker; a *clause* that indicates a reversal in outlook or result despite an adverse or promising condition. (This is more of a *semantic* interpretation of the *clause* than a separate *construction*. These *clauses* are *introduced* by the *concessive conjunctions*. Another *concessive conjunction*, *but*, follows the *concessive clause* and *introduces* a *clause* that is not a *concessive clause*. Note the contrast between *but* and the other *concessive conjunctions* in the examples. The examples show *concessive clauses* including *concessive conjunctions* in bold print.) □ *Even though he tried as hard as he could, he still came in second. He tried as hard as he could, but he still came in second.* □ *We suspect that the stock will rise, even though the market as a whole looks like a disaster. The stock market as a whole looks like a disaster, but we suspect that the stock will rise.* □ *Though everyone said bad things about her, she continued to try to do what she thought best. Everyone said bad things about her, but she continued do what she thought best.* □ *I will be there on time even if the sky falls in! The sky may fall in, but I will be there on time.*

concessive conjunction   a *conjunction* that *introduces* a *concessive clause*. (Namely, *although, but, even if, even though, though*, and *while*. See *concessive clause* for a comment on *but*. The examples show *concessive conjunctions* in bold print.) □ *Even though he tried as hard as he could, he still came in second.* □ *We suspect that the stock will rise, even though the market as a whole looks like a disaster.* □ *Though everyone said bad things about her, she continued to try to do what she thought best.*

concord   See definition and examples at *(grammatical) agreement*. See *number concord, person concord* for specific kinds of *concord*.

concrete noun   a *semantic subclass* of *nouns* including the names of physical things that can be seen, touched, smelled, measured, etc. (See also *abstract noun, proper noun, count(able) noun*. The examples show *concrete nouns* in bold print.) □ *Please put the box on the floor.* □ *Can I have some water, please?* □ *I can hardly smell the roses.* □ *Keep your hands to yourself!*

conditional clause AND clause of condition   a *dependent clause* in the *conditional (mood)* stating the conditions under which the adjacent *independent clause* will be true. (Such *clauses* are often *in-*

troduced by *if*. The examples show *conditional clauses* in bold print.) ☐ ***If you do that again, I'll scream.*** ☐ *I will be there a little late **if it rains.*** ☐ ***If she does, I won't.*** ☐ *I will **unless it rains.*** ☐ *We will be there on time, **assuming that there is not an earthquake or other similar disaster.***

conditional conjunction   a *word* or *phrase* used to *introduce* a *conditional clause*. (For instance: *although, as, as long as, assuming (that), given (that), if, in case, on the condition (that), provided (that), supposing (that), though, unless.* The examples show *conditional conjunctions* in bold print.) ☐ ***If** she does, I won't.* ☐ *I will **unless** it rains.* ☐ *I can manage it, **provided** it is not too heavy.* ☐ *We will be there on time, **assuming that** there is not an earthquake or other disaster.* ☐ *I will keep dancing **as long as** you keep clapping.*

conditional (mood)   a *semantic* state of a *sentence* or *clause* that tells the conditions under which a *proposition* is true. (The *conditional mood* is marked by the presence of a *conditional conjunction*. The following *conditional sentences* illustrate the *conditional mood*.) ☐ *Jane will handle the external matters, provided that you take care of everything concerned with the company.* ☐ *If you really tried, you could do it.* ☐ *Assuming that Bob is the one you pick, there should be no difficulty at all.* ☐ *I would sing with you, if I could sing at all.*

conditional sentence   a *sentence* made up of a *complex sentence* containing a *conditional clause* and an *independent clause* that expresses a hypothesis or hindsight rather than fact. (The following are *conditional sentences*.) ☐ *If it had rained, I might have come in sooner.* ☐ *If Ted had only paid attention to what he was doing, he might have avoided the accident.* ☐ *The meeting will be a success unless Sue is late.*

condition contrary to fact   a hypothetical, possible, or supposed condition or situation. (Part of the *metalanguage* of *grammar* concerned with the *conditional (mood)* and the *subjunctive (mood)*. The examples show the *condition contrary to fact* in bold print. Note that both *clauses* are contrary to fact, but only the one in bold print is stated as a condition.) ☐ ***If I had only known about***

your sore arm, I would have been more careful. ☐ **Had she been on time,** *none of this would have happened.* ☐ *I would* **if I could only get there on time.** ☐ **Even if you beg me,** *I will adamantly refuse to do it.*

conjoin   to connect or link *constituents* together, as with a *conjunction*. (*Conjoined* elements are shown in bold print in the examples.) ☐ *Peter sings with* **Paul and Mary.** ☐ **Jane will run** *and* **June will ride her bicycle.** ☐ *Bill will* **fish** *or* **cut bait.** ☐ *Sally will have to* **sink** *or* **swim.**

conjugate   to enumerate the various *tenses* and *aspects* of a *verb* in the various *numbers* and *persons.*

conjugation   **1.** a *formal subclass* of *verbs* based on unique sets of *inflections* for *tense, aspect, person,* or *number.* (A *verb* inflected for a particular *conjugation* is said to belong to the *conjugation.* English does not have any *verb subclasses* of this type. See, however, *strong verb, weak verb.*) **2.** a list of the *inflected forms* of a *verb;* the *paradigms* of the *verb.* (Here is the *conjugation* of the *present tense* of the *verb be* in all *persons* and both *numbers,* singular and plural: *I am, you are, he is, she is, it is, we are, you are, they are.* Compare to *declension.*)

conjunct   an *adverbial* that serves to link a *sentence* to other *sentences* in the same *discourse.* (The *conjunct* is not part of the basic *structure* of the *sentence* in which it is found. Typically: *be that as it may, in other words, nevertheless, nonetheless, therefore, without a doubt, in spite of that, finally, in conclusion,* etc. The examples show *conjuncts* in bold print.) ☐ **Nonetheless,** *I must ask you to be here on time for the rest of the term.* ☐ **In other words,** *you will not be able to deliver the goods by the time specified in the contract?* ☐ **Therefore,** *the entire committee recommends passage of the measure.* ☐ **Without a doubt,** *these are the tastiest chocolate chip cookies ever to end up in my mouth.*

conjunction   a *function word* that joins *words, phrases,* or *clauses.* (See comments at *connective.* See also *adversative conjunction, concessive conjunction, conditional conjunction, conjunct, coordinating conjunction, copulative (conjunction), correlative (con-*

junction), disjunctive (conjunction), illative conjunction, subdisjunctive (conjunction), subordinating conjunction.)

conjunctive (adverb) AND **linking adverb, (sentence) connector**
an *adverb* serving to link things in the manner of a *conjunction;* an *adverb* used as a *conjunction.* (Typically: *accordingly, also, as a result, besides, conversely, further, furthermore, hence, however, in addition, nevertheless, nonetheless, then, therefore, thus.* Compare to *conjunct.* The examples show *conjunctive adverbs* in bold print.) □ *I would be there;* ***however,*** *I will be in France at that time.* □ *She didn't turn in her paper;* ***hence*** *she failed.* □ *He cannot be depended upon to do it right;* ***besides,*** *he's always late.* □ *I will make the ice first,* ***then*** *I will start on baking the cake while the ice cream is freezing hard.*

conjunctive pronoun   a *relative pronoun* used to *introduce* a *relative clause.* (Typically: *as, who, which, what, that.* Only *who* can be *inflected* for its position in its own *clause.* The examples show *conjunctive pronouns* in bold print.) □ *I bought a tree* ***that*** *would look nice in my yard.* □ *I do not know* ***whom*** *you mean.* □ *Bill found out* ***what*** *everyone already knew.* □ *I do not know* ***who*** *should answer the door.*

connective   a very general term for any type of *grammatical form* that connects, *conjoins, introduces,* links, or relates *words, clauses,* or *sentences.* (The term is not usually rigorously defined. It includes *conjunctions,* obviously, but may also include any *construction* that leads into another *proposition. Adverbs* such as *finally, therefore, however,* and *on the contrary* are *connectives,* as well as *that* and *which* when used to *introduce* a *clause.* See the list at *conjunction.* The examples show a variety of *connectives* in bold print.) □ *You think I am crazy?* ***On the contrary,*** *it is you who are mentally infirm.* □ ***Finally,*** *I would like to introduce your friend and mine, Wallace J. Ott.* □ *Sticks* ***and*** *stones may break my bones....* □ ***Without a doubt,*** *I am usually regarded as a fairly even-tempered individual.* □ *I would be quite happy with one* ***or*** *the other.* □ *I want this one* ***and*** *that one.*

connector   See *conjunctive (adverb).*

connotation AND **emotive meaning**   a suggestion or association *conveyed* by a *word* in addition to its *denotation*. (The *words* in bold print in the following *sentences* have negative *connotations*.) ☐ *I can't bear to think about **death**.* ☐ *A female dog is called a **bitch**.* ☐ *Is that a **pimple** beside my nose?* ☐ *You should flush the **stools** away immediately.*

connote   [for a *word*] to suggest nuances, overtones, or associations in addition to the basic *denotation* of a *word*. (See examples at the previous entry.)

constituent   an element that is part of a larger *structure*. (A *verb* is a *constituent* of a *verb phrase*.)

constituent structure   the sequential and hierarchical organization of the *constituents*—on their various levels—of an *utterance*. (For instance, a *determiner*, *adjective*, and *noun* are *constituents* of the *noun phrase*. The *noun phrase* is a *constituent* of a *sentence*.)

construction   a set of *words, affixes, auxiliaries*, etc., assembled into a *grammatically* permissible sequence; a *structure*. (Many definitions of *construction* state that a *construction* is a meaningful *phrase* or *clause*. Usually, however, the elements that identify a particular *construction* are *grammatical*. See also *absolute construction, elliptical construction, free construction, partitive construction, subjunctive construction*. The examples show many different types of *constructions* in bold print. In brackets after the sentence is a *grammar* term that tells what kind of *construction* is in bold print.) ☐ ***The old dog*** *died very slowly.* [subject] ☐ ***The old dog died very slowly.*** [sentence] ☐ *The old dog **died very slowly**.* [predicate] ☐ *The old dog died **very slowly**.* [adverb(ial) phrase] ☐ *Please get **out of here**!* [prepositional phrase]

contentive   See the following entry.

content word AND **contentive, lexical word, naming word, notional word, vocabulary word**   a *word* that *conveys lexical meaning* as opposed to *grammatical meaning*, such as a *noun, verb, adjective,* *adverb* rather than a *preposition* or *particle*. (Compare to *function word*. The examples show *content words* in bold print.) ☐ *The **man** on the **fence** would **often sing**.* ☐ *Don't **stare**!* ☐ *The **woman** in **red sneezed** in her **soup**.* ☐ *Will you **keep quiet**!* ☐ *A **solitary cat** or even **lots** of cats would **cause** no **trouble**.*

[continuous] See *continuous (aspect)* at *progressive (aspect)* and see *future continuous (aspect)*, *future perfect continuous (aspect)*, *past continuous (aspect)*, *past perfect continuous (aspect)*, *present continuous (aspect)*, *present perfect continuous (aspect)*.

continuous (aspect) See *progressive (aspect)*.

continuous (tense) See *progressive (aspect)*.

conversion AND **functional change, functional shift** a type of derivation where the *part of speech* or other *word class* designation of a *constituent* is changed without the use of *affixes* or any other *formal* apparatus. (Very often this term accounts for nothing more than an expansion of the number of *parts of speech* that categorize a given *constituent*. In many instances, this should be viewed as a completed historical process rather than something that can be observed in everyday standard language. In slang, however, *conversion* is one of the most commonly used processes for creating new expressions. The examples show *conversions* in bold print. It should be assumed that these examples are of *conversion* that has been completed at some time in the past.) ☐ *Of course I use a hammer to **hammer** a nail! What else?* ☐ *Four men were there, **manning** the booth until closing time.* ☐ *Let's get just one more good **take**, and then we'll call it a day.* ☐ *The **red** on the cabinet isn't red enough.*

convey to signify or transmit a meaning; to mean. (A vocabulary item in the *metalanguage* of *grammar*.)

coordinate clause one of two or more *clauses* joined by *coordinating conjunctions*. (The examples show *coordinate clauses* in bold print.) ☐ ***Mary swam,** and **Bob kept watch**.* ☐ ***Should I fish,** or should I cut bait?* ☐ ***I did not want to,** but **I did**.* ☐ ***I fixed the computer,** and **Polly adjusted the printer**.*

coordinate sentence See *compound sentence*.

coordinating conjunction   a *conjunction* that links two or more elements of the same *grammatical category* or elements that have the same *grammatical structure*. (Typically: *and, but, for,* and *or.* Also includes *nor* and *and/or.* The examples show *coordinating conjunctions* in bold print.) ☐ *We ran **and** ran to get there on time.* ☐ *A dog **or** a cat would make a nice pet.* ☐ *Will you be driving **or** taking the train?* ☐ *The cat **and** the fox are similar in their craftiness.* ☐ *The frog jumped **and** the mouse scurried across the log.*

coordination   the linking of two or more elements of the same *grammatical category.* (This is accomplished by the use of a *coordinating conjunction.* The coordinated *constituents* are shown in bold print in the examples.) ☐ *We **ran** and **ran** to get there on time.* ☐ *A **dog** or a **cat** would make a nice pet.* ☐ *Will you be **driving** or **taking** the train?* ☐ *The **cat** and **the fox** are similar in their craftiness.* ☐ *The **frog jumped** and **the mouse scurried** across the log.*

copula AND **copulative verb, copular verb**   **1.** the *verb be* in any of its *inflected forms.* (This is one type of *linking verb.* The examples show various uses of the *copula.*) ☐ *She ought to have **been** more careful.* ☐ *It **was** the detective who wrested the ace of spades from the thug.* ☐ *Fred **is** taller than Bob.* ☐ *She **is** a golfer.* ☐ ***Am** I happy!* ☐ *The frogs will have **been** croaking since dawn.* ☐ *I will **be** here all day long.* ☐ *Our friend **was** wonderful.* **2.** See *linking verb.*

copular verb   See the previous entry.

copulative (conjunction)   **1.** a *particle* that serves to link or bond a *subject* to its *predicate nominative* or *predicate adjective;* a *copula* viewed as a *conjunction* rather than as a *verb.* (Typically: *be, become, feel, seem.* The examples show *copulative conjunctions* in bold print.) ☐ *I **feel** sick about the stock market.* ☐ *She **is** a golfer.* ☐ *It **seems** quite chilly today.* ☐ *Jane **became** totally impossible to deal with.* **2.** a *coordinating conjunction.* (Typically: *and, also, besides, both, likewise, moreover, then.* The examples show *copulative conjunctions* in bold print.) ☐ *She is difficult to work with; **moreover,** she smokes.* ☐ *He caught one, **then** he caught another.* ☐ *I think I'll stay home tonight; **besides,** I have a cold.* ☐ *Sally finds all of this quite tedious, **but** John is fascinated.*

copulative verb   See *copula.*

correlative (conjunction)   one of a set of pairs of *forms* that link similar *structures.* (Typically: *although—still; although—yet; both—and; either—or; if—then; neither—nor; not only—but also; since—therefore; though—still; though—yet; whether—or.* Correlative *conjunctions* can link pairs of *nouns, verbs, prepositional phrases,* and *sentences.* The linked pairs must be parallel or identical *structures* in that they are the same category of *constituent.* The examples show *correlative conjunctions* in bold print.)   ☐   ***Both*** *Fred* **and** *Tom can pilot an airplane.*   ☐   ***Either*** *fish* **or** *cut bait.*   ☐   *I didn't know* **whether** *to go* **or** *to stay.*   ☐   *The middle-size chair was* **neither** *large* **nor** *small.*   ☐   ***Either*** *I will ask for a raise,* **or** *I will find a new job.*

count(able) noun   a *noun* that can be preceded by a *cardinal numeral* that indicates how many. (In the third example, *bees* is a *count noun* because it *can* be preceded by a cardinal numeral, as in *two bees.* The direct opposite is *uncountable noun.* Compare to *noncount noun* or *mass noun.* Many *noncount nouns* also have countable counterparts that refer to a type, *class,* or species of the *nouns,* such as *rices, wheats, champagnes, rouges, waters,* etc. The *words* shown in bold print in the following examples are *countable nouns.*)   ☐   *Four* **cats** *leapt on the helpless* **puppy.**   ☐   *I found four* **grains** *of rice in my* **pocket.**   ☐   *We saw a thousand* **ants** *and some* **bees.**   ☐   *We tried three or four different* **wheats** *in that* **field** *and nothing worked.*   ☐   ***Ships*** *of that size cannot pass through the Panama Canal.*

D

dangling modifier   a *modifier* that has been placed in a position that makes it seem to *modify* the wrong *constituent* or no *constituent* at all. (There are many different types of *dangling modifier*. Only the *dangling participle* has its own term. See also *misplaced modifier*. The *dangling modifiers* are in bold print in the examples. Since each is incorrect it is a *starred form*.) □ *We spotted the mountain **coming around the bend**. □ ***When cooking pork**, the hands should be clean. □ ***While falling**, he suddenly caught it. □ ***Speaking too soon**, Bob appeared silently, but just on time.*

dangling participle AND **hanging participle**   a *participle phrase* in a *sentence* that does not contain a *noun* or *pronoun* that the *phrase* could *modify*. (See also *dangling modifier*. A *participle phrase* is in error when it functions as an *adverb* and is used to *modify* a *nominal*. The last two examples are classical "errors" in the use of *participle phrases* for this latter reason.) □ *Considering everything, what objection could possibly be raised?* □ *Knowing her as well as I do, there should be no difficulty.* □ *Remembering my manners, there were no problems.* □ *Facing the facts, little was left to do.* □ *Standing perfectly still, the huge lion ran quickly past.* □ *Having tarried too long over tea, the tour bus left immediately for its next destination.*

dative (case)   a *noun case* name applied to the English *indirect object*. (A grammatical *case* that *denotes* a receiver of something. From the Latin word *dativus*, "having to do with giving." There is no *formal* indication of the *dative case* in English, and the meaning associated with this "case" is *conveyed* in part by *word order* and the *forms* of the *personal pronoun*. *Common case* might be a more suitable term. See a brief description of the role of *case* in English at *case* and *case grammar*. The examples show in bold print *nominals* that can be said to be in the *dative case*.) ☐ *Please give it to* **me**. ☐ *They gave* **her** *a lovely silk scarf.* ☐ *Seven men brought* **John** *an enormous log for his woodworking project.* ☐ *The clerk promised he would send* **us** *some.*

declarative sentence AND **statement**   a type of *utterance* that states, affirms, or declares. (In terms of *mood*, a *sentence* in the *indicative mood*. *Mood* focuses on the intent of the speaker. *Sentence* types like *declarative sentence, imperative sentence,* and *interrogative sentence* focus on the *structure* of the *sentence*. The examples are all *declarative sentences*.) ☐ *The sky is blue.* ☐ *I'll be down to get you in a taxi, honey.* ☐ *Of course I will.* ☐ *Fred swam more than was necessary.* ☐ *We need to have a lot more just like this one.*

declension   **1.** a *class* of *nouns* the members of which behave in the same way. (Not all languages have such *classes* of *nouns*. Languages that have *grammatical noun class* often have *class* numbers, such as "first declension, second declension," etc. A sample *noun* from a specific *class* is shown in all its possible *grammatical forms* in a *declension*. English does not have *noun class inflections* that will appear in a *declension*.) **2.** a statement or list of the various *forms* of *nouns, pronouns,* or *adjectives; paradigms* of *nouns, pronouns,* or *adjectives* combining various categories, such as *case, number,* and *gender*. (Compare to *conjugation*.)

decline   to list or recite the various *forms* of *nouns, pronouns,* or *adjectives,* showing the combinations of various categories, such as *case, number,* and *gender*. (Since English lacks *inflection* for *case* and *gender,* this is not usually done for English.)

deep structure   an analytical and abstract version of a *sentence* that provides the *syntactic* and *semantic* information necessary to interpret the *sentence*. (Part of *transformational-generative grammar*. See also *surface structure*.)

defective verb   a *verb* that lacks a unique *past participle form*; a *verb* that lacks unique *past tense* and *past participle forms*. (The term is used primarily to refer to *modal verbs*. The *defective verbs* are *can, may, might, must, ought, shall,* and *will*. The *modal verbs* *ought* and *must* lack both a unique *past tense* and a unique *past participle form*. The examples show *defective verbs* in bold print.)   □ *I **may** go there. I don't know yet.*   □ *You really **ought** to, you know.*   □ *You **must** give it a try, no matter how frightened you are.*

defining relative clause   See *restrictive (relative) clause.*

definite article   a *particle* that points or refers to a *nominal* representing a specific entity. (The *form the* is used when both the speaker and the hearer recognize precisely which entity is being referred to. The examples show *definite articles* in bold print.)   □ *Give me **the** cookie, please.*   □ ***The** old man just sat there.*   □ *Put **the** big one on **the** desk, please.*   □ *This is **the** book I want.*

definitive (adjective)   one of a group of *adjectives* that typically stands first in a series of *adjectives*. (These adjectives are *a, an, the, my, your, his, her, its, our, their, this, that, these, those, what, which, any, each, every, either, neither, no, some, such, enough,* and any *possessive noun*. There are, of course, exceptions to the "first in a series" pattern. The examples show *definitive adjectives* in bold print.)   □ ***An** ancient castle stood on **the** crumbling cliff.*   □ ***Any** old book will do.*   □ *I just can't seem to get **enough** spending money these days.*   □ ***Every** single one of the children has had the measles.*   □ *We gave the coats to **those** older and more mature citizens.*   □ *Please place the pipes near **your** father's chair.*   □ *Please place the newspaper on **Tom's** favorite chair.*

definitive genitive AND **epexegetical genitive**   the *of-genitive* used to make the meaning of a *noun* more specific. (Some of these are *fixed phrases* or established *proper nouns*. The examples show *definitive genitives* in bold print.)   □ *You have turned this into a carnival **of a meeting**.*   □ *I spent four years in the city **of Chicago**.*   □ *Bob is a prince **of a gentleman**.*   □ *He attended the University **of Alaska** for four years.*

degree   an indication of the extent of *comparison* for *adjectives* or *adverbs*. (See *absolute degree, clause of degree, comparative (degree), positive (degree), superlative (degree).*)

demonstrative (adjective) AND **determinative**   a *demonstrative (pronoun)* that *modifies* a specific *nominal*. (These *words* have the *form* of a *pronoun* and function as an *adjective*. The examples show *demonstrative adjectives* in bold print.) ☐ *Give me **that** one.* ☐ ***These** hats are the best.* ☐ *Please put **those** sandwiches on **that** other tray and leave **these** little ones right here.*

demonstrative (pronoun)   The *pronouns that, this, these, those*. (*These* and *those* are *plural*; *that* and *those* refer to something distant. The examples show *demonstrative pronouns* in bold print.) ☐ ***These** are the best hats. Leave **these** right here. Put **those** on **that** and leave **these** here.*

denominal   See the following entry.

denominative verb AND **denominal**   a *verb* derived from a *noun* or an *adjective*. (The examples show *denominative verbs* in bold print.) ☐ *The cat **eyed** the snake with exceeding caution.* ☐ *She **fingered** the material casually and gave a little sneer of disapproval.* ☐ *Must you always **salt** your food before tasting it?* ☐ *One should **ready** everything before beginning.*

denotation AND **cognitive meaning**   the literal and explicit meaning of a *word* or *phrase;* the dictionary definition of a *word*. (A property of a *noun, phrase, verb,* or *sentence*. The opposite of *connotation*.)

denote   to *convey* a particular meaning; to *convey* a specific meaning or reference. (A property of *words, phrases,* and *sentences*. All *content words* must *denote* something.)

dental preterit   the *form* of the *past tense* of *regular verbs*. (Because the [t], [d], and [əd] of the *past tense marker* are consonants said to be articulated in the dental position. In fact, in American English, these consonants are typically articulated in the alveolar position.)

dependent   pertaining to a *constituent* that cannot stand or occur alone without the presence of another constituent. (Compare to *independent*. See *dependent clause*. See other entries concerned with "dependence": *dependent clause, independent, independent clause, independent possessive (pronoun).*)

dependent clause AND **collateral clause, subordinate clause   1.** a *sentence* functioning as an *adverb* or *adverb(ial) phrase embedded* in another *sentence*, and *introduced* by a *subordinating conjunction*. (It is the *subordinating conjunction* that prevents the *dependent clause* from standing on its own. The examples show *dependent clauses* in bold print.) □ *I went home **after I finished jogging**.* □ *I played the fiddle **while dinner burned**.* □ *She threatened to jump out the window **unless I agreed to the plan**.* □ *We danced a while, **then we all got to go home**.* **2.** a sentence functioning *adjectivally, embedded* in another *sentence*, and *introduced* by a *relative pronoun*. (The *relative pronouns* are *who, whose, whom, which, that*. See *adjective clause*. The examples show *dependent clauses* in bold print.) □ *The piano **that I play** needs tuning.* □ *I gave a rose to the lady **who works here**.* □ *The old woman **who lives in a shoe** filed for bankruptcy.* □ *An enormous flock of crows, **which we had spotted in the distance**, headed for the field.*

derivation   1. the process of forming a new *word* from an existing *word*, often changing the *part of speech* in the process. (This is usually accomplished by adding one or more *affixes*, although sometimes *phonological* changes are used in *derivation*. Compare to *inflection*. The examples show *derivations* in bold print.) □ *We decided to **modernize** our kitchen. It is not at all modern by today's standards.* □ *She tried to **visualize** what her blind date would look like.* □ *The light shone **brightly** on the snow.* □ *The **width** is fine. The problem is with the **length**.* □ *The **runner** fell from exhaustion.* **2.** a derived *form;* the product of an act of *derivation*.

derivational morpheme   See the following entry.

derivational suffix AND **derivational morpheme** a *particle* that indicates the change of one *part of speech* to another. (The examples show *derivational suffixes* in bold print.) □ *Let's modernize our kitchen.* □ *Why does the snow glisten so brightly?* □ *Suddenly, the runner turned around and started going the other way.* □ *Bobby asked why the spinning top didn't fall over.*

derivative a *word* of one *part of speech* made from another *part of speech*. (See *derivational suffix*. The *derivatives* are shown in bold print.) □ *They idolize rock stars.* □ *I love to swim, and my brother loves swimming even more than I do.* □ *The redness of his face faded quickly.* □ *The width is fine. The problem is with the length.*

descriptive adjective AND **qualifying adjective** an *adjective* that adds to the meaning of the *nominal* it *modifies* and helps identify a general kind, *class,* or type. (Compare to *limiting adjective,* which indicates which specific entity is being referred to. The examples show *descriptive adjectives* in bold print.) □ *Keep away from angry bulls.* □ *You can distinguish the successful man from the unsuccessful one by the way he walks.* □ *I really prefer a red one.* □ *They were charging me for a special telephone even though I had a plain one.*

descriptive adverb an expression that *modifies* a *verb, sentence, adjective,* or other *adverb*. (As opposed to *adverbs* that serve other functions, such as *interrogative (adverbs), relative adverbs, locative adverbs, etc. Descriptive adverbs* are often formed by the addition of -*ly* to *adjectives* that exhibit *gradability* as in the *positive (degree), comparative (degree),* and *superlative (degree).* The examples show *descriptive adverbs* in bold print.) □ *Please come here quickly.* □ *We felt strangely frightened by all this.* □ *I am very tired of all this.* □ *They were so sleepy, they could hardly keep their eyes open.*

descriptive clause See *nonrestrictive clause*.

descriptive genitive See *genitive of attribute*.

descriptive grammar a *grammatical statement* based on a *linguistic* description of a language. (Often cited in opposition to the notion of *prescriptive grammar*. A *descriptive grammar* is based on observable evidence, and the evidence is usually a record of the actual use of a language. It is meant to be unbiased in that the *grammarian* avoids making statements or judgments about the language being described and avoids claiming which *constructions* are better than others. See Quirk, *et al.,* in the bibliography for an example of a *descriptive grammar.* The writer of a *descriptive grammar* seeks not to judge the data, but only to record, analyze, and explain it. See also *proscriptive grammar.*)

descriptive linguistics   a type of *linguistic* study characterized by describing and categorizing the elements of a specific language rather than analyzing language to learn about language in general. (See *prescriptive grammar* and *proscriptive grammar.* There is no "prescriptive linguistics" counterpart to this kind of *linguistics.*)

descriptivist   a *linguist* or *grammarian* who produces or, more frequently, favors *descriptive grammars.* (As opposed to a *prescriptivist.*)

desiderative mood   a *mood* of a *sentence* or *clause* that *conveys* desire, want, or need on the part of the speaker. (This *mood* uses special *forms* in Greek, and it is *periphrastic* in English. Compare to *benedictive mood.* The example *sentences* are in the *desiderative mood.*)   □ *Let this one suffice; there are no more.*   □ *May you rot in hell!*   □ *May all good things come your way.*   □ *Let luck be on my side for once!*

det   the usual abbreviation of *determiner.*

determinative   See *demonstrative (adjective).*

determinative clause   See *restrictive clause.*

determinative mood   a *mood* that *conveys* consent or acceptance on the part of the speaker. (The example *sentences* are in the *determinative mood.*)   □ *Have no fear, I will pay you back everything I owe you.*   □ *I will see to it immediately.*   □ *I will do as you ask.*   □ *If that's the way you want it, that's the way it will be.*

determinative possessive pronoun AND **possessive adjective** a *personal* pronoun that functions as a *determiner.* (Specifically: *my, your, his, her, its, our,* and *their.* Compare to *independent possessive (pronoun).* The examples show *determinative possessive pronouns* in bold print.) □ *Please put* **my** *packages on the table.* □ *Where are* **our** *tickets?* □ *I keep* **my** *books in this cabinet.* □ *Is this* **your** *desk?*

determiner AND **det** a *function word* that appears before a *nominal* and distinguishes the *referent* of the *nominal* from other *nominals.* (The typical determiners are *a, an, one, no, the, this, that,* and *any.* The examples show *determiners* in bold print.) □ **This** *one is better than* **that** *one.* □ **The** *old woman does not want* **any** *soup.* □ *There was* **no** *porter in* **the** *station.* □ *Do you have* **a** *match?*

diagram **1.** to *parse* a *sentence* into its *constituents* and draw a *sentence diagram* showing the *constituents* of the *sentence.* **2.** See *tree diagram.* **3.** See *(sentence) diagram.*

diminutive suffix in English, a *form* indicating small size, endearment, or condescension. (These are *-en, -ette, -ie, -kin, -let, -ling, -ock, -y.* Some of these *suffixes,* such as *-kin, -ling, -ock,* are seen typically in fixed combinations, such as *munchkin, gosling,* and *hillock.* Examples of these *suffixes* are in bold print in the examples.) □ *Come here, Billy.* □ *The little lamb***kins** *cavorted in the meadow.* □ *A few rabbits sat near the hill***ock.** □ *Take this steak***let** *away and bring me a hunk of meat!* □ *We took a room***ette** *on the train and were quite comfortable.*

direct discourse AND **direct speech** an instance where the speech of someone is reported in the *form* of a *direct quotation.* (Compare to *indirect discourse.* See comments on the *form* at the individual *sentences* at *direct quotation.* The example *sentences* show *direct discourse.*) □ *Polly said,* **"I hope you will be able to get the kind of job that you are looking for."** □ *John asked,* **"Will we ever finish this project?"** □ **"Oh, my severe goodness gracious!"** *spouted Robert.* □ **"Piffle!"** *was the reply.*

direct object a *nominal* that names the "receiver" of the *action of the verb;* an *object(ive) complement.* (Compare to *indirect object.*

The examples show *direct objects* in bold print.) ☐ *The dog ate some of the salad.* ☐ *The lady bought **an apartment building.*** ☐ *The doctor placed **the minister** in the hospital.* ☐ *Henceforth, the students will do **their own work.***

direct quotation   a *sentence* constructed to indicate that certain *words* are quoted directly from the speech or writing of someone. (The actual quotation is the *direct object* of a *transitive verb.* A comma follows the *transitive verb,* the first *word* of the quoted *sentence* is capitalized, and the entire quoted *sentence* is enclosed in quotation marks. The examples are all *direct quotations.*) ☐ *Bob asked, "What kept you so long?"* ☐ *"It is really very good of you to come over on a night like this," said Bill in a consoling voice.* ☐ *"Jee whillikers!" cried Martha.* ☐ *"Nope!" I said, "Nope!"*

direct speech   See *direct discourse.*

disconjunctive   the combination *and/or.* (Typically used in legal documents. The examples show *disconjunctives* in bold print.) ☐ *The party of the first part agrees never to enter **and/or** inhabit the premises again.* ☐ *The insurance company requires the form to be signed by the victim **and/or** a lawyer.* ☐ *The parents **and/or** grandparents, if living, shall receive one-half of the estate.* ☐ *Your car **and/or** other vehicle cannot remain on the street overnight.*

discontinuous constituent   a *constituent* or *grammatical structure* that straddles another *constituent.* (The members of the *discontinuous constituent* are shown in bold print in the examples.) ☐ ***Will** he **be able to do** it?* ☐ ***Had** he only **given** more thought to it, things would have gone better.* ☐ ***Are** you ever **going**?* ☐ ***Do I have to call** all these different people **up**?*

discourse   an *utterance* or a sequence of meaningful and semantically connected *utterances.*

disjunct   an *adverbial* or a *sentence adverb* that reveals the speaker's evaluation of the *propositions* or implications of the rest of the *sentence.* (Compare to *adjunct* and *conjunct.* The examples show *disjuncts* in bold print.) ☐ ***Hopefully,*** *I will be there right on the dot.* ☐ ***Of course*** *I will!* ☐ ***Gleefully,*** *she swept into the room.* ☐ ***Naturally,*** *I would expect full payment in advance.*

disjunctive (conjunction) AND **adversative conjunction** a *conjunction* that *introduces* an opposition or contrast between the elements it joins. (These are *although, but, either, except, lest, neither, nor, notwithstanding, or, provided, save, than, though, unless, whereas, whether, yet.* The examples show *disjunctive conjunctions* in bold print.) ☐ *I would,* ***but*** *I just can't.* ☐ *Is this a great cat* ***or*** *what?* ☐ *Did she scream* ***or*** *did she keep her head?* ☐ *They held on tightly,* ***yet*** *they fell.*

ditransitive verb a *verb* that can take two *objects,* a *direct object* and an *indirect object.* (Compare to *monotransitive verb.* In the examples, the "|" separates the two *objects.*) ☐ *My grandfather bought* ***me*** *|* ***an ice cream cone.*** ☐ *Will you please give* ***her*** *|* ***the money you owe her?*** ☐ *Please pass* ***your brother*** *|* ***the salt.*** ☐ *The company presented the* ***retiree*** *|* ***a gold watch.*** ☐ *He gave* ***it*** *to* ***me.***

divided infinitive See *split infinitive.*

double adverb a sequence of two *adverbs* that end in *-ly.* (Viewed as bad style. The examples show *double adverbs* in bold print.) ☐ **You need to get this done* ***really quickly.*** ☐ **This kind of thing is* ***scarcely likely*** *to help matters.* ☐ **You will* ***really likely*** *be the winner.*

double comparative AND **redundant comparative** the use of both the *-er marker* of the *comparative degree* and the *periphrastic more.* (Viewed as an error. The examples show *double comparatives* in bold print.) ☐ **Now, this is* ***more better.*** ☐ **This one is the* ***more fresher*** *of the two.* ☐ **See if you can find a pair that is* ***more smaller.***

double genitive AND **double possessive** a *construction* consisting of the *possessive form* of a *noun* or *pronoun* and a *genitive construction* formed with *of.* (This *construction* is usually used with *animate nouns* and their corresponding *pronouns.* A *word* following the *of* cannot show possession if the *word* is not made possessive. The *double genitive* is not an error.) ☐ *Can you help with this spe-*

*cial problem **of mine**?* ☐ *If you don't keep that ugly dog **of yours** out of my yard, I'm going to call the police.* ☐ *We set out to buy an expensive painting, but had to settle for the painting **of Fred's** that we had turned our noses up at for so long.* ☐ *This jacket **of yours** always seems to find its way to the floor.*

double negative   two *negative words* in the same *clause.* (Common in various English dialects. In some languages the *double negative* is used for emphasis. Each of the following examples illustrates a *double negative* and is incorrect in *standard English,* as indicated by the *. [See *starred form.*] This is *nonstandard* and considered *substandard* by many people. A corrected *sentence* follows.) ☐ **I **don't** want **no** more trouble out of you. / I don't want any more trouble out of you.* ☐ **She **isn't no** friend of mine. / She isn't any friend of mine.* ☐ **I **can't** see **nothing** in this fog. / I can't see anything in this fog.* ☐ **She **doesn't** do **none** of those things. / She doesn't do any of those things.*

double passive   a sequence of two *verbs* in the *passive voice.* (Viewed as an error. The examples show the *verbs* making up the *double passive* in bold print.) ☐ **We were **expected** to have been finished at noon.* ☐ **He had been **hoped** to be **located** by now.* ☐ **Earlier, it had been **thought** that to have been **born** with a caul was a bad omen.* ☐ **It was **said** to have been **perverse.***

double plural   a *noun* bearing two indications of plurality. (Typically both a *regular* and an *irregular* indication. An error. The examples show *words* exhibiting the *double plural* in bold print.) ☐ **These **geeses** have made an awful mess.* ☐ **Good evening, ladies and **gentlemens**.* ☐ **No one could deserve more **kudoses** than Walter.* ☐ **We sent letters to all the **medias**.*

double possessive   See *double genitive.*

double superlative AND **redundant superlative**   the use of both the *-est* marker of the *superlative degree* and the *periphrastic most.* (Viewed as an error. The examples show *double superlatives* in bold print as *starred forms.*) ☐ **We saw the horse that had run **most fastest**.* ☐ **This is the **most freshest** fish I ever ate.* ☐ **What is the **most ugliest** car you can name?*

dual number   the *grammatical number* that indicates two. (As opposed to *singular* or *plural*. In English, this number survives in the *word both*, which serves to *modify* or restrict the *plural* to mean only two. Also, *between* can be said to show *dual number* when compared to *among*. This *grammatical category* is used more extensively in some other languages. True *dual number* does not exist in modern English. The examples show in bold print the *dual number* that survives in English.)   ☐ ***Both*** *women just stood there and stared.*   ☐ *Give some to* ***both*** *of them.*   ☐ *I have to do* ***both*** *things before dawn.*   ☐ ***Both*** *cats refused to eat.*   ☐ ***Both*** *my sister and I were starved, but we divided the tomato equally* ***between*** *us.*

dubitive mood   a *mood* used to *convey* doubt on the part of the speaker. (The examples are *sentences* in the *dubitive mood*.)   ☐ *She may have been here earlier.*   ☐ *I don't know. She might have been here.*   ☐ *Maybe Jane was here.*   ☐ *It is entirely possible that she was here then.*

dummy subject   See *expletive*.

durative (aspect) AND **durative (tense), continuous (aspect), continuous (tense)**   a *verb aspect* indicating that the *action of the verb* continues unbroken for some time. (This is the same *construction* as the *imperfective (aspect)*, but this term emphasizes the ongoing nature of the action rather than the incomplete nature of the action. Compare to *iterative aspect*, where the *action of the verb* is repeated. Many different elements may contribute to the understanding of the *durative aspect*. See also *continuous (aspect), imperfect(ive) (aspect)*. See comments on naming *aspects* at the entry for *aspect*. The example *sentences* are in the *durative aspect*.)   ☐ *I am* ***thinking***. *Please don't bother me.*   ☐ *He is* ***working*** *on it right now.*   ☐ *She* ***has been doing*** *it for ages.*   ☐ *We won't be* ***thinking*** *about it until we have had supper.*

durative (tense)   See the previous entry.

E

edited English AND **school English, standard English** the type of English taught in schools; English used and written with conscious attention paid to the previously existing standardized patterns of literate English usage. (These terms are as close to the notion of *good English* as one can get. The term *good English* is not accepted by some scholars because it allows one to infer the existence of "inferior English." See remarks at *substandard English*. *Standard English* implies that there is only one fixed and widely agreed upon variety of English that is accessible to everyone.)

effected object AND **object of result** an *object* of a *transitive verb* that achieves its form or is produced or created by the *action of the verb*. (This refers to achieving its present state, not changing its state. Compare to *affected object*. The examples show *effected objects* in bold print.) □ *John set out to build a* ***house.*** □ *If Sally had had all the ingredients, she would have baked a* ***cake.*** □ *Someday I will write a* ***book.*** □ *This is a fine* ***mess*** *you've made!*

effective aspect a type of *point-action aspect* that focuses on the final point of an act, the exact time at which the act was completed. (This is usually evident in the *verb* itself. See comments on naming *aspects* at the entry for *aspect*. The examples show *verbs* in the *effective aspect* in bold print.) □ *We* ***ate*** *all our roast beef.* □ *The cat just now* ***died.*** □ *She* ***completed*** *her recital with four songs by Strauss.* □ *They all* ***arrived*** *at once.*

ellipsis a deleted part of an *utterance*, the meaning of which is understood and can be recovered from the remainder of the sentence. (These examples show *ellipsis*. The "deleted" part of the *utterance* is shown in square brackets.) □ *I can do it as well as you [can do it]*. □ *Jane didn't do it as well as she ought [to have done it]*. □ *Joe works as hard as Steve [works]*.

elliptical construction a *grammatically well-formed construction* where *constituents* are omitted, but *understood*. (Most of these omissions are governed by *grammatical rules*. See *understood*. In the examples, the omitted elements are restored in bold print and placed in square brackets.) □ *When [it becomes] convenient, please close the window*. □ *Fred is taller than Bob [is tall]*. □ *Joe works as hard as Steve [works]*. □ *What are you doing? [I am doing] The dishes*.

elliptical genitive the use of the s-*genitive form* of the possessor alone to indicate the possessor and the entity possessed. (The possessed entity that has been omitted is shown in brackets. This often refers to someone's home.) □ *Where is Tom? At his aunt's [house] again*. □ *I'll be at Ted's [house], if you want me*. □ *Is this my orange or Jane's [orange]?* □ *My bucket is empty, so I will see if there is any in Bob's [bucket]*.

embed to insert one *constituent* inside another. (See the following entry.)

embedded sentence a *sentence* within a *sentence*. (Note that the introductory *relative pronoun* is not part of the *embedded sentence*. The examples show *embedded sentences* in bold print.) □ *The news that **Walter had finally found a job** came as a complete surprise*. □ *No one was very pleased to learn how **the officer had taken away all the people at the party***. □ *When **we found out what had really been going on all those years**, we were totally disgusted*. □ *More than anything, the boys wanted to hear that **there were still some tickets available for the hockey game***.

emotive meaning See *connotation*.

[emphatic]   See *emphatic appositive, emphatic auxiliary, emphatic mood, emphatic pronoun, emphatic tense, past emphatic, present emphatic.*

emphatic appositive   See *intensive (personal) pronoun.*

emphatic auxiliary AND **intensive *do***   the *verb do* inflected for the *present tense* or *past tense*, used to make some other *tense* or *aspect emphatic.* (See *emphatic mood.* The examples show the emphatic auxiliary in bold print.) ☐ *He **did** walk, I tell you.* ☐ *He **did** not walk!* ☐ *Oh, yes. In spite of the accident, he **does** walk.* ☐ ***Do** please sit down.* ☐ *I **do** hope you'll come again soon.* ☐ *He really **did** sell all his stock.*

emphatic mood AND **emphatic tense**   a *mood* of a *sentence* or *clause* that makes the *verb* emphatic by the addition of the *emphatic auxiliary do.* (This *construction* is not a *tense* as defined here, nor is it an *aspect.* The examples show various *tense* and *aspect constructions* made emphatic through the use of the *emphatic auxiliary.*) ☐ *He did walk, I tell you.* ☐ *He did not walk!* ☐ *Oh, yes. In spite of the accident, he does walk.* ☐ *Do please sit down.* ☐ *I do hope you'll come again soon.* ☐ *He really did sell all his stock.*

emphatic pronoun   See *intensive (personal) pronoun.*

emphatic tense   See *emphatic mood.*

empty word   See *expletive.*

enclitic   a *word* that has been included into a preceding or following *word*, forming a type of *compound.* (Generally, it loses its stress in the process. The examples show *enclitics* in bold print.) ☐ *This is no job for a layman.* ☐ *The chairman is late.* ☐ *I cannot agree.*

ending   See *(word) ending.*

epexegetical genitive   See *definitive genitive.*

epicene gender   See *common gender.*

equational verb   See *linking verb.*

equative (sentence)   a *sentence* where the *subject* and its *nominal complement* have the same *referent.* (The examples show the main *noun* of the *subject* and the *nominal complement* in bold print.) ☐ **Mr. Stone** *is* **the man** *I talked to on the train.* ☐ **Chuckles** *was* **the clown** *on the Bob Brown Show.* ☐ **That television set** *seems to be* **the one** *that fell off my nightstand.* ☐ **Ethelred** *is* **king**.

essential clause   See *restrictive clause.*

essive (case)   a *grammatical case* denoting a state of being at a place. (From the Latin word *esse*, "to be." There is no true *essive case* in English, and the meanings associated with the *essive case* are *conveyed* by the *prepositions in, at, on,* etc. See a brief description of the role of *case* in English at *case* and *case grammar.* The examples show the way English expresses the *semantic* relationship *conveyed* by this *case.*) ☐ *He is* **at this place.** ☐ *We found a lot of them* **in the kitchen.** ☐ *The chair that is* **in the corner** *is mine.*

ethical genitive   the *pronoun your* used to mean "the, the one, the one at hand, etc." (Viewed as poor style or rural. See also *impersonal pronoun.* The examples show *ethical genitives* in bold print.) ☐ **Now, this one is* **your** *hybrid variety.* ☐ **Take* **your** *typical everyday kid at school, for instance.* ☐ **He is* **your** *hyperactive kind of guy.* ☐ **I showed her my book and said, "This is* **your** *typical textbook."*

exclamation   See *exclamatory sentence.*

exclamatory interrogation   an *interrogative sentence* used with the *force* of an *exclamatory sentence.* (There is a problem in deciding which punctuation to use. In the examples, although the form of the *sentence* is that of an *interrogative sentence*, the exclamation point is used, because it is the only way to show in writing that the *sentence* is an *exclamatory interrogation.*) ☐ *How dare you!* ☐ *Can you believe it!* ☐ *Are you kidding!* ☐ *Would you believe!*

exclamatory sentence AND **exclamation**   a *sentence* that is to be uttered as a forceful ejaculation. (Almost any *phrase* or *word*—that would not otherwise be a *complete sentence*—can be made an *exclamatory sentence* in writing by the use of capitalization and an exclamation point. See also *exclamatory interrogation.* The ex-

amples are all *exclamatory sentences.*) □ *No!* □ *Yes!* □ *Your father's mustache!* □ *Give it to me!* □ *Well!* □ *So it goes!* □ *Of all the nerve!*

exclusive (person)   a *grammatical person* of the *first person plural* that excludes the person being addressed. (There is no special *form* for the *exclusive (person)* in English. It can be identified only by the context of the *utterance*. The *exclusive pronouns* that represent the *exclusive (person)* are in bold print.) □ *Putting his arm around Sally, Tom said, "**We**'re going to the mall and you're not!"* □ *We have discussed your proposal and have determined that you are entirely correct.* □ *Oh, Tom! Come join us.*

exclusive pronoun   a *pronoun* in the *first person plural* that excludes the person being addressed; a type of *we* that excludes the person being addressed. (There is not a special *form* of *pronoun* with this meaning in English. The examples show the way the *exclusive pronoun* is implied in English.) □ *We miss seeing you at **our** house.* □ *I'm glad you came to visit **our** neighborhood for the day.* □ *Please come over to **our** side.* □ *Our neighbor put his cows into **our** field.*

existential sentence   a *sentence* that asserts that an entity exists, is located in a particular place, or possesses certain properties. (The examples are all *existential sentences.*) □ *There is a small cottage just by the foot of the road.* □ *My car has power seats.* □ *The university has an enormous library.* □ *There are four squirrels in the tree.*

experiencer case   the *dative case* in *case grammar;* the *case* of the *indirect object.* (In *case grammar,* the element in the *experiencer case* actually "experiences" the *action of the verb.* A *constituent* in the *experiencer case* is a *direct object* in *traditional grammar,* when the verb is active. See a brief description of the role of *case* in English at *case* and *case grammar.* The examples show the way English expresses the *semantic* relationship *conveyed* by this *case.* The *words* in bold print can be said to be in the *experiencer case.*) □ *We convinced **Ralph** to do it.* □ *The **cat** was terrorized by the dog.* □ *Someone brought **the candy** to Jane.* □ *Who appointed **Bob** manager?* □ *The **watch** was repaired by the jeweler.*

expletive AND **dummy subject, empty word, impersonal pronoun, prop word** 1. *It* or *there* as a dummy or filler *subject,* that precedes the actual *subject,* which appears after the *verb.* (Sometimes there appears to be no real *subject* at all. See also *anticipatory subject.* The examples show *expletives* in bold print.) □ *There were twenty of them altogether.* □ *It looks as if it will snow today.* □ *It's going to rain.* □ *There is nothing left for us to do.* 2. an exclamation, especially one that seems to fill space. (The examples show *expletives* in bold print.) □ *Wow! I like it!* □ *That's the one. Yes!* □ *Stupendous! The movie was superb.* □ *Wow! This is great!* 3. an oath or *exclamation* that fills a space in a *sentence.* (A euphemistic term for a vulgar oath. The examples show *expletives* in bold print.) □ *Oh, poop!* □ *Where is that damn jerk?* □ *Damn! I want it now! Damn!* □ *Oh, hell! It's too late.*

extraposition the shifting of an element of an *utterance* to a position other than its usual location for the purpose of emphasis. (The examples show first the normal *utterance,* and then an instance of *extraposition.* See also *anticipatory subject* and *postponed subject.*) □ *Leaving the country without a passport can be dangerous. / It can be dangerous leaving the country without a passport.* □ *My face was red as I explained the embarrassing situation. / Red was my face as I explained the embarrassing situation.* □ *I expect my clocks to keep good time. / To keep good time is what I expect from my clocks.*

F

factitive case AND **result(ative) case**   the *grammatical case* of an entity that has been created by the *action of the verb*. (From *case grammar*. Typical with the *verbs make, create, build, erect, fabricate, manufacture*, etc. *Verbs* that describe doing things to entities that already exist do not take the *factitive case*. See *effected object*. See a brief description of the role of *case* in English at *case* and *case grammar*. The examples show the way English expresses the semantic relationship conveyed by this case.)   □ *Fred spent all afternoon making **a cake**.*   □ *The workers erected **the building** in no time at all.*   □ *What **a mess** you have made here!*   □ *Martin walked right in and built **a little house** out of playing cards.*

factitive verb   a *verb* of calling, choosing, naming, or thinking that takes both a *direct object* and a *complement*. (The *complement* is a *predicate objective* or an *object* in the *factitive case*. See *objective complement*. Typical *factitive verbs* are *elect, make, call, name, appoint*, and *choose*. The examples show *factitive verbs* in bold print.)   □ *We **elected** her our representative.*   □ *The entire city council **appointed** Sally mayor.*   □ *We **called** Sally Babs just to irritate her.*   □ *Bob and Bill **appointed** Jane their representative in court.*

factive verb   a *verb* that takes a *complement* in the *form* of a *clause* wherein the meaning of the *verb* implies that the speaker believes that what is stated in the *clause* is a fact. (For instance, *know, agree, realize, regret, remember, deplore*, etc. The examples show *factive verbs* in bold print.)   □ *I **regret** that she has managed to escape.*   □ *Tom* *finally **realized** that his dog had left for good.* ☐ *I didn't **remember** how I did it.* ☐ *The mayor **deplored** the way the council ignored the problem.*

feminine (gender)   **1.** the *grammatical subclass* of the *noun* found in languages where all *nouns* are *inflected* for *gender,* such as *feminine, neuter,* and *masculine.* (In such languages, the actual biological sex or lack thereof is often irrelevant. This kind of *feminine gender* is found in English only in a few loan *words.* The examples show *words* having *feminine gender* in bold print.) ☐ *Sue is an **alumna** of Yale.* ☐ ***"Die Frau** Ohne Schatten" is a famous opera.* ☐ *We saw it performed at **La Scala.*** **2.** a special idiomatic category found in a few English *nouns,* such as the names of ships and wheeled vehicles. (The pronouns in the examples demonstrate this use.) ☐ ***She**'s a fine vessel, isn't **she?*** ☐ *Head **her** into the pier!* ☐ *Give **her** some more gas and maybe **she**'ll start this time.* **3.** a reflection in some *nouns* and *pronouns* of actual female biological sex. In English certain *nouns* are associated with the female biological sex and *pronouns* in the *feminine gender* are used to refer to these *nouns.* (See *natural gender.* Compare to *arbitrary gender.* The examples show *words* in the *feminine gender.*) ☐ *Martha will become the **executrix** of the estate.* ☐ ***She** put **her** hat on.* ☐ *The **princess** put **her** hat on.* ☐ *His **mother** was looking for him.*

final preposition   a *preposition* used to end a *sentence.* (Viewed by some as an error in *edited English.* See *proscriptive grammar.* The examples show *final prepositions* in bold print.) ☐ **A preposition is indeed a bad thing to end a sentence **with.*** ☐ **Why am I the one who always has to clean the house **up?*** ☐ **This wine is to die **for.*** ☐ **Are you going to come **with?***

finite verb   a *verb* used in a *form* that exhibits *number, tense, aspect,* etc.; the *form* of the *verb* that can take *inflection.* (As opposed to a *nonfinite verb,* a derived *form* of a *verb.* Definitions of *finite verb* often refer to the "restrictions" or "limitations" of *tense, number,* and *person* as a way of incorporating the notion of "finiteness." *Finite verbs* are simply *verbs* behaving as *verbs.*) ☐ *The cheetah **ran** ever so fast.* ☐ *The door **opened** slowly.* ☐ *We all **wanted** to go with her.* ☐ *The children **spilled** their glasses of milk, one by one, until we ran out of paper towels.*

first person   the *grammatical person* that refers to the speaker or writer; the *grammatical person* expressed as *I* or *we*. (*Pronouns* display *person* in either of two *numbers, singular* and *plural*. The *verbs be, have,* and *do* have unique *first person forms* that must agree with a *first person subject*. See also *second person, third person*. The examples show *pronouns* in the *first person* in bold print.) ☐ *Am **I** happy!* ☐ ***Our** trees died.* ☐ ***I** shall sing.* ☐ ***We** are all happy that **my** mother made cookies for **us**.*

fixed phrase   a multiword *lexeme;* a frequently used *phrase*— sometimes including *noun compounds*—whose meaning may not be the *semantic* sum of its component *words;* an *idiomatic phrase;* a *collocation*. (This is a fairly loose concept that cannot be rigidly defined. The examples show *fixed phrases* in bold print.) ☐ ***Be that as it may**, you must continue.* ☐ *And now, **without further ado**, I give you Wallace J. Ott!* ☐ *Bob really wanted to go home and **hit the hay**.* ☐ *Please **call me up** when you get a chance.*

flat adjective   See *adjectival (noun)*.

flat adverb   an *adverb* derived from an *adjective* without the addition of the *-ly suffix*. (Some *adverbs* occur both as *flat adverbs* and non*flat adverbs*, such as *slow*. The term means essentially "lacking" *inflection*. Compare to the use of *flat* in *flat verb*. The examples show *flat adverbs* in bold print.) ☐ *This is a **fast** horse. It can really go **fast**.* ☐ *What a **slow** day! Things are going so **slow**!* ☐ *That kite is very **high** in the sky. It is really flying **high**.* ☐ *Are you ready for an **early** day? I just love to get up **early**.*

flat infinitive   See *bare infinitive*.

flat verb   See *bare infinitive*.

force   the function or qualities [of some other *constituent*]. (Often collocated with *have*. Part of the *metalanguage* of *traditional grammar*. Does not refer to the exercise of power, but to one *class* of *constituent* behaving as some other *constituent*.)

form   **1.** a *word;* a *string* of sounds comprising a *word* or *affix;* a *morpheme* (or *allomorph*). (A generic term for referring to individual *morphemes, words,* or *compounds*. Compare to *part*. See also *base (form), bound form, combining form, form class, form word, formal, formative, free form, pro-form, simple form (of the verb), s-form, starred form.)* **2.** a specific variant of a *word* or *morpheme.*

formal   **1.** having to do with the *forms* of a language. (This is the sense used in this dictionary unless indicated otherwise.) **2.** of a highly structured social significance or order. (As in *formal* English, or the *formal* use of English.)

formative   **1.** an *inflection.* **2.** a *morpheme;* a *form* from which larger *constituents* can be formed. (The "|" separates the *formatives* in the examples.) □   *The | old|er | cow|s | lumber|ed | slow|ly | home.* □   *We | will | leave | when|ever | we | want.* □   *The | juggl|er|s | travel|ed | with | many | circus|es.* □   *Continue | to | try | wall|paper|ing.*

form class   a functional category embracing a number of *words* whose *grammatical* behavior is identical. (*Function words* do not fall into this category. A replacement for the traditional *part of speech* designation for *nouns, verbs, adverbs,* and *adjectives.* Far more limited than *part of speech* or *word class.*)

form word   a *grammar word* or a *function word.* (*Form word* contrasts directly with *content word.* See the comments and list of near synonyms at *function word.* Of course, all *words* are *forms. Form words* include *verbal auxiliaries, pronouns, conjunctions, prepositions, modal auxiliaries, articles,* etc. The examples show *form words* in bold print.) □   **The** oldest **of the** octogenarians kept cats **and** dogs. □   **Her** uncle put seven **of them under the** couch. □   **These** words contrast **with** content words. □   Fred kept sitting **there,** smiling **and** singing.

fragmentary sentence   See *sentence fragment.*

frame   a *sentence pattern* designed to determine the similarity in *grammatical* behavior of a series of *words* or *forms.* (See the discussion and examples at *slot and filler grammar.*)

free construction   See *absolute phrase.*

free form   a *form* that is able to stand alone without having to be accompanied by some other *form;* a *form* that is not an *affix* or a *combining form.* (Here, this definition is interpreted to include any *form* that can serve as a one-word answer to a question, other than an *either/or* question. That is, "Did you say *a* or *the?*" would not qualify *a* or *the* as a *free form.* The question "What was his general age?" would qualify the answer *old,* however. The opposite of *bound form.* In the examples, the *free forms* are shown in bold print.) □ *The **old man climbed** the stairs.* □ *The **little girl** fled.* □ *We **do** not **like your manager.*** □ ***Sam did nothing** to **help.***

free variation   the condition of two or more variant *forms* that alternate freely and unpredictably. (A great deal of *free variation* is *phonological,* but there are also some instances relating to *grammar.* The examples show pairs of *sentences* that are in *free variation.* The *constituents* that vary are shown in bold print.) □ *Did you **call** the dentist **up?** / Did you **call up** the dentist?* □ ***Can** you do it? / **Are** you **able** to do it?* □ *I **learnt** the whole thing. / I **learned** the whole thing.* □ *Heavens, I **shrank** my shirt. / Heavens, I **shrunk** my shirt.*

full verb   See *lexical verb.*

functional change   See *conversion.*

functional shift   See *conversion.*

function class   a view of the classification of *constituents* on the basis of function rather than form. (Some *nouns* such as *house* are viewed as members of the *form class noun* because they take the *inflections* that *nouns* take. Other *forms,* for instance *gerunds,* are not usually considered to be members of the *noun form class,* but they are members of the *function class* "noun," because they function as *nouns.*)

function group   a group of *function words,* such as *pronouns, prepositions, determiners, auxiliaries, intensifiers, conjunctions, interjections,* etc.

function verb   a *verbal auxiliary* used without the *head* of its *verb phrase* and its associated *complements,* when the said *head* has occurred before in the same or a previous *utterance.* (The omitted *head* is shown in square brackets in the examples. The *function* *verb* is in bold print. See also *elliptical construction*.) □ *He asked me to go, and I know I should [go].* □ *I will do it only if I must [do it].* □ *Sally really didn't want to just come right out and say it, but she felt as if she ought to [come right out and say it].* □ *I certainly wouldn't want you to drop everything you are doing and come over here to look at this mess, but you may have to [drop everything you are doing and come over here to look at this mess].*

function word AND **form word, functor, grammar word, grammatical word, relating word, structural word** an *affix, auxiliary, conjunction, modal, preposition,* or some other *indeclinable word,* usually indicating a *grammatical* meaning or function. (*Function words* do not normally take *affixes.* There is no contrast in the *classes* of *words* or *particles* referred to by the main entry head and the alternate entry heads. Any differences are due to a particular point of view being emphasized by the speaker or to differences in schools of *grammatical* thought. See *particle.* Compare to *content word.* The examples illustrate a wide variety of *function words.*) □ *Hit it for me.* □ *I would like another cup of coffee.* □ *Put it there, please.* □ *The cat crept slowly out from under the bed.* □ *If we had been able to drive, we would have been able to get here much earlier.*

functor the same as *form word.* (See the comments and list of near synonyms at *function word.*)

fused sentence two or more *sentences* run together with no punctuation or *conjunctions* separating them. (The examples, being incorrect, are given as *starred forms.*) □ **We just love to be here we can smell the fresh sea air.* □ **Fred and Mary left Bill arrived.* □ **Bob fell over the stone he was not hurt.* □ **Keep on trying do not give up.*

future continuous (aspect) See *future progressive (aspect).*

future perfect aspect See *future perfect (tense).*

future perfect continuous (aspect) See the following entry.

future perfect progressive (aspect) AND **future perfect continuous (aspect)** an *aspect* of the *verb* indicating that an activity that will be progressing in the future will continue to happen up to some point in the future. (This aspect is formed with *have* in *future time* plus the *past participle* of *be*, plus a *verb* with an *-ing* suffix. See comments on naming *aspects* at the entry for *aspect*. The examples show *verb phrases* in the *future perfect progressive aspect* in bold print.) ☐ *I **will have been looking** for you by then.* ☐ *When they realize they are sunburnt, they **will have been riding** their bikes for too long.* ☐ *By the time you first hear them, the frogs **will have been croaking** since dawn.* ☐ *When we return, our weeds **will have been growing** like wildfire for a month.*

future perfect (tense) AND **future perfect aspect** a *verbal aspect* that asserts that the *action of the verb* will be completed by a time that is in the future relative to the time of *utterance*. (It is formed by *will* (or *shall*), plus *have*, plus the *past participle*. See comments on naming *aspects* at the entry for *aspect*. The examples show *verb phrases* in the *future perfect tense* in bold print.) ☐ *I **will have gone** by noon.* ☐ *Our ship **will have come in** by the time we retire.* ☐ *Bob **will have met up** with Jane by noon.* ☐ *Don't worry. Nothing **will have happened** by then.*

future progressive (aspect) AND **future continuous (aspect)** an aspect formed with *be* showing *future time* plus the *present participle* of another *verb* indicating that the *action of the verb* will be happening at a time in the future. (Semantically, this aspect *conveys the meaning that at a future point in time, an action will be incomplete, in progress, or developing. See comments on naming *aspects* at the entry for *aspect*. The examples show *verb phrases* in the *future progressive aspect* in bold print.) ☐ *When we are in Bermuda, Sally **will be shopping** the whole time.* ☐ *I **will be sweeping up** this mess forever.* ☐ *You **will be taking** these pills for the rest of your life.* ☐ *The cats **will be catching** all the mice that run out of the burning barn.* ☐ *It **will be raining** by then.*

future (tense) a *tense* that indicates that an action is to be begun or completed at some future time; *future time*. (If *tense* is a category of *verb inflection*, there is no *future tense* in English because there is no *inflection* of the *verb* in the *future tense*. There is instead a category called *future time*. From another point of view, the *fu-*

ture tense, or *future time*, is indicated by a *periphrastic future tense* in English. This uses *auxiliaries, present* and *past tense forms,* and *adverbs of time* to denote *future tense.* In the examples, the device used to indicate *future tense* or *future time* is shown in bold print.) □ *I **shall** sing.* □ *He **will** buy a cake.* □ *She **will** have done it by then.* □ *The new term begins **tomorrow.*** □ ***Will** we be dancing there?* □ *My ship comes in **at noon.***

future time AND **futurity**   a term for the English system of expressing what is called *future tense* in some other languages. (See comments at *future (tense)* above and at *periphrastic future tense.* The examples express *future time* without using what is recognized as a *tense marker.* The *phrase* that indicates *future time* is in bold print.) □ *They are set to take possession of the apartment **tomorrow.*** □ *He leaves **on Wednesday.*** □ *Finish **by noon** and you can leave.*

futurity   See the previous entry.

G

[gender]   See *arbitrary gender, common gender, epicene gender, feminine (gender), (grammatical) gender, masculine (gender), natural gender, neuter (gender).*

generate   to produce or create *sentences* through the rules of a *generative grammar.*

generative grammar   generally, a type of *grammar* that produces or creates *sentences* through a sequence of *rules* and in doing so assigns a *syntactic* description to each *sentence.* (This refers to the form of the *grammar,* rather than to a specific grammar. *Generative grammars* are of great theoretical value but are not practical as *pedagogical grammars.* See also *transformational generative grammar.*)

generative-transformational grammar   See *transformational-generative grammar.*

generic noun   a *noun* used to indicate a general category of entities rather than a specific entity or just any entity. (The *plural, articles,* or *determiners* indicate that a *noun* is generic. There is no special *form* for a *generic noun.* The examples show *generic nouns* in bold print.)   □ ***The leopard*** *shall lie down with* ***the lamb.***   □ ***All men*** *must die.*   □ ***The otter*** *is very playful.*   □ ***Otters*** *are very playful.*   □ ***The dog*** *is man's best friend.*   □ ***Cleanliness*** *is a virtue.*

genitive   having to do with the *genitive (case)*; having to do with possession or possessors. (See *absolute genitive, adverbial genitive,* *definitive genitive, descriptive genitive, elliptical genitive, epexegetical genitive, ethical genitive, genitive of attribute, genitive of kind, genitive of measure, genitive of origin, genitive of source, Norman genitive, objective genitive, of-genitive, partitive genitive, possessive genitive, predicate genitive, Saxon genitive, s-genitive, subjective genitive.*)

genitive (case) AND **possessive case**   a structural indication of a broad class of *grammatical* and *semantic* relationships usually characterized as possession or ownership. (Ultimately from Greek *genos,* "a class" through mistranslation. In terms of *form,* this is indicated in English by a *possessive pronoun* standing for the owner, by the *-'s suffix* attached to the owner, or by placing the *preposition of* before the owner. Since, in some instances, the *genitive* is indicated by the addition of a *suffix*—in the manner of true *cases*—the use of the term *genitive case* is common. There are various *semantic subclasses* of the *genitive case.* See the list at *genitive.* See *absolute genitive, adverbial genitive, descriptive genitive, genitive of attribute, genitive of measure, genitive of origin, objective genitive, partitive genitive, possessive genitive, subjective genitive.* See examples of these varieties of the *genitive case* at their own entries. See also *common case, possessive.* See a brief description of the role of *case* in English at *case* and *case grammar.*)

genitive of attribute AND **classifying genitive, descriptive genitive**   a *semantic subclass* of the *genitive case* used to describe a *construction* consisting of a possessor and a quality or attribute that applies to that possessor. (In the examples, the first *utterance* shows the *modifier* as a *predicate adjective,* and the second *utterance* shows the *modifier* as a *genitive of attribute* in bold print. The quality or attribute is also shown in bold print.) □ *Frank is* **stubborn.** / ***Frank's stubbornness*** *embarrassed us all.* □ *You are* **diligent.** / *Without* **your diligence** *this whole matter would have lapsed.* □ *They are* **inquisitive.** / *Please ask them to keep* **their inquisitiveness** *to themselves.* □ *The manuscript is* **authentic.** / *The* **manuscript's authenticity** *has yet to be proven.*

genitive of kind   an s-*genitive* form that tells what kind, as opposed to possession. (The examples show *genitives of kind* in bold print.)

☐ *I would like to purchase a pair of* **children's** *shoes.* ☐ *How much should I expect to pay for* **men's** *gloves?* ☐ *They made some kind of dish using a* **cow's** *stomach.* ☐ *The king fanned himself with an* **elephant's** *tail.*

genitive of measure   the *genitive case form* used to express amount of time, distance, quantity, or value. (A *semantic subclass* of the *genitive case*. The examples show *genitives of measure* in bold print.) ☐ *After* **ten years'** *absence, she finally returned.* ☐ *After an* **absence of ten years,** *she finally returned.* ☐ *They took a* **journey of seven miles** *on foot.* ☐ *I haven't seen her in* **donkey's years.**

genitive of origin AND **genitive of source**   a *semantic subclass* of the *genitive case* used to describe a *construction* consisting of the object of a *transitive verb* possessed by the *subject* of the *verb.* (Each example shows a *sentence* followed by a derived *genitive of origin.*) ☐ *Frank built a lovely house. /* **Frank's house** *turned out to be quite unsafe.* ☐ *Sally wrote an exciting book about elves and monsters. /* **Her book** *was panned by the critics, who found it dull and puerile.* ☐ *Francine baked a cake that contained an enormous amount of sugar, cream, and butter. / As unhealthy as it was,* **her cake** *was the best I have ever eaten.* ☐ *Jane composed an ode and recited it before the queen. /* **Jane's ode** *failed to amuse the queen.*

genitive of source   See the previous entry.

gerund AND **participial noun**   a *verb* ending in *-ing* that functions as a *noun* or *nominal;* a *verbal* made from a *present participle* functioning as a *nominal.* (This is analogous to a Latin *form. Gerund* emphasizes *form,* while *participial noun* emphasizes function. See also *gerundial adjective, predicate gerund.* The examples show *gerunds* in bold print.) ☐ *That constant* **ringing** *drives me crazy.* ☐ *I am tired of your* **bickering.** ☐ **Swimming** *is her favorite sport.* ☐ **Fishing** *for catfish is boring to most people I know.* ☐ **Trying** *and* **succeeding** *are two different things.*

gerundial adjective   a *gerund* functioning as an *adjective.* (The examples show *gerundial adjectives* in bold print.) ☐ **Flying** *birds* *are among nature's most elegant sights.* □ *I love the sound of **running** water.* □ *Please turn off that **dripping** faucet.* □ *He just stood there and let the **smoking** gun fall to the floor.*

gerund phrase   a *gerund* and its associated *modifiers,* all of which function as a *nominal.* (Complete *gerund phrases* are in bold print in the examples.) □ *I am tired of **your constant bickering**.* □ ***The old man's snoring** is loud.* □ ***Your trying** and **my succeeding** are two entirely different things.* □ ***Fixing up broken-down and worn-out old clocks** is my hobby.*

good English   English that follows the *traditional grammar rules*; *edited English.* (See comments under *edited English.*)

govern   [for a *grammatical constituent*] to influence some other *grammatical constituent,* usually by determining the choice of *inflection* on the other *constituent.* (See *government.*)

government   the apparent "influence" of one *form* over another *form* in the same *clause* or *sentence;* one *form's* "causing" another *form* to acquire a particular *inflection.* (The result of *government* is *agreement* or *concord.* In the examples the first *form* in bold print exhibits *government* of the second *form* in bold print.) □ *Please give me **four apples**.* □ ***She runs** extremely fast.* □ ***They have** not yet gone.* □ ***Roger** put **his** own hat on.*

gradability   a *semantic* characteristic of an *adjective* or an *adverb* that is a member of a series. (Such as with *warm* in the series *cold, tepid, warm, hot, scalding,* where all five *words, cold, tepid, warm, hot, scalding,* are *gradable.* The concept includes, but is broader than, the concept of *comparative (degree).* See also *superlative (degree), comparative (degree).* The examples show *gradable words* in bold print.) □ *I prefer my soup **hot** rather than just **warm**.* □ *They felt that the child was **smarter** than he acted, and was certainly not **stupid**.* □ *Put the **big** one inside the **smaller** one.* □ *This pool is **shallow**, and that one is **deep**.*

gradable   pertaining to a *grammatical form* that can exhibit *gradability.*

gradable adjective   an *adjective* that exhibits *gradability.*

gradable adverb   an *adverb* that exhibits *gradability.*

gradable pair   a pair of *words* with opposing meanings that exhibit *gradability.* (Such pairs are not exclusive opposites—there are grades of difference. Such *words* are *hot, warm; hot, cold; hot, blazing.* The examples show *gradable pairs* in bold print.)   ☐   *If you think this is **hot** now, you won't believe how much **hotter** it gets in August.*   ☐   *Well, I think I am **well-to-do**, but I'm certainly not **rich**.*   ☐   *This one is **red**, but I would like one just a little bit **redder**.*   ☐   *This coffee is only **lukewarm** and I prefer my coffee **blazing**.*   ☐   *Have we gone **far** enough, or should we go **farther**?*

grammar   1. the instructions that are assumed to be resident in the human brain that allow creating and interpreting *sentences.* (This kind of *grammar* is learned by the developing child. It has nothing to do with the *rules* of *pedagogical grammar.* It is more like an ability or competence with a particular language. Presumably, each speaker has one *grammar* of this type for each language known. The description of the knowledge associated with this kind of *grammar* is a major goal of modern *linguistics.*) 2. a model, analog, or statement of the knowledge and abilities described in sense 1; a modern, written *linguistic* description of the *linguistic* knowledge resident in the brains of the speakers of a given language. (Such a *grammar* must be able to account for everything the speaker can do with language—create and understand an indefinite number of *sentences* and make judgments as to the *grammaticality* of *sentences.* No complete or satisfactory *grammar* of this type has yet been produced.) 3. a *pedagogical grammar* of the type used in the schools; a partial set of *grammatical* rules, as in a *prescriptive grammar* or a *proscriptive grammar.* (This type of *grammar* does not necessarily have any descriptive goals of its own. Its goals are related to literacy training and language standardization. The details of the *grammar* used for pedagogical purposes may be derived from or influenced by the descriptive work described in sense 2. See also *case grammar, descriptive grammar, generative grammar, generative-transformational grammar, grammar word, pedagogical grammar, phrase-structure grammar, prescriptive grammar, proscriptive grammar, reference grammar, slot* *and filler grammar, traditional grammar, transformational grammar, transformational-generative grammar.)*

grammarian someone who specializes in *grammar;* someone who writes *grammars.*

grammar word a *word* or *particle* without *lexical meaning,* used to indicate *tense, aspect,* and all other *grammatical relationships.* (This term emphasizes the difference between indicators of *grammatical function* and *content words.* See the comments and list of near synonyms at *function word.* The *grammar* words appear in bold print in the examples.) □ ***Please** do **it** quickly **or not at all.*** □ *Keep **your** car **to the** right side **of the** road.* □ ***The** ostrich does **not** stick **its** head **into** the sand.* □ ***There** are **no** penguins **in** Alaska.*

grammatical **1.** having to do with *grammar.* (See the term used in the entries that follow.) **2.** *grammatically well-formed;* in keeping with *grammatical* rules; accounted for by a *grammar* or by the intuition of a competent speaker of the language being examined. (Essentially, this means "correct." In part, the term is a reaction against the terms *correct* or *right.* For some people, *utterances* can be *grammatical* even if they make no sense, or if they are not true, as long as the *utterances* in question conform to *grammatical rules.* Compare to *ungrammatical.* All the following *utterances* are *grammatical,* but they are not necessarily logical or sensible.) □ *Put it there, chum.* □ *Seven badgers fled into the night.* □ *Suddenly, the green sea rose up and came down on the little kitten.* □ *Colorless green ideas sleep furiously.*

(grammatical) agreement AND **concord** a correspondence or mutual dependency between two or more *forms* involving some *grammatical* characteristic or *grammatical category.* (A *third person singular subject* and its *present tense verb* must agree. *Nouns* and *adjective numerals* must agree in *number.* Compare to *government.* The *constituents* that are in *grammatical agreement* are shown in bold print in the examples.) □ ***He** runs a record shop.* □ *The **man** who lives next door raises dogs.* □ ***Three** ducks swam into view.* □ ***All** cats have soft fur.*

grammatical ambiguity   the property of a *phrase, clause,* or *sentence* that has two or more distinct meanings that are not due solely to *lexical ambiguity.* (Compare to *lexical ambiguity,* which operates only on the *word* level, and *sentential ambiguity,* which operates on the *sentence* level. The *sentence* "Spending money pleases me" displays *grammatical ambiguity* because there are two interpretations: "I am pleased by the act of spending money" and "Money [that can be spent] pleases me." *Constituents* exhibiting *grammatical ambiguity* are in bold print.) □ *Flying planes can be dangerous.* □ *She sat out **drinking in the moonlight**.* □ *The turkey is **ready to eat**.* □ ***Spending money** pleases me.*

grammatical category   a designation of *grammatical* type, *class, subclass, part of speech, word class,* or *form class.*

grammatical function   the function of a *constituent* or an *inflection* in the context of an *utterance.* (From one point of view, a *form* classified as a *preposition* may have a number of different *grammatical functions.*)

(grammatical) gender   a property of eight English *pronouns* and some *nouns* indicating, in general, either the sex of the creatures signified or the sexlessness of the things signified. (The *pronouns* displaying *gender* are *he, she, it, his, her, its, hers,* and *him.* The feminine *forms, she, her, hers* are reserved for female *antecedents* and boats or ships. Traditionally, the *forms he, his, him* are used with male *antecedents* and when the sex of the *antecedent* is clearly not solely female, undetermined, or irrelevant. Currently, for this latter instance, there is considerable substitution of *they, them, their,* and *theirs* for *he, him,* and *his*—despite the *number* violation—to make it impossible to construe the use of the *masculine gender* as exclusively male. The *phrase he or she* is also used in the last instance. The *neuter gender* is used for things, animals of undetermined sex, and, rarely, for human babies of undetermined sex. See also *feminine (gender), masculine (gender), neuter (gender).* *Pronouns* exhibiting *grammatical gender* are in bold print in the examples.) □ ***He** put **his** hands in **his** pockets and went on **his** way.* □ ***She** found a cute little dog and put **her** hat on **its** head.* □ *It's **hers**, not **his**.* □ ***He** put **her** hat on **his** head and **she, his** on **hers**.*

grammaticality 1. the quality of being *grammatically well-formed* or *grammatically ill-formed.* 2. the measure of how *grammatically well-formed* or how *grammatically ill-formed* an *utterance* or *constituent* is.

grammatically ill-formed not following *grammatical rules;* not conforming to the *rules* of a *grammar; grammatically* incorrect. (The opposite of *grammatical* or *grammatically well-formed.*)

grammatically well-formed AND **grammatical** following *grammatical rules;* conforming to the *rules* of a *grammar; grammatically* correct. (In *grammar,* particularly the kinds of *grammar* that language scientists concern themselves with, the notion of "correctness" is expressed by *grammatically well-formed.* This contrasts with notions of "complete thoughts," "logic," or "truth." The opposite is *grammatically ill-formed.* The rather technical concept embodied in *grammatically well-formed* does not include the notions of appropriateness, logic, or good style that might be thought of as part of correctness. See also *sentence, sentence fragment,* and *well-formed.* The following *utterances* are *grammatically well-formed,* but they are not all logical, sensible, or true.) □ *We sold all the computers in one second.* □ *Grass is blue.* □ *The bird flew deep into the water and gobbled up a few tadpoles.* □ *I thought to myself, "I really want to go out and get a . . . , well, I forgot."* □ *Wilted fish grind square bubbles.*

grammatical meaning the meanings of *affixes, particles,* and *function words.* (Compare to *lexical meaning.* The *words* in bold print have *grammatical meaning* rather than *lexical meaning.*) □ ***The old man sat under the*** *tree smoking.* □ *Stick **this** package **down there under the** chair.* □ ***You just** made **that up**!* □ ***What** kinds **of** cheeses are **you** expecting **to** find **up there**?*

(grammatical) number the indication of *one* or *more than one* in the *inflection* and *agreement* system of a language. (English has two *grammatical numbers: singular,* indicating *just one,* and *plural,* indicating *more than one.* See also *dual number.* They are evident in the *pronouns.* This has nothing to do with the numbers used in counting. See *cardinal numeral* and *ordinal numeral*. See also *count noun*. The examples show *singular* and *plural forms* in bold print.) □ *Did you want one* **hamburger** *or two of* **them?** □ **They** *did not seem to care a* **bit.** □ **We** *fled with* **our** *lives.* □ **Mice** *were everywhere* **we** *looked.*

(grammatical) person   a *grammatical* quality of *nominals* that indicates the relationship of the speaker or writer to the rest of the *sentence*. (*First person* refers to the speaker or the speaker's group [*I, me, we, us, my, mine, our, ours*]. *Second person* refers to whomever is being spoken to [*you, your, yours*]. *Third person* refers to the entity being spoken about [*he, him, his, she, her, hers, it, its, they, them, their, theirs*]. Other *forms*, such as *verbs*, may be *inflected* to agree with the *person* of a *subject*. In English, *grammatical person* is evident in the *personal pronoun* system. English *verbs* are *inflected* to agree with *third person* singular subjects. Other *verb inflections* reflect *number*. In the examples, *words* having *grammatical person* are in bold print.) □ **I** *am talking to* **you** *about* **her.** □ **My** *cat is ignoring* **you.** □ **They** *came home at last.* □ *Is this one* **yours?**

grammatical relationship   the linkage between the *constituents* of an *utterance* that can be said to be determined by *grammatical rules;* a pattern of *government, agreement,* or *word order* observable between the *constituents* of a *sentence* as indicated by *inflection* or *function words.*

grammatical subclass   a grouping together of *constituents* exhibiting similar *grammatical* behavior. (*Grammatical subclasses* cannot be identified satisfactorily by meaning. Compare to *semantic subclass*.)

grammatical subject AND **apparent subject**   the *subject* of a *transitive verb* or *object* of a *passive transitive verb*. (As opposed to the *logical subject*. The *grammatical subject* is shown in bold print in the examples.) □ **The cows** *expended a lot of energy traveling to the pasture.* □ **One of the older men** *was injured by the flying glass.* □ **Money** *talks.* □ **The entire farm and all the equipment** *was bought by* a consortium of big-city investors.

grammatical word   a *function word*. (Has nothing to do with the judgment of *grammatically well-formed vs grammatically ill-formed.*)

H

habitual action   See the following entry.

habitual aspect AND **habitual action**   an *aspect* of the *verb* that shows the repetition of an action. (The notion of *habitual aspect* is evident in the *past tense*, expressed with *used to*. *Adverbs* also help convey this notion. Otherwise, there is no unique *marker* of this aspect. See comments on naming *aspects* at the entry for *aspect*. The *marker* of *habitual aspect* is shown in bold print in the examples.)   □   *We **used to** play there all the time.*   □   *They don't now, but they **used to**.*   □   *Jane's father **used to** run a little cafe on North Main Street.*   □   *They still do it as they **used to**.*   □   *Bob **sees** the peridontist twice a week.*   □   *Tom **flees** whenever he **sees** me coming.*

hanging participle   See *dangling participle*.

having the force of   See *force*.

head clause   See *main clause*.

head(word)   the main or central *word* of a *phrase* or *compound*; the central or core element of a *phrase*: the *verb* in a *verb phrase*, the main *noun* in a *noun phrase*, the *adjective* in an *adjective phrase*, etc. (The examples show the *headwords* of various *phrases* in bold print.)   □   *The bird**house** became very busy early in the spring.*   □   *We prefer the gentle rolling **hills** of Kentucky to the deathly flat **plains** of Illinois.*   □   *The accident was very **serious** indeed.*   □   *I really wish you had **thought** of that earlier.*

helping verb   See *auxiliary verb*.

historical present   a *present tense* used in a narrative in place of the *past tense* to encourage a listener to experience the events told about as if they were happening at the time of the narration. (Regarded as *colloquial English* or even *nonstandard English* in certain settings or with certain speakers. Not normally used in writing. The examples show *verbs* in the *historical present* in bold print.) □ *Then this guy **comes** in and **says** to me, "Hey, dude!"* □ *Fred **walks** into the room and **turns** on the light.* □ *She **says** to me, "Bag it!" and I just **walk** away.* □ *Even as a child, he **keeps** to himself.*

hortative   See *cohortative mood.*

hypotaxis   the connecting of a *dependent clause* to a *main clause* by the use of a *subordinating conjunction.* (Compare to *parataxis.* The examples show *subordinating conjunctions* in bold print.) □ *We profited **because** we invested wisely.* □ ***Although** we invested nothing, we profited handsomely.* □ *She left **so that** we could take her place.* □ *Dorothy always knew **when** Mickey was on vacation.* □ *I will gladly do it **unless** you want to.* □ *Harriet goes fishing every Saturday **unless** there is reason not to.*

I

idiom a pattern or *construction* whose meaning is not predictable from the meanings of the individual *words*. (Sometimes *phrasal verbs* are included in this category, because in constructing *utterances* containing *phrasal verbs,* the selection of the proper *preposition* is *idiomatic,* sense 1. In the examples, the part of the *utterance* that is an *idiom* is in bold print.) □ *It's time to* **hit the hay.** □ *By smiling at the wrong time, he* **gave himself away.** □ *I will do it* **when the time is ripe.** □ *That broccoli* **went right through me.**

idiomatic **1.** peculiar to a specific language; peculiar to a certain variety of a language; peculiar to a specific language *construction.* (For instance, in American English, to "knock someone up" means to impregnate, and in British English, it means to rouse someone by knocking on the door.) **2.** pertaining to a *construction* that is not capable of regular, normal, or predictable *semantic* interpretation; pertaining to a *construction* that has a nonliteral *semantic* interpretation. (The examples contain *idiomatic* expressions in bold print.) □ *Well, I guess it's about time to* **hit the hay.** □ *I have* **half a mind** *to tell him what I really think.* □ *Do it now!* **Strike while the iron is hot!** □ *That last thing you said seems to* **ring a bell.** *Now I think I remember the name you wanted.*

illative (case) a *grammatical case* denoting direction into or toward. (Ultimately from the Latin word *latus,* "carried" when used as a participle of *inferre* "to infer." There is no true *illative case* in English, and the meaning associated with the *illative case* is *conveyed* by the *prepositions to, toward, at, into,* etc. See a brief description of the role of *case* in English at *case* and *case grammar.* The examples show the way English expresses the *semantic* relationship *conveyed* by this *case.*) □ *Shall we walk **to the store?*** □ *The woman moved slowly **toward the door.*** □ *They all went **into the little room.***

illative conjunction   a *conjunction* that leads or carries one from a premise to a conclusion. (These are *accordingly, consequently, hence, then, therefore, wherefore.* The examples show *illative conjunctions* in bold print.) □ *The council has ordered it; **consequently** it will be done.* □ *He brought all the right instruments; **hence** the operation will begin.* □ *You have committed a grave crime; **accordingly** you will be punished.* □ *You are the one; **therefore** you must come with me.*

ill-formed   not *grammatically well-formed;* not *well-formed.*

immediate constituents   [in a hierarchical set of *constituents*] the next lower level of *constituents.* (The lowest level of *structure* has no *immediate constituents* and is called an *ultimate constituent.* The term is from *structural linguistics.*)

imperative mode   See the following entry.

imperative (mood) AND **imperative mode**   the meaning or intent of the *verb* in an *imperative sentence;* a *verb* in a *sentence* that gives an order or a command. (The term *imperative mood* focuses on the *verb,* while the term *imperative sentence* focuses on the entire *sentence.* In these examples, the *verb* in bold print is in the *imperative mood.*) □ ***Close*** *the door!* □ *Come on, **hit** that ball!* □ ***Drop*** *dead!* □ ***Stop*** *that silly laugh, if you please!* □ *No! No! **Take** it away!*

imperative sentence   a *sentence* expressing a command, request, or encouragement, often ending with an exclamation mark. (Such a *sentence* is usually addressed to a specific person, and the *you* that represents that person is absent and said to be *understood.* It must be noted that not all the examples are synonymous to identical *sentences* that include the so-called *understood* form. "You please close the door!" may not even be *grammatical*. Compare to *exclamatory sentence*. The examples are all *imperative sentences*.) □ *Go home!* □ *Come on, hit that ball!* □ *Please close the door!* □ *Take it away instantly!*

imperfect   See the following entry.

imperfect(ive) (aspect) AND **imperfect(ive) (tense)**   a *verb construction* consisting of an *auxiliary* and a *verb* in the *progressive aspect*, indicating that the *action of the verb* continues with no indication of terminating. (In the term *progressive aspect*, the focus is on the continuity of the *action of the verb*. In the term *imperfect(ive) (aspect)*, the focus is on the fact that at a specific time, the *action of the verb* is determined not to be completed or terminated. See also *continuous (aspect), durative (aspect)*. See comments on naming *aspects* at the entry for *aspect*. The examples show *verb phrases* in the *imperfect aspect* in bold print.) □ *He* **was running** *when last I saw him.* □ *She* **will be sailing** *before the day is out.* □ *Even tomorrow, the engine* **will** *still* **be running**. □ *They cannot still* **be eating!**

imperfect(ive) (tense)   See the previous entry.

impersonal pronoun   1. See *expletive*, sense 1. 2. the *pronoun you* meaning "everyone" or "one" and the use of *your* meaning "the." (See also *ethical genitive, indefinite pronoun*. The examples show *impersonal pronouns* in bold print.) □ **You** *always have to put this little thing right in here, or it won't work.* □ *First take* **your** *butter and eggs and mix them in* **your** *bowl.* □ *In order to graduate,* **you** *have to take seven courses from this list.* □ *Now, reach down and turn on* **your** *radio.*

impersonal verb   a *semantic subclass* of the *verb*, indicating a state of weather or the earth's position relative to the sun, that takes the *subject it*. (It is more likely the use of the *verb* than a particular *subclass* that is represented by this term. *Verbs* used in this way can include *darken, lighten, brighten, rain, snow, blow, grow, get, become, turn*, etc. The examples show *impersonal verbs* in bold print.) □

*When it **rains**, it **pours**.* ☐ *It's **snowing** out.* ☐ *I believe I heard it* ***thunder***. ☐ *It's **getting** dark earlier these days.*

inactive voice   See *passive voice*.

inanimate noun   a *semantic subclass* of *nouns* containing the names of things that cannot move and things that are not or never were alive. (Compare to *animate noun*. The examples show *inanimate nouns* in bold print.) ☐ ***Stones** are found in great **numbers** in Montana.* ☐ *The **sand** was too hot to walk on.* ☐ *The **corpse** lay still except for the jostling of the **wagon**.* ☐ *Please put the **bowl** on the **table**.*

inceptive verb   See the following entry.

inchoative verb AND **inceptive verb**   a *semantic subclass* of *verbs* that indicate the beginning or onset of an action. (See also *ingressive aspect*. The examples show *inchoative verbs* in bold print.) ☐ *The cup **broke** into a dozen pieces.* ☐ *The aged cow finally **died**.* ☐ *The apple **fell** from the tree.* ☐ *The cattle somehow **opened** the gate by themselves.*

indeclinable word AND **invariable word**   a *word* whose *form* is invariant; a *word* not subject to *formal* changes. (This includes *affixes* and *particles*. The *indeclinable words* are in bold print in the examples.) ☐ *We profit**ed** because we invest**ed** wise**ly**.* ☐ ***Although** we invest**ed** **nothing**, we profit**ed** handsome**ly**.* ☐ *She left **so that** we could take her place.* ☐ *Dorothy **always** knew **when** Mickey was **on** vacation.* ☐ *I will glad**ly** do it **unless** you want **to**.*

indefinite adjective   an *indefinite pronoun* used to *modify* a *noun*. (These are *both, each, either, neither,* and *some*. The examples show *indefinite adjectives* in bold print.) ☐ ***Each** fish was cooked and served with a little bit of lemon.* ☐ ***Neither** child was pleased with the event.* ☐ ***Either** one is fine with me.* ☐ *Give some to **each** person.*

indefinite article AND **nonspecific determiner**   the *particles a* and *an*. (They are used when not referring to specific things or people. Compare to *definite article*. The examples show *indefinite articles* in bold print.) ☐ *Please peel me **a** grape.* ☐ ***An** apple **a** day keeps the doctor away.* ☐ *Put **an** X next to the one that you just read.* ☐ *Please give me **a** pear, just any pear, but not the one with **a** bruise on it.*

indefinite pronoun   a *pronoun* that does not refer to a specific person or thing; a *pronoun* whose *antecedent* is unknown. (The following may be used as *indefinite pronouns: all, any, anybody, anyone, anything, both, each, either, everybody, everyone, everything, few, many, more, most, much, neither, nobody, none, no one, nothing, one, other, others, several, some, somebody, someone, something, whatever, whoever.* These *pronouns* contrast to *personal pronouns, reflexive pronouns, possessive pronouns,* and *demonstrative pronouns.* See also *collective pronoun.* The examples show *indefinite pronouns* in bold print.) ☐ *Is **anyone** at home?* ☐ ***No one** seemed to know the answer.* ☐ ***Many** will see this as a great honor.* ☐ ***Neither** smiled at us, and soon **both** were glowering fiercely in our direction.* ☐ ***Few** were aware of what was soon to happen.*

(indefinite) quantifier   a *word* or *phrase,* other than a *numeral,* that shows the quantity of a *noun.* (Note that when the *quantifier* is part of a *prepositional phrase,* the *noun* whose quantity is specified is the *object of the preposition,* not the *head* of the *prepositional phrase.* Typically: *few, few of, many, lots of, slews of, hunk of, piece of, ounces of, bushel of, little, several, much, plenty of, loaf of,* etc. The examples show *indefinite quantifiers* in bold print.) ☐ *Give me a **few** radishes, please.* ☐ *And I'll need a **bushel of** acorn squash, too.* ☐ *How about another **hunk of** that cake?* ☐ *The governor presented **several** new ideas.* ☐ *How much is a **loaf of** bread these days?*

independent   pertaining to a *constituent* that can stand on its own without the presence of some other *constituent.* (See *free form.* Compare to *dependent.* See list at *dependent.*)

independent clause   a *clause* that can stand on its own as a *complete sentence.* (Usually used in reference to a *sentence* containing more than one *clause.* Compare to *dependent clause, subordinate clause.* The *independent clause* is shown in bold print in the examples.) ☐ ***It's raining.*** ☐ ***Keep on running!*** ☐ ***I have sev-***

eral books, but none is by James Joyce. □ *When we get there, I'll cook you the finest dinner you've ever had!*

independent possessive (pronoun) AND **absolute genitive, absolute possessive** a *form* of the *possessive pronoun* that functions as a *nominal.* (There are eight such *forms* in English: *mine, ours, yours, his, hers, its, theirs,* and *whose.* These *pronouns* do not stand for a particular person or persons, but for something owned by a particular person or persons. Compare to *determinative possessive pronoun.* The examples show *independent possessive pronouns* in bold print.) □ *Mine has a larger engine than yours.* □ *Hers is the one with the enormous red feather.* □ *We will finish theirs as soon as we can find the time.* □ *Ours is not to reason why.*

indicative mode See the following entry.

indicative (mood) AND **indicative mode** the meaning or intent of the speaker uttering an *indicative sentence;* the state of a *sentence* that advances an assertion or states a fact. (The term *indicative mood* focuses on the *verb,* while the term *indicative sentence* focuses on the entire *sentence.* Compare to *subjunctive mood.* In these examples, the *verb(al) phrase* in bold print is in the *indicative mood.*) □ *She speaks Chinese.* □ *None of us will leave tomorrow.* □ *John is not one to complain.* □ *I will lean this against the wall.*

indicative sentence a *sentence* in the *indicative mood;* a *sentence* that advances an assertion or states a fact; a *sentence* that indicates something. (The same as *declarative sentence.* The examples are all *indicative sentences.*) □ *The corn is green.* □ *London remains the largest city in the U.K.* □ *She speaks Chinese.* □ *I spy a smokestack in the distance.*

indirect discourse AND **indirect quotation, indirect quote, indirect speech, reported speech** speech summarized or paraphrased; speech reported rather than being quoted directly. (Compare to *direct discourse.* A writing style rather than a *grammatical form.* The part of the *sentence* that constitutes *indirect discourse* is in bold print.) ☐ *Polly told me that she hoped I would be able to get the kind of job that I was looking for.* ☐ *John asked whether we would ever finish this project.* ☐ *He said to go home.* ☐ *Nancy said that she had changed Rachel's diaper.*

indirect object AND **object of reference, object of service, remoter object, secondary object**   a *nominal* that names the entity that is affected by the *action of the verb;* a *nominal* that tells to or for whom or what the *action of the verb* is performed. (A type of *complement.* Compare to *direct object.* The examples show *indirect objects* in bold print.) ☐ *I need to give **my dog** a bath.* ☐ *I gave **her** three dollars.* ☐ *Bring it **to me**, please.* ☐ *Please buy **me** an ice cream cone.*

indirect question   a *declarative sentence* that reports a question in the *form* of a *dependent clause.* (There is no question punctuation or intonation with *indirect questions.* In the examples, the *dependent clause* that contains the "question" is in bold print.) ☐ *I wondered **when the train would arrive**.* ☐ *Oliver asked **if he might have some more**.* ☐ *She asked us **if we were satisfied**.* ☐ *Bob sought to learn **what we were doing**.*

indirect quotation   See *indirect discourse.*

indirect quote   See *indirect discourse.*

indirect speech   See *indirect discourse.*

inessive (case)   a *grammatical case* denoting "place in which." (From the Latin word *inesse,* "to be at, in, or on." There is no *inessive case* in English, and the meanings associated with the *inessive case* are *conveyed* by the *prepositions at, behind, in, in back of, on, under, within,* etc. See a brief description of the role of *case* in English at *case* and *case grammar.* The examples show the way English expresses the *semantic* relationship *conveyed* by this *case.*) ☐ *The mayonnaise is **in** the refrigerator, of course.* ☐ *The cat lay **in back of** the chair, plotting.* ☐ *Everyone was **within** the enclosure, waiting to be called.*

infinitive   an unmarked *verb form,* which, when preceded by *to,* functions as a *noun.* (Sometimes, such as after *let, make, dare,* the *to* can be omitted, yielding a *bare infinitive.* The *verb* is "infinite" in the sense that it is not limited by—or marked by—*tense, person,* or *number.* Compare to *finite verb.* See also *bare infinitive, cleft infinitive, divided infinitive, flat infinitive, infinitive clause, infinitive marker, infinitive phrase, object of an infinitive, passive perfect infinitive, passive progressive perfect infinitive, perfect infinitive, predicate infinitive, present infinitive, present perfect infinitive, progressive perfect infinitive, sign of the infinitive, split infinitive, subject of an infinitive,* to-*infinitive.* The examples show various uses of the *form* of the *infinitive.*) □ ***To breathe** is **to be alive.*** □ *He just wanted **to die.*** □ *Are you ready **to go** yet?* □ *I really need **to get** some exercise.*

infinitive clause   a *construction* treated as a *clause* wherein the *subject* is in the *objective case* and the *verb* is an *infinitive* or *infinitive phrase.* (See also *infinitive phrase, object of an infinitive.* In the examples, the *infinitive clause* is in bold print.) □ *We thought **him to be older.*** □ *They ordered **us to leave the boxes on the porch.*** □ *For **Fred to bake all those cookies on such short notice** pleased us.*

infinitive marker AND **infinitive sign, sign of the infinitive**   the *to* that occurs before the *verb* in an *infinitive.*

infinitive phrase   a *phrase* made from an *infinitive* functioning as a *nominal, adjective,* or a *complement.* (It is formed from a *verb* preceded by *to* and includes the *verb's auxiliaries* and *complements.* See also *infinitive clause.* The examples show *infinitive phrases* in bold print.) □ ***To be able to cut down her own Christmas tree** was all she wanted in the whole wide world.* □ *We all wanted **to go.*** □ *The cold wind caused me **to shiver violently.*** □ ***To be honest,** I don't know.* □ *The yellow brick road is the only path **to follow.*** □ *I play **to win.*** □ *Do you really think we ought **to stay here?***

infinitive sign   See *infinitive marker.*

infix   **1.** an *affix* inserted into an otherwise indivisible *word;* a *morpheme* that is inserted into another *morpheme.* (This *form* is rare in English, except in slang and low colloquial speech. Compare to *prefix* and *suffix*. The examples are in *colloquial English* or slang. The *infix* is in bold print.) □ *You are abso-**bloody**-lutely right about that, chum.* □ *I have never seen such a con-**screwing**-sarned stubborn mule.* **2.** an *affix* inserted between two other *morphemes*. (Some language scholars view this as a misunderstanding of *infix*. This results in either a sequence of *suffixes* or, less commonly, a sequence of *prefixes*. The examples show *infixes* in bold print.) □ *Thank you for your **helpfulness**.* □ *Cleanliness is next to godliness.* □ *I live a pretty **citified** life.* □ *Would you be so kind as to direct me to children's wear?*

inflected   exhibiting a *grammatical marker* of some type; having a *grammatical inflection* of some kind.

inflection   **1.** a *grammatical marker*, such as an *affix*, that is used as a signal of a *grammatical property*. (*Inflections* are used to alter the *grammatical form* of *words*. *Inflections* in English are typically *affixes*, but a change in *phonology* is sometimes employed to serve as a *grammatical marker*. Compare to *auxiliary*. The examples show *inflections* in bold print.) □ *We **walked** all the way home!* □ *She **runs** every day to keep fit.* □ *This one is **redder** than that one.* □ *We should have **been** there earlier.* **2.** the use of, or process of adding, *affixes* to other *forms* to indicate a *grammatical* or *syntactic* category or function. (English favors *word order* rather than *inflection*. Compare to the term *derivation*, which is used to refer to a change in *part of speech*.)

ingressive aspect   a type of *point-action aspect* where the meaning focuses on the beginning or inception of an act. (See comments on naming *aspects* at the entry for *aspect*. See also *inchoative verb*. The *verb* that can be said to be in the *ingressive aspect* is in bold print.) □ *The minute he got home he **went** to sleep.* □ *It just **started** to snow.* □ *We **began** the game.* □ *The other shoe **dropped**.*

instructive (case)   a *grammatical case* denoting "by means of." (There is no *formal* indication of the *instructive case* in English, and the meaning associated with this "case" is *conveyed* by the prepositions *by, by means of,* and *via*. See also the following entry.

See a brief description of the role of *case* in English at *case* and *case grammar.* The examples show the way English expresses the *semantic* relationship *conveyed* by this *case*.) □ *She accomplished it by gentle persuasion.* □ *They entered by means of a rear door.* □ *They left via the main entrance.* □ *We will contact you by means of this little signaling device.*

instrumental (case)   a *grammatical case* denoting "through the use of" or "with." (There is no *formal* indication of the *instrumental case* in modern English, and the meaning associated with this *case* is *conveyed* by the *prepositions by, by means of, with.* This is very close to the previous entry. See a brief description of the role of *case* in English at *case* and *case grammar.* The examples show the way English expresses the *semantic* relationship *conveyed* by this *case*.) □ *Can you fix it with that little thing?* □ *She put it together with a screwdriver.* □ *Everything worthwhile is accomplished by hard work and luck.* □ *It is held on by means of glue.*

intensifier AND **intensive**   an *adverb* that increases the *degree* or intensity of certain *adjectives* or *adverbs*. (The examples show *intensifiers* in bold print.) □ *We all got very sick.* □ *The bear is extraordinarily powerful.* □ *I arrived much too late.* □ *All the cowboys were mighty tired.* □ *I am dreadfully sorry.*

intensifying adjective   See *intensive (personal) pronoun.*

intensive   See *intensifier.*

intensive *do*   See *emphatic auxiliary.*

intensive (personal) pronoun AND **emphatic appositive, emphatic pronoun, intensifying adjective**   a *reflexive pronoun* used to emphasize a *personal pronoun* by repeating a reference to the same *grammatical person* that immediately precedes it. (They are *myself, yourself, himself, herself, itself, ourselves, yourselves, themselves.* The examples show *intensive personal pronouns* in bold print.) □ *I myself will see that it is done on time.* □ *Bravo! Even Shakespeare himself could not have put it better.* □ *I'm sorry. You yourself are re-*

sponsible. □ *This was such an important occasion and security was so strict that the queen* **herself** *had to undergo a brief search.*

interjection   an exclamatory or emotive *form* that is inserted or "thrown" into a stream of speech; a *word* or expression often given emotive value in the stream of speech. (These *forms* usually have no meaning other than that of their emotive force. In print, separated *interjections* are usually followed by an exclamation mark, whereas included *interjections* are followed by commas. Typical of such *forms* in literary use: *o, oho, ah, aha, lo, alas.* Numerous *forms* that occur frequently in *colloquial English* conversation are also classified as *interjections: boy, congratulations, good grief, great, groovy, help, hey, hooray, hurry, like, my goodness, never, no, no way, ouch, outstanding, ugh, wow, y'know, yes, yikes.* The examples show *interjections* in bold print.) □ *Oh! I cut my finger!* □ *Oh, you can't be serious.* □ *O, give me a home where the buffalo roam.* □ *I want,* **like,** *a place to live where there are these,* **like,** *big cow things, y'know.*

internal accusative   See *cognate object.*

interrogative   pertaining to the asking of a question. (See *interrogative (adverb), interrogative (pronoun), interrogative sentence, interrogative (word).*)

interrogative (adverb)   a *question word* that *introduces* a question, the answer to which is assumed to be *adverbial* in function. (Typically: *where, why, how, when,* which are *interrogative adverbs* when used to ask a question. The examples show *interrogative adverbs* in bold print.) □ *When do you expect to arrive?* □ *Why do you keep doing that even when I have asked you politely to stop?* □ *How can geese fly so far without resting?* □ *Where will we find a place where we can buy some cough syrup?*

interrogative (pronoun)   a *question word* that *introduces* a question, the answer to which is assumed to be a *nominal.* (Typically: *who, what, which, whom, whose,* and some would include *where.* See also *interrogative adverb.* The examples show *interrogative pro-*

nouns in bold print.) ☐ ***What** do you mean by that?* ☐ ***Who** says?* ☐ ***Whom** did you say you wished to see?* ☐ ***Which** do you want?*

interrogative sentence a *sentence* that asks a question. (An *interrogative sentence* is followed by a question mark in writing and either begins with a *question word* or ends in a rising intonation in speech. The examples are all *interrogative sentences.*) ☐ *Who says?* ☐ *Where did you come from?* ☐ *How can you say that?* ☐ *Did you want just any old book?* ☐ *He's arriving now?*

interrogative (word) AND **question word** an *interrogative (adverb)*, *interrogative (pronoun)*, or any *auxiliary* that serves to mark a *sentence* as a question. (The examples show *interrogative words* in bold print.) ☐ ***When** will you finish?* ☐ ***Why** on earth did you do that?* ☐ ***What**'s going on here?* ☐ ***Did** he really do it?* ☐ ***Have** you any bananas?*

intransitive verb a *verb* with no *direct object*. (See also *active voice, passive voice*. Compare to *transitive verb*. The examples show *intransitive verbs* in bold print.) ☐ *The children **talked** and **giggled** through the movie.* ☐ *Dogs **bite**.* ☐ *The rain **fell** hard.* ☐ *The trees are **dying**.* ☐ *Both of them were **deteriorating** rapidly.* ☐ *What causes things like that to **deteriorate** so quickly?*

introduce [a *constituent* serving] to identify the beginning of some other *constituent*. (This is not really a *grammar* term, but only part of the basic *grammar metalanguage* used in definitions and *rules*.)

invariable word See *indeclinable word*.

inversion an apparent change in *word order* from typical or normal to some other *grammatical* sequence. (The examples show pairs of *sentences*, the second of which is an *inversion* of the first.) ☐ *You are here. / Are you here?* ☐ *He will go. / Will he go?* ☐ *He left running like a deer. / Running like a deer, he left.* ☐ *We have never known such pain. / Never have we known such pain.*

irregular not conforming to the typical or general pattern of behavior for a particular *form class*. (The *starred form* after each example shows what the regular pattern might produce. See more examples at *irregular plural* and *irregular verb*. The *starred forms* are incorrect.) □ *Three* **geese** *waddled across the road.* *gooses □ *This one* **cost** *an arm and a leg.* *costed □ *The speaker lauded him with* **kudos** *over and over.* *kudoses □ *He* **bought** *two of them.* *buyed.

irregular plural   a *plural form* of a *noun* that is formed by some means other than by adding the (spelling) *suffixes -s* or *-es.* (These *plural forms* must be learned individually. Compare to *regular plural.* The examples show *irregular plurals* in bold print.) □ *The* **geese** *ran among the* **oxen,** *causing them to snort with immense displeasure.* □ *The* **children** *were late for school because of the weather.* □ *Get your* **feet** *out of the way!*

irregular verb AND **strong verb**   a *verb* whose *past tense* and *past participle* are formed in some manner other than by just adding the (spelling) *suffixes -ed* or *-en* or their variants. (In the Germanic languages, including English, these *verbs* form their *principal parts* by a change of vowels rather than by adding an *affix.* Compare to *regular verb.* The examples show *irregular verbs* in bold print.) □ *Four of them* **ran** *faster than the others.* □ *He* **broke** *his promise.* □ *The sun* **shone** *brightly on our little crew.* □ *I already* **ate** *my dinner.* □ *The chorus had* **sung** *half the oratorio by the time we arrived.*

iterative aspect   an *aspect* of the *verb* that focuses on a continuing repetition of the same act. (There is no *formal* indicator of this *aspect.* Certain *adverbs* can indicate iteration, however. See comments on naming *aspects* at the entry for *aspect.* The examples show *verbs* that can be said to be in the *iterative aspect.*) □ *She* **talks** *against almost everything.* □ *He sat there and* **giggled** *through the speaker's presentation.* □ *Must you* **tap** *your foot like that?* □ *The child* **fell** *down repeatedly.*

J

joint possession an instance of two or more owners of the same entity. (When the joint owners are expressed by *nouns* [not *pronouns*] in *edited English,* the *possessive marker* is often placed on the last *noun.* In *colloquial English,* the *possessive marker* may appear on each *noun.* When the joint owners are expressed as *pronouns,* the *possessive pronoun* is used in each instance in *edited English.* In *colloquial English,* the *independent possessives mine, yours, his, hers, its, ours,* and *theirs* are often used [except for the final member of the series], and these may be mixed with the other *possessive pronouns: my, your, his, her, our, their.* The examples show the components of *joint possession* in bold print.) □ *We sent the flowers to **Bob, Tim, and Ralph's** apartment.* □ *We are going to **Sally and John's** place for supper.* □ *Is this **her, my, and your** office for the next two weeks?* □ *Is this house both **yours and his?***

K

kernel   See *stem*.

kernel sentence   a basic, simple *sentence pattern*. (In the earliest *forms* of *transformational-generative grammar* the first stage of the *grammar* generated a set of *kernel sentences* that were further acted upon (*conjoined, embedded,* etc.) by *transformational rules* to produce the more-complex *sentences*. This term appears occasionally in *grammar* discussions, usually with the definition given here.)

L

lexeme   the smallest meaning-bearing unit of language that can be distinguished from other meaning-bearing units. (This includes *word roots* and *idioms*. *Inflection* is never part of a *lexeme*. The items in bold print in the examples are *lexemes* that are *verbs*.) ☐ *I had already **eaten** when you **called**.* ☐ *When can we **eat**?* ☐ *We were **eating** fried chicken and country gravy, and did not **wish** to be **interrupted**.* ☐ *I **thought** that the story would have been completely **forgotten** by now.*

lexical   having to do with *words* and their meanings. (See *lexical ambiguity, lexical item, lexical meaning, lexical verb, lexical word, lexicon*.)

lexical ambiguity   the property of a *word* or *compound* that has two or more distinct meanings. (Compare to *grammatical ambiguity* and *sentential ambiguity*. The *constituent(s)* exhibiting *lexical ambiguity* are in bold print.) ☐ *The archer—complaining that her hair was being pulled—had entangled her **bow** in her **bow**.* ☐ *When you said **rock** group, I thought you meant musicians, not a collection of **stones**!* ☐ *I'm going to make that crook **sing** if it's the last thing I do.*

lexical item   a *content word*, as opposed to a *function word* or larger *constituent*.

lexical meaning   **1.** the meanings of *content words:* the meanings of *nouns, verbs, adjectives,* and *adverbs*. (Compare to *grammatical* *meaning*. See also *denotation*.) **2.** the meanings of *words* as compared to the meanings of *sentences*. (Compare to *sentential meaning*.)

lexical verb AND **full verb**   a *verb* that can be used as the only *verb* in a *sentence*, as opposed to an *auxiliary verb*; a *verb* that is a *lexical word* and not a *function word*. (See also *notional verb*. The examples show *lexical verbs* in bold print.) ☐ *Please **keep** your hands to yourself.* ☐ *I would never have been able to **do** this by myself.* ☐ *We are **having** turkey again tonight.* ☐ *I would **jump** for joy if you would **put** it over there.*

lexical word   See *content word*.

lexicon   **1.** a list of *words* and their meanings; a vocabulary; a dictionary. **2.** the *words* and *idioms* peculiar to a particular language; the composite of all the *words* and *idioms* belonging to a particular language. **3.** the part of a *formal grammar* of a language, such as a *transformational-generative grammar*, where the information about *words* is found.

limiting adjective   an *adjective* that points to or selects a specific entity; an *adjective* having the *force* of a *definite article*. (Compare to *descriptive adjective*. The examples show *limiting adjectives* in bold print.) ☐ *He chose **the older** puppy, because he said it smiled at him.* ☐ *This batch is gritty, and I prefer **the smooth** peanut butter we have at home.* ☐ *I want **the red** one, please.* ☐ *Look at that **big** bird over there!*

linguist   a language scientist; a practitioner of *linguistics*.

linguistic   **1.** concerning language and the study of language *structure*. **2.** concerning language *form* or *structure*.

linguistics   the scientific study of language; the study of form, structure, and meaning in language.

linking adverb   See *conjunctive (adverb)*.

linking verb AND **equational verb**   a *verb* that serves to bond a *subject* to its *predicate nominative* or *predicate adjective*, typically, the *verb be*. (Others are *act, appear, become, grow, remain, stay, keep, turn* in contexts where they can be replaced with *seem*, and all the *verbs* that refer to a particular sense: *feel, look, taste, smell, sound.* See also *copula, copulative (conjunction).* The examples show *linking verbs* in bold print.) □ *The lady **is** a clerk.* □ *Our friend **was** wonderful.* □ *After the rain, the day **became** warm and amber in the autumn haze.* □ *He **seemed** happy enough.* □ *Sally always **feels** depressed on Mondays.* □ *This stuff **smells** bad, so I will throw it out.*

locative adverb AND **adverb of place**   a *word* or *phrase* that indicates "in what place"; an *adverb* answering the question *where?* (*Locative adverbs* may follow *forms* of the *copula be*. The examples show *locative adverbs* in bold print.) □ *The dog sleeps **over there**.* □ *The dog's bed is **behind the door**.* □ *Please lay the mat **under the table**.* □ *My Uncle Wallace is **in China**.* □ *He said that he lost the kite **somewhere down the road in a tree**.*

locative (case)   a *grammatical case* denoting "place at which or in which." (Ultimately from the Latin word *locare*, "to place." There is no *formal* indication of the *locative case* in English, and the meaning associated with this *case* is *conveyed* by *structures* called *locative phrases* and *locative adverbs*. See a brief description of the role of *case* in English at *case* and *case grammar*. The examples show the way English expresses the *semantic* relationship *conveyed* by this *case*.) □ *The case for the computer is **in the closet**.* □ *No, it is **over here**.* □ *The man **in the bus** was signaling to us.* □ *Just leave them **here**, thanks.*

locative phrase   a *phrase* indicating place. (Often refers to a *prepositional phrase* that indicates location. This term focuses on the meaning of the *construction* rather than the function as in *locative adverb*. The examples show *locative phrases* in bold print.) □ *Please put it **in the closet**.* □ *The man **by the kitchen table** sang too loud.* □ *Put it **in a bag**, please.* □ *The ferry took us all **across the lake**.*

logical subject   the *author* of the *action of a verb*, as opposed to the *grammatical subject* of a *verb*. (The *logical subject* of a *passive* *transitive verb* is found in the *by phrase*. See *agent* for more examples. These examples show *logical subjects* in bold print.) ☐ ***The dog*** *bit the man.* ☐ *The man was bitten by **the dog**.* ☐ ***She*** *is the meanest person I have ever met.* ☐ *It was Charlie whom **John** struck with the golf ball.*

M

main clause AND **principal clause, head clause**   the primary *clause* in a multiclause *sentence;* the primary *independent clause* in a multiclause *sentence.* (Sometimes referred to as the *clause* expressing the main idea. The examples show *main clauses* in bold print.) □ ***I wanted to sing,*** *but I didn't have the voice for it.* □ *As I stepped on the cat's tail,* ***I prepared myself for a feline complaint.*** □ ***She wanted to keep it,*** *but it wouldn't have been right.*

main verb   the *verb* that is the *headword* in a *verb phrase;* the *lexical verb* in a *verb phrase;* a *verb* that is not being used as an *auxiliary.* (In the examples, the *main verbs* are shown in bold print.) □ *Please* ***put*** *your hands on the table.* □ *I would never have been able to* ***do*** *this by myself.* □ *They will not be able to have* ***given*** *any of this much thought by then.* □ *I would* ***be*** *very happy if you would* ***leave*** *it alone.*

mandative mood   a *mood* that uses a *sentence* in *future time* with the *force* of an *imperative sentence.* (The example *sentences* are in the *mandative mood.*) □ *You will bring me what I ask!* □ *This will be done tomorrow!* □ *You will go at once!* □ *Everyone will do whatever is asked!*

marked   having a *grammatical marker* of some kind; *inflected.*

marker   an indicator of a *grammatical* property, *grammatical category,* or *grammatical relationship,* either an *inflection* or an *auxiliary.*

masculine (gender)   **1.** the *grammatical subclass masculine* found in languages where *nouns* are inflected for *gender*. (For *nouns* in such languages, the actual biological sex or lack thereof is irrelevant. Compare this sense to the first sense of *feminine (gender)*.) **2.** a reflection in some *nouns* and *pronouns* of actual male biological sex. (In English certain *nouns* are associated with males, and *pronouns* in the *masculine gender* are used to refer to these *nouns*. Sometimes, it is the *pronoun* that indicates what the sex of the *referent* actually is. See *natural gender*. The examples show *words* exhibiting *masculine gender* in bold print.) ☐ *He put his coat on his shoulder.* ☐ *Give him his due.* ☐ *The football player hung his coat in his locker.* ☐ *The coach gave the dickens to his players.*

mass noun   See *noncount noun*.

metalanguage   the vocabulary, typical phrascology, and *idiomatic* expressions used in describing or discussing language; language about language. (This dictionary is designed to help understand the *metalanguage* of *grammar* as well as specific *grammar* terms.)

middle voice AND **reflexive voice**   a *voice* wherein the *agent* and the recipient of the action of the verb refer to the same entity. (In some instances, the *middle voice* is shown by a *reflexive verb*. This concept is borrowed from Greek. This definition is the most general one, and many modern *pedagogical grammars* ignore the term. The examples show verbs in the *middle voice*.) ☐ *I pride myself on my humility and sensitivity to others.* ☐ *Stop kidding yourself!* ☐ *I always shave myself, and I have never been shaved by a barber.* ☐ *You will have to serve yourself because the cook is too busy.* ☐ *The door opened.*

misplaced modifier   a *modifier* placed so that it *modifies* the wrong *constituent*. (See also *dangling modifier* and *dangling participle*. There are many different *structures* that are covered by this term. The result of such *constructions* is humor, *grammatical ambiguity*, or nonsense. The examples show the faulty *sentence* as a *starred form* followed by an improved version.) ☐ **She tripped on a log and broke her leg, which must have been six feet long. / She*

*tripped on a log, which **must have been six feet long,** and broke her leg.*
☐ **He answered the embarrassed woman **with a foolish smile.** / **With a foolish smile,** he answered the embarrassed woman.* ☐ **They **almost** finished building all the bridges. / They finished building **almost** all the bridges.* ☐ **Throw Aunt Flo **from the train** a kiss. / Throw Aunt Flo a kiss **from the train.*** ☐ **He thought of taking his own life **often.** / **Often,** he thought of taking his own life.*

modal (auxiliary)   any one of a set of *verbal auxiliaries* indicating necessity, possibility, capability, permission, or obligation. (Specifically: *can, could, would, should, ought, might, may, must, have to,* and *had to.* See comment at *modal verb* and *mood.* The examples show modal auxiliaries in bold print.) ☐ *She **could** have done more and **would** have if the clock hadn't suddenly gone awry.* ☐ *Sue **might have** caught a tiger swallowtail, but her net was damaged.* ☐ *You **ought** to go inside, because you **might** catch cold.* ☐ *You simply **must** do something with this room!* ☐ *We all **had to** be there before noon.*

modality   See *mood.*

modal verb   a type of *verbal auxiliary* that indicates the *mood* or *mode* of the *verb phrase.* (This term refers to the same phenomenon as the *modal (auxiliary).* It is noted, however, that these *forms* do not ever function as *verbs* in English. Typical *modal verbs* are *can, will, shall, may, might, must, ought.* See also *defective verb.* The examples show *modal verbs* in bold print.) ☐ *You simply **must** do it.* ☐ *I know I **ought** to.* ☐ *I **will** try to do it tomorrow.* ☐ *I **may** not bother to inquire again.*

mode   See *mood.*

modifier AND **qualifier**   a *word, phrase,* or *clause* that restricts, limits, or more specifically identifies some other *constituent.* (The terms may or may not include *articles* or *determiners,* depending on the views of the *grammarian* discussing them. See *adjective, adverb.* The examples show *modifiers* in bold print.) ☐ *The **red** barn burned **quickly** to the ground.* ☐ *A student **in my French class** is a **licensed** pilot.* ☐ *Give me a friend **whom I can depend on.*** ☐ *Put **this** thing over there.*

modify   to provide additional information about the *constituent modified*. (This does not refer to a change in *form* of the *constituent modified*. See *modifier*.)

monomorphemic   having only one *morpheme*, as with *bliss, yes, stop, strong*.

monotransitive verb   a *transitive verb* used with only one *object*, a *direct object*. (This may refer to *verbs* that never take more than one *object* and is also used to refer to *verbs* appearing in an *utterance* with only one *object*. Compare to *ditransitive verb*. The examples show *monotransitive verbs* in bold print.) □ *Polly burst the balloon.* □ *Bob refused to kill the fly.* □ *Jane did not have time to paint the bedroom.* □ *Put it over there, please.*

mood AND **modality, mode**   the categories of potentiality, probability, necessity, reality, or obligation *conveyed* in a *clause* or *sentence*. (The *moods* of importance to modern English *grammar* are the *imperative mood*, the *indicative mood*, and the *subjunctive mood*. The term itself is named for a supposed "mood" or frame of mind of the speaker who may express an attitude about the reality, necessity, probability, etc., of what is being said. See various *moods* or *modes* at *apodictive mood, benedictive mood, cohortative mood, conditional (mood), desiderative mood, determinative mood, dubitive mood, emphatic mood, imperative (mood), indicative (mood), mandative mood, necessitative mood, obligative mood, permissive mood, subjunctive (mood)*.)

morpheme   a *word* or part of a *word* that cannot be broken down into smaller, meaningful parts. (In *linguistics*, the *morpheme* is represented phonologically by one or more *allomorphs* that would normally be expressed in *phonological* symbols or in *phonetics*. In the examples, each of the items in bold print consists of a single *morpheme*. The items not in bold print represent two *morphemes*.) □ *He put a small hat on the dog.* □ *I see it.* □ *They crawled away without any more fuss.*

morphology   **1.** the *linguistic* study of *word formation*. **2.** a statement of the analysis of *word formation;* a statement of the *constituents* of a specific *word*.

N

naming word See *content word.*

natural gender biological sex, as opposed to *grammatical gender.*

necessitative mood a *mood* indicating need or necessity through the use of *must* and its *past tense had to*, the *present tense* with *have to,* and the *future tense* with *(will) have to.* (The example *sentences* can be said to be in the *necessitative mood.*) ☐ *This must be done now.* ☐ *We told Jane that she must keep trying.* ☐ *You must see a doctor about that.* ☐ *I know I have to do it.* ☐ *You will have to do something about that.*

negative **1.** a *particle, word,* or *phrase* meaning *no* or *none.* (Other terms concerned with negating are *double negative, negative adverb, negative aspect, negative particle, negative pronoun, negative question, negator.* The examples show various types of negatives.) ☐ *I have **no** oranges, **nor,** indeed, has anyone else.* ☐ *Arthur has **no** such thing.* ☐ *There are **no** more red ones.* ☐ *We have **no** fruit at all.* **2.** a particle, word, or phrase serving as an *adverb* expressing negation or denial. (The examples show *negatives* in bold print.) ☐ *The Chinese do**n't** have enough automobiles.* ☐ *I can**not** believe that there is a global oil shortage.* ☐ *I do **not** do that anymore.* ☐ *We **no longer** go there.*

negative adverb See *negator.*

negative aspect the general meaning of a *verb* that denies a *proposition.* (The opposite of *affirmative aspect.* There is no special as-

110

pect marking in this *construction*. Unlike other *aspects,* this one does not have a time element. See comments on naming *aspects* at the entry for *aspect*. In the examples, the *verb(s)* and the element causing negation are in bold print.) ☐ *I will **not** be there on time.* ☐ *You **are** anything **but** courageous.* ☐ *The elephant **did not uproot** the farmer's crops.* ☐ *We **are no longer able to read** such small print.*

negative particle an *affix* or *indeclinable word* indicating denial or negation. (Typically *no* or *not*. The examples show *negative particles* in bold print.) ☐ *This problem is proving **intractable**.* ☐ *That is **not** desirable.* ☐ *I am **unable** to find what I was looking for.* ☐ *This **isn't** fun anymore.* ☐ *There is **no** such animal.*

negative pronoun an *indefinite pronoun* whose *antecedent* is expressed as *negative* or nonexistent. (Typically: *nobody, no one, none, neither, nothing.* The examples show *negative pronouns* in bold print.) ☐ ***Nobody** went to the concert, and the performers were devastated.* ☐ *I told **no one**!* ☐ *I asked for a lot and received **none**.* ☐ ***None** were saved from the horrendous flood.* ☐ *I put both fried chicken and french fried potatoes on the list, but I ended up with **neither**.* ☐ *I heard a terrible noise in the attic, but when I went up there, I found **nothing**.*

negative question a question (or *interrogative sentence*) that includes a *negative particle*. (Typically, *negative questions* are asked with contractions. The full *forms* may seem literary or stilted unless they are being used for emphasis. The examples show the *words* that signal *negative questions* in bold print.) ☐ ***Haven't** you done your homework?* ☐ ***Have** you **not** done your homework?* ☐ ***Didn't** you enjoy yourself at the party?* ☐ ***Did** you **not** enjoy yourself at the party?* ☐ ***Won't** you please give me a ring the next time you are in town?* ☐ ***Can't** I have some too?*

negator AND **negative adverb** a *form,* other than a *negative particle,* that makes a *sentence negative* to a greater or lesser degree; an *adverb* that gives a *negative* cast to a *sentence*. (These forms are *hardly ever, never, seldom, nothing, neither.* The examples show *negators* in bold print.) ☐ *She **hardly ever** comes to the office gatherings.* ☐ *I **never** said that I did.* ☐ *I really like broccoli, but I* *seldom eat cabbage.* ☐ *After all our preparation, the entire conference came to* **nothing**.

neuter (gender)   a *gender* denoting an entity that is neither *masculine gender* nor *feminine gender,* or which may be either or both. (Evident in English primarily in *pronouns* that have *antecedents* that are neither biologically masculine or feminine. Compare to *common gender.* The examples show *pronouns* having *neuter gender* in bold print.) ☐ *The machines ran as fast as* **they** *could.* ☐ *I picked up a box and put* **it** *on the table.* ☐ *The crystal was already broken when* **it** *was delivered.* ☐ *When you finish with these papers, please put* **them** *in the wastepaper basket.*

nominal   **1.** pertaining to a *word* or *structure* functioning as a *noun.* (Other terms related to this entry are *adnominal, denominal, denominative verb, nominal clause, nominalization, nominalize, pronominal adjective.*) **2.** any *word* or *structure* that functions as a *noun.* Often used in preference to terms such as *noun, pronoun, gerund, noun phrase,* and *infinitive phrase.* (Compare to *substantive,* where the emphasis is on meaning rather than function. The first *nominal* in each example is in bold print.) ☐ ***The endless beating of the drums late into the night*** *annoyed me.* ☐ ***She*** *kept beating the drum late into the night.* ☐ ***To be able to sleep through the night*** *became her only goal.* ☐ ***Finding food*** *was our first task.*

nominal clause   a *dependent clause* functioning as a *nominal.* (See also *noun clause.* The *nominal clause* does not behave exactly like a *noun* in that it does not occur in the *plural,* nor can it take all the *noun's determiners* and *complements.* The examples show *nominal clauses* in bold print.) ☐ *We knew* ***how he did it.*** ☐ *Bill saw* ***that Polly was attended to.*** ☐ *Jerry reiterated* ***what he had said before.*** ☐ ***That Fred kept pigeons*** *is well known.* ☐ ***Who sat here*** *is* ***what I want to know.***

nominalization   the process of changing a *verb, adjective,* or *adverb* into a *nominal.* (See the following entry.)

nominalize   to make a *nominal* from any *part of speech* or *constituent* that is not already a *nominal.* (See also *derivation.* The examples show *words* that have been *nominalized* in bold print.) ☐

*The **runner** tripped over the log.* ☐ *The **tripping** slowed her down.* ☐
*The **poor** have yet to be heard from.* ☐ ***Wellness** is a state of mind.*

nominative **1.** See *nominative (case)* and other terms containing
nominative: *absolute nominative, nominative absolute, nominative (case), predicate nominative.* **2.** a *form* in the *nominative case*; a *nominal*. (The *nominatives* in these examples are in bold print.) ☐ ***Keeping track of expenses** is time-consuming.* ☐ ***She*** *just came in.* ☐ ***The white rhinoceros** is almost extinct now.* ☐ *Jane said she was getting tired of **having to do all the tidying-up for everyone**.*

nominative absolute AND **absolute nominative** a *construction* consisting of a *subject* and a *participle* along with any other parts of the *verb phrase*. (The *construction* serves as a parenthetical comment *modifying* an adjacent *sentence*. The *nominative absolute* is not linked by a *conjunction* to its adjacent *sentence*. Compare to *ablative absolute*. The examples show *nominative absolutes* in bold print.) ☐ ***The lecturer having finished**, Paul left.* ☐ ***The cat having died**, it was buried immediately.* ☐ ***The paint being dry**, he hung the portrait on the wall.* ☐ ***Our ship being tied to its moorings at last**, we disembarked.*

nominative (case) AND **subject(ive) case** an *inflection* indicating a *grammatical subject*; the state of a *constituent* serving as a *grammatical subject* or a *predicate nominative*. (In English, any *nominal* serving as a *grammatical subject* can be said to be in the *nominative case*. Ultimately from the Latin word *nomen*, "name." There is no *formal* indication of the *nominative case* in English, except in the *personal pronouns*. See a brief description of the role of *case* in English at *case* and *case grammar*. The *nouns* and *pronouns* in bold print in the examples are in the *nominative case*.) ☐ ***He** fled.* ☐ *The **mice** ate the cake while the **cat** sat there like a bump on a log.* ☐ ***He** is the **one** of whom **we** spoke.* ☐ ***I** spy it.*

noncount noun AND **mass noun, uncountable noun** a *noun* that does not occur after a *cardinal numeral* or an *article* indicating a particular quantity of the things named by the *noun*. (Typically refers to things that are not in countable units—a mass or continuum—or things that are usually too numerous to count conveniently. Also used for clearly separate entities that are treated as a group or collection. It is the inability to accept a preceding *cardinal numeral* that characterizes the *noncount noun*. Many of the *noncount nouns* also have countable counterparts that refer to a type, class, or species of the *nouns*. For instance: *rices, wheats, champagnes, rouges, waters,* etc. See *count(able) noun* for examples of these *words*. The examples show *noncount nouns* in bold print.) □ *She had* **rouge** *on her cheeks and two cheap plastic bracelets on her wrists.* □ *They drank* **champagne** *to celebrate.* □ *I found some* **rice** *in my pocket.* □ *They say there is some* **lead** *in our drinking water.*

nondefining relative clause See *nonrestrictive relative clause.*

nonessential clause See *nonrestrictive clause.*

nonfinite verb a *verb* that cannot stand as the *main verb* of a *clause;* a *verbal.* (Refers to *verbs* expressed as *infinitives, participles,* and *nominals* derived from *verbs. Nonfinite verbs* or *verbals* function as *parts of speech* other than *verbs* and cannot take *verb inflections.* The examples show *nonfinite verbs* in bold print.) □ *Robert intends* **to return** *to school.* □ *Patricia is* **running** *for office.* □ **Finding** *food became our most immediate concern.* □ *Jake was badly* **beaten** *by the gang of thugs.* □ *The swiftly* **running** *water concealed many sharp and dangerous rocks.*

nonpast (tense) a *verb tense* that can be used to express any time except the *past tense.* (Essentially an alternate term for *present tense* that embraces the various uses of the *present tense* other than to indicate present time. These include the expression of general or eternal truths and expressions of future reference. This term excludes the use of the *present tense* to express past time as with the *historical present.* The *verbs* in bold print in the examples are in the *nonpast tense.*) □ *Grass* **is** *green.* □ *Helium* **is** *a gas.* □ *I* **have** *an appointment in an hour.* □ *She* **leaves** *for Berlin next Wednesday at noon.*

nonrestrictive clause AND **additive clause, descriptive clause, nonessential clause, nondefining relative clause** a *clause* in a *sen-*

tence that is loosely attached semantically to its *main clause* and is not essential to its *main clause; a clause* that adds information but is not intended to specify or select a particular entity. (Such *clauses* are described as parenthetical and nonessential, and can be omitted. They are thus set off, usually by commas, from the rest of the sentence. Compare to *restrictive clause* and *parenthetical clause*. The examples show *nonrestrictive clauses* in bold print.) □ *The old man, **whom we had seen there often**, died in the flood.* □ *Molly—**determined to make herself loved**—floated gracefully into the room.* □ *Sue's father, **who is a doctor**, took me home.* □ *The baseball player, **who ultimately ended up raising chickens for a living**, struck out for the second time in the game.*

nonspecific determiner 1. *adjectives* such as *all, any, many, some,* which do not refer to specific people or things. (The examples show *nonspecific determiners* in bold print.) □ ***Some** people don't care for real chocolate.* □ ***Many** pieces were taken, but **all** the rest were mine.* □ ***All** things are not equally well made.* □ *I would be happy to have **any** cake at all.* 2. See *indefinite article*.

nonstandard English a type of English that deviates systematically from *standard English*. (This term includes everything that the term *substandard English* includes, but has no value judgment.)

Norman genitive See *of-genitive*.

notional verb the *main verb* in a *verb phrase; a content word* that is a *verb*. (This is essentially the same as *main verb*, except that this emphasizes the content or meaning of the *verb* rather than its functions. See also *lexical verb*. The examples show *notional verbs* in bold print.) □ *If this had been **fixed** earlier, we would have been able to **complete** our work on time.* □ *I really ought to have been able to **present** my thoughts without constant interruption.* □ *Ted should have **done** it before this time.* □ *By this time next week all the students will have **left**.*

notional word See *content word*.

noun a *word* that names a person, place, thing, or idea; a *word* that can be inflected for *(grammatical) number* and can come after *adjectives* and *determiners*. (See also *nominal*. See *abstract noun,* *action noun, adjectival (noun), adverbial noun, animate noun, collective noun, common noun, compound (noun), concrete noun, count(able) noun, generic noun, inanimate noun, mass noun, noncount noun, noun adjunct, (noun) class, noun clause, (noun) compound, noun phrase, noun substitute, participial noun, predicate noun, proper noun, uncountable noun, verbal noun.* The examples include *nouns* and *derived forms* functioning as *nouns*.) ☐ *An old **man** bought the **house**.* ☐ ***Fred** cooked a **pot** full of **rice**.* ☐ ***Honesty** is the best **policy**.* ☐ *I really enjoy **running**.* ☐ *Please give me some more of that excellent **cake**.*

noun adjunct   in a *noun compound,* the first of the two *nouns* that delimits or restricts as an *adjective* would; a *noun* that *premodifies* another *noun.* (The *noun adjunct* could be omitted without damaging the *grammaticality* of the *sentence.* See comments at *adjunct.* See also *adverbial adjunct.* The examples show *noun adjuncts* in bold print.) ☐ *The **window** shade suddenly rolled up.* ☐ *A **police** car came upon the scene.* ☐ *The dirty dishes are in the **kitchen** sink.* ☐ *Who left the **corn**cob on the floor?* ☐ *There were a number of **cattle** cars standing on the **rail** siding.*

(noun) class   in some languages, a property of the *noun* that calls for *agreement* between the *noun* and other elements of the *sentence.* (In English, *nouns* are subclassified to show a number of *semantic* differences, but there is not any *formal* indication of *noun class* in English.)

noun clause   a *dependent clause* functioning as a *nominal.* (See also *nominal clause.* Note that the *noun clause* does not behave exactly like a *noun* in that it does not occur in the *plural,* nor can it take all the *noun's determiners* and *complements.* The examples show *noun clauses* in bold print.) ☐ ***That Mary was quite ill** was well known.* ☐ *We knew **who did it**.* ☐ *She felt **that she had heard enough**.* ☐ ***That the French had revolted in 1789** was news to Eric.* ☐ *Jerry reiterated **what he had said before**.* ☐ ***Who is ringing the bell** is **what I want to know**.*

(noun) compound AND **compound noun**   a *nominal* composed of two *nouns,* the first of which is called a *noun adjunct.* (See also *compound adjective, compound object, compound sentence,* *compound subject, compound verb, compound word*. Various *forms* of this type may appear in print spelled as two *words*, hyphenated, or solid. For many *noun compounds*, dictionaries do not agree on a preferred spelling. The examples show *noun compounds* in bold print.) □ *The **window shade** suddenly rolled up.* □ *A **police car** came upon the scene.* □ *The dirty dishes are in the **kitchen sink**.* □ *There were a number of **cattle cars** parked on the **rail sidings**.*

noun phrase a *constituent* functioning as a *noun*. (The examples show *noun phrases* in bold print.) □ ***An old man** bought **the house**.* □ *Someone bought **those ugly old dresses**.* □ ***That the French had revolted in 1789** was news to Eric.* □ *We want **everything you can possibly get**.*

noun substitute a *pronoun*.

NP a *noun phrase*. (This convenient abbreviation was *introduced* in early *transformational-generative* grammar writings and has become used in other discussions of *grammar*. In its earliest form, it was a single symbol with the vertical line of the P overlapped onto the right leg of the N. See also *VP*.)

number See *(grammatical) number*.

number concord *agreement* in *number*. (This applies to *verbs* with *third person singular subjects*; *singular* and *plural nouns* and the *forms* of the *verbs be, do, have*; various *determiners* such as *many, both*, etc.; and *nouns* used with numerals. The examples show *constituents* exhibiting *number concord* in bold print.) □ ***He** has **one**.* □ ***They have** none.* □ *Please give me **many gifts**.* □ ***I** need only **four pairs**.* □ *Take **these books** with you.*

numeral adjective See *adjective numeral*.

object   a *nominal* that is affected by or receives the *action of a verb* or follows a *preposition*. (Specifically a *direct object,* an *indirect object,* and an *object of a preposition.* See also *adverbial objective, affected object, agentive object, cognate object, compound object, direct object, effected object, indirect object, object complement, object(ive) case, object(ive) complement, objective genitive, objective pronoun, object of an infinitive, object of a possessive, object of a preposition, object of reference, object of result, object of service, predicate object(ive), prepositional object, remoter object, resultant object, secondary object, second object, two-object verb.* The examples show a variety of different kinds of English objects.)   ☐ *I am weary of **all this.***   ☐   *Give **a bigger piece** to **me.***   ☐   *I would really like **to chop down that old tree.***   ☐   *Don't chop down **that old tree!***

object complement   See *object(ive) complement.*

object(ive) case   the *grammatical* state of a *nominal* that is the *direct object* of a *transitive verb,* an *indirect object,* or the *object of a preposition.* (In English, the *objective case* covers the historical *accusative case* and *dative case.* There are only six *words* in the English language that are uniquely marked to show this case: *me, him, her, us, them,* and *whom.* There is no other indication of the *objective case* except *word order.* See a brief description of the role of *case* in English at *case* and *case grammar.* The examples show the *pronouns* listed above and other *nominals* in the *objective case.*)

☐ *I see **him**.* ☐ *We fought **them** repeatedly.* ☐ *Please give **Oliver** some more **porridge**.* ☐ *My uncle wouldn't buy **me** any ice cream.*

object(ive) complement 1. a *noun, adjective,* or *pronoun* used to *complete* a *factive verb,* i.e, a *verb* of choosing, naming, or thinking, or a *modifier* of a *direct object.* (This *nominal* complements the *object* of a *transitive verb.* Some *verbs* require *objective complements.* The idea of "completing" is a *semantic* one. The examples show *objective complements* in bold print.) ☐ *Let's make Sally **queen for a day**.* ☐ *They named me **executor**.* ☐ *The officer appointed Sam **deputy**.* ☐ *They made him **a ruler**.* ☐ *We voted her **the most friendly one of all**.* 2. a *complement* that is a *direct object* or an *indirect object.* (This is not the most widespread use of this term.)

objective genitive a *semantic subclass* of the *genitive case* that consists of the *object* of a *transitive verb* and a *nominalized form* of the *transitive verb,* possessed by the *object.* (Compare to *subjective genitive.* Each example shows first the *sentence* with the *transitive verb* followed by its *object,* and then one or more derived *object genitives* included in a different *sentence.*) ☐ *The old gentleman **carved the meat** elegantly. / The **meat's carving** was carried out quickly.* ☐ *He **carved the meat**. / The **carving of the meat** was a botched-up job if I ever saw one.* ☐ *The posse **captured the robbers** after a long chase. / The **robbers' capture** was a messy affair. / The **capture of the robbers** took place in broad daylight.* ☐ *Tom **painted the fence**, tempting everyone to join in. / The **painting of the fence** was a total disaster.*

objective pronoun one of a special set of *pronouns* used as the *direct object* of a *transitive verb,* an *indirect object,* or the *object of a preposition.* (There are six of these *pronouns: him, her, me, us, them,* and *whom.* Typically in English, however, *who* is often used in a position before the *verb* even when *whom* would be *grammatical.* The examples show the various *pronouns* in their various uses. Compare to *subjective pronoun.* The *personal pronoun you* is the same whether it is a *subjective pronoun* or an *objective pronoun.* The examples show *objective pronouns* in bold print.) ☐ *Please* *give **them** to her.* □ *She said it wasn't very nice of **me**.* □ *You gave **them** to **whom**?* □ *Come on. Give **us** a break.* □ *We brought **him** a lovely filet of the salmon we caught.* □ *Come sit by **us**.*

object of an infinitive the *object* of the *verb* in an *infinitive clause* or *infinitive phrase* when the *verb* in the *infinitive clause* is a *transitive verb*. (See remarks at *infinitive clause*. The examples show *objects of an infinitive* in bold print.) □ *Do you really want me to feed **him**?* □ *I would really like to chop **that old tree** down.* □ *We were not able to do **it** on time.* □ *Please keep trying to fix **it**.*

object of a possessive the entity that is possessed. (Not widely known. The examples show *objects of a possessive* in bold print.) □ *Bill's **hand** was bandaged quickly and professionally.* □ *My **cat** fled from the dog in terror.* □ *The hole was bored deep into the earth's **crust**.* □ *I fell into the **bottom** of the pit.*

object of a preposition the *nominal* that follows a *preposition*; the *nominal* that is combined with a *preposition* to form a *prepositional phrase*. (In some ways, the *object of a preposition* seems to function similarly to the *object* of a *transitive verb* in that both require the use of the *objective case* in the *pronouns* that have an *objective case form*. The examples show *objects of a preposition* in bold print.) □ *What an enormous piece of **pie**!* □ *Would you kindly put this stack of towels into **the cupboard**?* □ *Give it to **me**!* □ *The huge hot air balloon flew directly over **us**.* □ *Let's not argue about **what needs to be done**.* □ *Of course, I will look through **whatever you want**.* □ *The boys fought over **how to do it**.* □ *They ought never to have heard about **it**.*

object of reference See *indirect object*.

object of result See *effected object*.

object of service See *indirect object*.

obligative mood a *mood* that indicates an obligation to do something, usually *marked* by *should*. (The example *sentences* can be

said to be in the *obligative mood*.) □ *Jane should keep trying.* □
You really should get some new clothes. □ *Everyone should brush after each
meal.* □ *My door should be kept closed at all times.*

oblique case   in English, any *case* but the *nominative (case)*; any
case but the *common case*. (Typically used in the *plural* to cover all
the *uninflected* cases in English. The meaning of the term, when
used, must be stipulated. Since general *case inflection* is not part
of Modern English, the term is of limited use. Generally, the term
refers to the *genitive (case)*, but for those who use the existence of
the six English *pronouns* marked for an *object(ive) case* as evidence for an *object(ive) case* in English, *oblique case* may also include the *object(ive) case*. See a brief description of the role of *case*
in English at *case* and *case grammar*.)

***of*-genitive** AND **Norman genitive**   a *genitive case* formed with the
preposition of. (Assuming that this *construction* was borrowed
from French after the Norman Conquest. See also *Saxon genitive*,
s-genitive. The examples show *of-genitives* in bold print.) □ *I
have never been in the city **of New York** in my life.* □ *You are no friend **of**
mine!* □ *He lived for many years at the home **of his aunt**.* □ *Put it in
the trunk **of the car**.*

open class AND **open set**   a group of a particular *word* type (such as
a *part of speech*) that can contain an infinite or at least indefinite
number of members. (As opposed to a *closed class* or *closed set*,
which has a small, fixed number of members. *Nouns, verbs, adjectives,* and *adverbs* are found in *open classes,* while *prepositions,*
determiners, modal auxiliaries, etc., belong to *closed classes.* The
expansion of the vocabulary of a language takes place within the
open classes.)

open set   See the previous entry.

operator   in an English *verb phrase,* the first *verbal auxiliary.* (When
the *utterance* is recast as, or transformed into, a question, the *operator* becomes the first element of the *interrogative sentence.* The
examples show *operators* in bold print.) □ *You **can** help me with*

*this. / **Can** you help me with this?* □ *Mr. Wallace and Tom **have** been to France and Germany. / **Have** Mr. Wallace and Tom been to France and Germany?* □ *I **will** have to have had my breakfast before the flight. / **Will** I have to have had my breakfast before the flight?* □ *They **ought** to have known what they were getting into. / **Ought** they have known what they were getting into?*

order See *word order.*

ordinal number See the following entry.

ordinal (numeral) AND **ordinal number** a *word* that behaves as a *noun* or an *adjective* and indicates order or rank. (The examples show *ordinal numerals* in bold print.) □ *I was the **first** one there.* □ *Who was **second**?* □ *Our team captured the **first**-, **second**-, and **third**-place medals.* □ *We were the **tenth** ones in line.*

orthographic word a written *word*, spelled in standard spelling, identified by a preceding and following space or punctuation. (This is the conventional definition of *word*, which is in contrast with *formal* or structural *linguistic* units such as *base, root, stem, morpheme,* etc. In the examples, every other *orthographic word* is in bold print.) □ *What **is** this **all** about?* □ *Is **it** an **elephant**?* □ *Everyone **should** brush **after** each **meal**.*

orthography the spelling system of a language; correct spelling. (Compare to *phonetics*, which uses a special alphabet to represent speech sounds on a one-for-one basis.)

P

paradigm   a list of a *declension* or a *conjugation*. (A full account of the *declensions* of *nouns* or *adjectives* or the *conjugations* of *verbs* may require many *paradigms*. *Paradigms* are used to show the patterns of *inflection* in highly inflected languages, especially for pedagogical purposes.)

parataxis   the joining together of *constituents* without the use of a *conjunction*. (Compare to *hypotaxis*. The examples show the *constituents* in *parataxis* in bold print.) ☐ *I came, I saw, I conquered.* ☐ *I'll have coffee, eggs, bacon*...that's all. ☐ *I bought coffee, bread, eggs, margarine, and yogurt.* ☐ *I know it, you know it, she knows it, but does anybody care?*

parenthetical clause   a *clause* that gives additional or supplemental information; a *nonessential clause* that provides supplemental information. (This *clause* could be deleted without affecting the *grammaticality* or basic meaning of the remaining *clause*. The *clause* has a *subject* and a *predicate*. This is a specific type of *parenthetical expression*. The examples show *parenthetical clauses* in bold print.) ☐ *Jim, **the man you just met**, is my brother.* ☐ *Our cat, **the one we just bought**, is getting to be annoying.* ☐ *My Uncle George, **who became a farmer**, just adores our cat.* ☐ *We gave another one to Melissa, **the one who has the curly hair**, because she looked so much like Shirley Temple.*

parenthetical expression   a *construction* giving extra or supplemental material in a *sentence*. (This expression could be deleted without affecting the *grammaticality* or basic meaning of the remaining part of the *sentence*. This term includes what is covered by the term *parenthetical clause*. The examples show *parenthetical expressions* in bold print.) ☐ ***Granted,*** *I was late.* ☐ *I hope to be early—**very early**—next time.* ☐ *Keeping track of our investments,* ***as we must do from time to time,*** *is much easier with a computer.* ☐ *We all arrived on time,* ***of course.***

parse to divide a *sentence* into its constituent *grammatical* parts and apply the appropriate *grammatical* terms to the parts. (*Parsing* is the central feature of *traditional grammar*. All *traditional grammar rules* make reference to the parts of the *sentence* by name, and *parsing* is the means of identifying the specific parts of the *sentence*. These *grammar rules* and terms are typically patterned on Latin *grammar*. A typical *parsing* exercise would involve dividing a *sentence* into *subject* and *predicate*, and then into a number of *parts of speech*. *Parsing* is also a central feature to natural language processing, especially as it involves computers. The examples are *parsed* into *subject* and *predicate* with the division between them indicated by "|.") ☐ *She | could no longer bend over to pick things up.* ☐ *The old cat, which had given birth to more than fifty kittens, | finally died.* ☐ *I | spy.* ☐ *She | stopped very suddenly.*

part a *word* in the *grammar metalanguage*, a *form* meaning a representative *form* of a particular *word* or member of a *word class*, as in *part of speech*. (In this sense, *part* does not mean *constituent* or "subpart.")

participial pertaining to a *participle*. (See also *dangling participle, participial noun, participial phrase, participle, participle phrase, past participle, present participle*.)

participial noun See *gerund*.

participial phrase AND **participle phrase** a *phrase* functioning as an *adjective phrase*, composed of a *present participle* or a *past participle* and its *modifiers* or *complements*. (The examples show *participial phrases* in bold print.) ☐ *The lady **bringing in the***

packages tripped over the rug. □ *You waste more time **trying to save money** than anyone I know.* □ *The little man **wringing his hands furtively** is the manager.* □ *We found him there in the meat locker, **frozen half to death.***

participle an *adjectival* derived from the *present participle* or *past participle form* of the *verb*. (See *present participle* and *past participle*. See also *gerundial adjective*. The examples show *participles* in bold print.) □ ***Flying** planes can be dangerous.* □ *Poorly **cooked** rice can be really sticky.* □ *She served very thinly **sliced** country ham on **beaten** biscuits.* □ *They searched endlessly for the **downed** plane.*

participle phrase See *participial phrase*.

particle an *affix* or *indeclinable word,* usually indicating a *grammatical* meaning or function. (*Prepositions* are usually considered to be *particles*. *Particles* that are *free forms* are usually called *function words*. See *negative particle* and *adverb particle*. The examples show *particles* in bold print.) □ *I absolutely will **not** do what you ask.* □ *Cleanliness is essential **to** our procedures.* □ *Call me **up** about nine tonight.* □ *Why did you have to bring **up** the matter?*

particle with verb See *phrasal verb*.

partitive pertaining to a *constituent* that indicates some part of a whole. (Typically: *some,* but also *half, most, much, part,* etc. The examples show *partitive constructions* in bold print.) □ *Please give me **some** of the cake.* □ *I want **half** of it.* □ *You already have **most** of it!* □ *Who has **some** money I can borrow?*

partitive construction a *partitive genitive* and the nominal it *modifies*; a *partitive phrase* and the nominal it *modifies*. (See *partitive genitive*. The examples here show the entire *partitive construction*.) □ *Please give me **a glass of water**.* □ ***Four square miles of swampland** are totally worthless.* □ *Just **a tiny bit of cake**, if you don't mind.* □ *These pages are **part of that book**.* □ *Both Spain and France are in **a beautiful region of Europe**.* □ *They hold **some of Europe's loveliest sights**.*

partitive genitive   a *semantic subclass* of the *genitive case* showing that one thing is a subpart or "some" of another. (See also *partitive construction, partitive phrase*. In some instances, it is possible to exchange the of-*genitive* with the s-*genitive*, but usually this sounds awkward or wrong. The *partitive genitive* is used to show measure, serving, or subpart. Compare to *definitive genitive*. The examples show *partitive genitives* in bold print.) □ *Please give me a glass **of water**.* □ *All these acres **of swampland** are totally worthless.* □ *Just a tiny bit **of cake**, if you don't mind.* □ *These pages are part **of that book**.* □ *Both Spain and France are in a beautiful region **of Europe**.* □ *They hold some **of Europe's** loveliest sights.* □ *This is one of the finest examples **of our modern art collection**.*

partitive phrase   a *phrase* indicating a part of a whole. (The *partitive phrase* is *introduced* by the *preposition of* and usually *modifies* one of the following list: *both, some, much, most, half, part, many*, etc. The examples show *partitive phrases* in bold print.) □ *He counted on getting most **of the cake**.* □ *Jane kept half **of it** for herself.* □ *Much **of what you hear on the radio** is not too pleasant.* □ *Many **of my friends** had been there and left.*

part of speech   a member of a list of *grammatical* classifications of individual *words*. (There are many such lists, and they typically list eight items. Sometimes *parts of speech* are referred to as the "eight" *parts of speech*, perhaps suggesting that there is a fixed number of *grammatical classes*. The most common such list of terms is *verb, noun, pronoun, adjective, adverb, preposition, conjunction*, and *interjection*. In *traditional grammar* pedagogy, the elements of a *sentence* that bear these terms are identified in the *parsing* process. Dictionaries contain lists of *parts of speech* that very often differ considerably from those named above. Many dictionaries further divide *verbs* into *transitive verbs* and *intransitive verbs*. Some dictionaries subdivide the *parts of speech* so that the list may be quite extensive, including perhaps *affirmation, negation, interjection, modifier, infix, prefix, suffix, phrase, sentence, present participle, past participle, combining form, plural noun, auxiliary verb, article, definite article, indefinite article*, etc.)

passival a *construction* wherein the *object* of a *transitive verb* becomes the *subject* of the *verb* and no *agent* is mentioned or implied. (In the examples, the *subject* and its *verb* are shown in bold print.) ☐ *All of our **products sold** quite well.* ☐ *Now, you will find that these larger **cars drive** very smoothly and comfortably.* ☐ *It rained and rained, day after day, and every single **basement flooded**.* ☐ *This **breed of cow does not milk** very easily.*

[passive] See *double passive, passival, passive auxiliary, passive perfect infinitive, passive progressive perfect infinitive, passive voice.*

passive auxiliary a *form* of the *verb be* and the *-ed* or *-en* that marks the *past participle* of a *verb*. (When the *verb* in question is *irregular*, (e.g., *cost, cost, cost*) the *passive auxiliary* as described here is not used. This definition simply provides a name for the normal *auxiliary*. It does not provide complete instructions for forming the *passive*. The examples show *passive auxiliaries* in bold print.) ☐ *The seeds **were** eaten by the birds.* ☐ *The deer **had been** killed by the car.* ☐ *You **were** reminded of this early enough.* ☐ *This **was** carried to the governor's office by a clerk.*

passive perfect infinitive a *nominal construction* consisting of *to* plus *have* plus the *past participle* of *be* plus the *past participle* of a *verb*. (See also *passive progressive perfect infinitive, perfect infinitive, progressive perfect infinitive.* The term is not in wide use, but if one encountered this *construction* and were obliged to name it, this term is appropriate. The examples show *passive perfect infinitives* in bold print.) ☐ ***To have been loved** so deeply and so long is more than I deserve.* ☐ ***To have been honored** in this fashion has always been my desire.* ☐ ***To have been called** at that hour must have been very annoying.* ☐ ***To have been treated** so shabbily by a mere child was more than I could bear.*

passive progressive perfect infinitive a *nominal construction* consisting of *to* plus *have* plus the *past participle* of *be* plus the *past participle* of a *verb*. (The likelihood of encountering this frequently is very small. See also *perfect infinitive, passive perfect infinitive, progressive perfect infinitive.* The term is not in wide use, but if one encountered this *construction* and were obliged to name it, this term is appropriate. The examples show *passive progressive perfect infinitives* in bold print.) □ ***To have been being dragged*** *repeatedly over the rough desert floor just to make a movie was ridiculous.* □ ***To have been being beaten*** *for such a long time must have had a deep and lasting effect on your thinking as well as your body.* □ ***To have been being driven*** *for hours was all the horse could look forward to.* □ ***To have been being held*** *under water for so long must have been terrifying.*

passive voice AND **inactive voice** a *semantic* state of the *verb* where the *agent* of a *sentence* is optional and, if present, follows the *verb*, and is *introduced* by the *preposition by*. (The *verb* requires a *passive auxiliary*. *Transitive verbs* can be in the *passive voice*. See also *active voice*. The examples show *verbs* in the *passive voice* in bold print.) □ *A fine dinner **was cooked** by Andy.* □ *The barn **had been painted** red.* □ *The horse **was ridden** until it dropped.* □ *Our house **was built** by excellent carpenters.*

[past] See *nonpast (tense), past continuous (aspect), past emphatic, past indicative, past participle, past perfect aspect, past perfect continuous (aspect), past perfect progressive (aspect), past perfect (tense), past progressive (aspect), past subjunctive (mood), past tense, simple past (tense), strong past tense, weak past tense.*

past continuous (aspect) See *past progressive (aspect).*

past emphatic See *emphatic mood.*

past indicative having to do with a *sentence* in the *past tense* and the *indicative (mood)*. (See also *present indicative*. The examples are all *sentences* in the *past indicative*.) □ *We all ate dinner on deck.* □ *She brought her husband to the company picnic.* □ *The owner wept as the boat sank.* □ *The bird flew away.*

past participle a *form* of the *verb*, often ending in *-ed* or *-en*, which, when combined with an *auxiliary*, forms the *perfect aspect*. (A *participle* functioning as an *adjective* is called a *verbal*. The first example is of a *verbal*. The remaining examples show the *past* *participles* as part of the *verb phrase.* The examples show *past participles* in bold print.) ☐ *The **broken** vase was my father's favorite.* ☐ *The birds have **eaten** the seeds.* ☐ *Had I **known** you were here, I would not have **left** home!* ☐ *She had **marked** all the errors.*

past perfect aspect See *past perfect (tense).*

past perfect continuous (aspect) See the following entry.

past perfect progressive (aspect) AND **past perfect continuous (aspect)** an *aspect* of the *verb* indicating that an activity that began in the past was still progressing at some point in the past and had not terminated. (This *aspect* is formed with *have* in the *past tense* plus the *past participle* of *be,* plus a *verb* with an *ing suffix.* See comments on naming *aspects* at the entry for *aspect.* The examples show *verbs* in the *past perfect progressive aspect* in bold print.) ☐ *I **had been looking** for you all morning, until the storm.* ☐ *They **had been riding** their bikes that day.* ☐ *The frogs **had been croaking,** but they were quiet now.* ☐ *Our weeds **had been growing** like wildfire and had destroyed the yard.*

past perfect (tense) AND **past perfect aspect** an *aspect* of the *verb* expressing action that was completed at some time in the past, formed by the *past tense* of *have* plus the *past participle* of another *verb.* (See comments on naming *aspects* at the entry for *aspect.* The examples show *verbs* in the *past perfect tense* in bold print.) ☐ *I **had eaten** dinner earlier.* ☐ *He looked as if he **had had** a pretty bad day.* ☐ *We had no idea as to who **had been** there before.* ☐ *I wish I **had sent** it on earlier.*

past progressive (aspect) AND **past continuous (aspect)** an *aspect* formed with the *past tense* of *be* plus the *present participle* of another *verb* indicating that the *action of the verb* was going on at a time in the past. (This is a combination of the *past tense* and the *progressive aspect.* Semantically, this *aspect conveys* the meaning that at a previous point in time, an action was incomplete, in progress, or developing. See comments on naming *aspects* at the entry for *aspect.* The examples show *verbs* in the *past progressive* *aspect* in bold print.) □ *Yesterday, the farmer* **was plucking** *chickens from dawn to dusk.* □ *He* **was running** *as fast as he could.* □ *They* **were not keeping** *track well.* □ *This morning, Mary* **was buying** *shoes for the children.*

past subjunctive (mood) a type of *subjunctive mood* wherein a conditional statement is expressed in a *past tense construction* to refer indefinitely to the present or future. (It is formed either with the *were past tense* of *be* plus a to-*infinitive*, indicating present or future, or with the *main verb* in the *past tense*, indicating present only. Some people regard the *construction* obsolete and its use pedantic. In the examples, the *conditional conjunction* is in bold print to show that it is a necessary part of the *construction*.) □ *If Ed* **were to come** *tomorrow, we wouldn't be ready for him.* □ **Unless** *you* **were to do** *it right now, it would be too late.* □ *If Sally* **were to see you,** *you would be ashamed.* □ *If we* **were to go there,** *what would we find?*

past tense a *verb tense* indicating that the *action of the verb* took place at some time previous to the *utterance*. (The examples show *verbs* in the *past tense* in bold print.) □ *We* **ran** *home as fast as we could.* □ *Sue* **did** *all her work and then* **went** *home.* □ *I* **did** *it well, I think.* □ *I* **spied** *it over there.*

pedagogical grammar a *grammar* intended to be suitable for teaching and learning a language. (Most such *grammars* are by nature *prescriptive grammars*. A *descriptive grammar* can be used as a *pedagogical grammar*, but there have been few attempts at producing large-scale *descriptive grammars* for this purpose. *Pedagogical grammars* are typical of what is found in school textbooks. They are designed to be useful to the student, not to exemplify *linguistic* theory. See Pratt, Corbin and Perrin, or Hodges and Whitten in the bibliography for an example of a *pedagogical grammar*.)

[perfect] The following entries include the *word perfect*: *future perfect aspect, future perfect continuous (aspect), future perfect progressive (aspect), future perfect (tense), imperfect, imperfect(ive) (aspect), imperfect(ive) (tense), passive perfect infinitive, passive* *progressive perfect infinitive, past perfect aspect, past perfect continuous (aspect), past perfect progressive (aspect), past perfect (tense), perfect auxiliary, perfect infinitive, perfect(ive) aspect, perfect (tense), pluperfect (tense), present perfect aspect, present perfect continuous (aspect), present perfect infinitive, present perfect progressive (aspect), present perfect (tense), progressive perfect infinitive.*

perfect auxiliary   a *form* of the *verb have* and the *-ed* or *-en* that marks the *past participle* of a *verb*. (When the *verb* in question is *irregular*, e.g., *ring, rang, rung*, the *perfect auxiliary* as described here is not used. This definition simply provides a name for the normal *auxiliary*. It does not provide complete instructions for forming the *perfect (aspect)*. The examples show *perfect auxiliaries* in bold print.)   □   *They will **have** tried it by tomorrow.*   □   *I couldn't possibly **have** completed it by the time you said.*   □   *I **had** studied already.*   □   *By then, we **had** driven enough.*

perfect infinitive   a *construction* consisting of *to* plus *have* plus the *past participle* of a *verb*. (See also *passive perfect infinitive, passive progressive perfect infinitive, progressive perfect infinitive*. The examples show *perfect infinitives* in bold print.)   □   ***To have loved** someone as much I have loved that child is something that few humans can experience.*   □   ***To have fallen** so far and survived is a miracle.*   □   ***To have known** much joy is my only goal.*   □   *We all wanted **to have seen** a whale before we left.*

perfect(ive) aspect AND **perfect (tense)**   an *aspect* of the *verb* that shows that the *action of the verb* is "perfected" or completed in relation to some point in time. (When combined with *tenses* the resultant combinations are often called *tenses*. See *present perfect tense, past perfect tense, future perfect tense* for comments on how these *tenses* are formed. See comments on naming *aspects* at the entry for *aspect*. See also *past participle*. The examples show different types of *perfect(ive) aspect*.)   □   *He **has done** it.*   □   *I have not heard that she **has succeeded**.*   □   *We **have reached** home at last.*   □   *When we **have finished** this one, we will start on the next.*

perfect (tense)   See *perfect(ive) aspect* for a definition and examples.

periphrasis   **1.** the obligatory use of *words* or *phrases* rather than *inflections* to indicate a *grammatical function* or a *grammatical construction*. (It is obligatory where there is no other way to express the *grammatical functions* in question. Many *grammatical functions* that might be indicated by *case* are handled by some type of *periphrasis* in English. See also *comparison of adverbs, comparison of adjectives, future time,* and *prepositional phrases*. The examples show various types of *periphrasis* in bold print.) □ *She fixed it **with a screwdriver.** * □ *The queen was **most pleased.** * □ *All of us **had to** put our own luggage on the bus.* □ *She **will go** there soon.* **2.** the optional or unnecessary use of *words* or *phrases* resulting in wordiness. (This is viewed as a stylistic flaw. In the examples, the first *sentence* shows *periphrasis* in bold print. In the second *sentence,* a less wordy replacement for the *periphrasis* is shown in bold print.) □ *He **did sing.** / He **sang.** * □ *She **would have been able** to do it. / She **could have** done it.* □ *Why, whatever do you mean? / **What** do you mean?* □ *Oh, oh, yes I do, **really awfully!** / **Oh, yes I do!** *

periphrastic comparison   a type of *comparative (degree)* or *superlative (degree)* of *adjectives* and *adverbs* where the *degree* is indicated by additional *words* such as *more, less, most, least*. (The examples show *periphrastic comparison* in bold print.) □ *I was not the **least** bit troubled by it.* □ *I do not know which of us was **more** frightened.* □ *Wallace was the **most** disturbed of all.* □ *This one is far **less** rough than that one.*

periphrastic conjugation AND **periphrastic tense**   a type of *verbal construction* where the *tense* of the *verb* can be determined only from the *tense* of the *verbal auxiliaries*. (Although this *construction* is not uncommon in English, these terms are. In English there is very little *inflection* for *tense* on the *verb* itself; most *tense* and *aspect* is indicated periphrastically. See *phrasal tense*. See examples at *periphrastic verb phrase*.)

periphrastic future tense   **1.** a *verbal construction* expressing *future time* by the use of some *form* of the *auxiliary be* plus *going to* rather than the usual *will* (or *shall*). (This is simply an alternate way of expressing *future time*. See *periphrasis*. The examples show *verbs* in the *periphrastic future tense* in bold print.) □ *I am going to sing.* □ *We are going to leave tomorrow.* □ *When are you going to get that thing taken care of?* □ *Jane said that she is just going to die if she doesn't get the job.* **2.** any expression of *future time*, including the use of *will* or *shall* or the use of the *present tense* with *adverbs* that imply *future time*. (These *future time* formations clearly fit the definition of *periphrasis*.) □ *I will do it.* □ *I leave tomorrow.* □ *Sally will be there when you least expect her.* □ *I know I will manage it.*

periphrastic genitive   a *genitive construction* formed by making the possessor the *object* of the *preposition of*, while the entity possessed is a *nominal* that the resultant *periphrastic genitive modifies; the of-genitive.* (See also *double genitive*. These *constructions* show a kind of affinity or relationship that is not exactly the same as the normal *genitive* that shows ownership. The examples show the *periphrastic genitive* in bold print.) □ *The door of the barn swung slowly on its hinges.* □ *One good hard push and Wallace found himself king of the mountain again.* □ *Seeing how rude the townspeople had become, Bill sensed that it was the end of an age.* □ *You smell as though you just got too close to the business end of a skunk.*

periphrastic tense   See *periphrastic conjugation*.

periphrastic verb phrase   a *verb phrase* where the *tense* or *aspect* of the *phrase* is represented by a *periphrastic conjugation*. (The examples show the part of the *verb phrase* that exhibits *periphrasis*.) □ *They will go whenever they get a chance.* □ *He did try as hard as he could.* □ *Sally ought to have been able to do it.* □ *Did you not keep one for yourself?*

permissive mood   a *mood* indicating the granting of permission, usually through the use of *can, may,* or *might*. (These *sentences* can be said to be in the *permissive mood*.) □ *You may if you wish.* □ *You can have just a tiny bit more.* □ *You can borrow the car if you put some gas in it.* □ *You and Sally may go to the prom only if you promise to be home by midnight.*

[person]   See *(grammatical) person* and see *anaphoric pronoun, conjunctive pronoun, demonstrative (pronoun), determinative possessive pronoun, emphatic pronoun, exclusive pronoun, impersonal pronoun, indefinite pronoun, independent possessive (pronoun), intensive (personal) pronoun, interrogative (pronoun), negative pronoun, objective pronoun, personal, personal pronoun, possessive pronoun, reciprocal pronoun, reflexive pronoun, relative pronoun, subjective pronoun.*

personal   having to do with *grammatical person*. (See *personal ending, personal pronoun, personal suffix, personal verb.*)

personal ending AND **personal suffix**   a *suffix* on a *verb* indicating *grammatical person*. (There is only one such ending in English. It indicates that the *subject* of the *verb* is *third person singular* and that the *verb* is in the *present tense*. It has two spelling *forms*: *s* and *es*. Other verb *forms*, *am, is, are, have, has, was, were*, are *inflected* to show person, but they do not utilize *suffixes*. The examples show *personal endings* in bold print.) ☐ *He fixes up old cars.* ☐ *She runs a bank.* ☐ *The old cow no longer gives milk.* ☐ *Tom and Charles swim while Jane stands on the shore cheering.*

personal pronoun   a *pronoun* that varies in *form* depending on its *grammatical person*. (See *(grammatical) person*. English has three *persons, first person, second person*, and *third person*. These *persons* are evident in the English *pronoun* system and in the *inflection* of *present tense verbs* with *third person singular subjects*. Some languages have additional *persons*, the most common being dual person. See *dual number*. The examples show *personal pronouns* in bold print.) ☐ *He keeps his book in her room.* ☐ *Please put my coat on your friend's chair.* ☐ *Those are our books in their car.* ☐ *You simply must be more careful with your possessions.*

personal suffix   See *personal ending.*

personal verb   a *verb* that has different *forms* for the *grammatical persons*. (There are only three: *be, do, have*. These *verbs* have *forms* that are specific to various *tenses, aspects*, and *grammatical rela-*

tionships. Additionally, *be* has the same unique *forms* as a *copula,* and *be, do, have* are used as *verbal auxiliaries.* The examples show *personal verbs* in bold print.) ☐ *He is a real handful.* ☐ *They were rarely on time.* ☐ *You have put it away.* ☐ *No, he has put it away.* ☐ *She does needlepoint.* ☐ *We do needlepoint.* ☐ *Your skirt is so lovely!*

person concord *agreement* between a *verb phrase* and the *grammatical person* of the *subject.* (*Agreement* can be observed in a *personal verb* serving as an *auxiliary.* Also found on the *main verb,* only for *third person singular subjects.* The elements in bold print show *person concord* with the preceding *nominal.*) ☐ *We have seldom seen so many cats.* ☐ *The cat runs fast and escapes those who might do it harm.* ☐ *They were exactly right about where Jane went.* ☐ *John sneezes whenever he gets near pine trees.*

philology the early *linguistic* study of language involving the study of the history of *words;* the study of historical and comparative *linguistics* concerned with the determination of the relationships between the languages of the world.

phoneme the basic contrastive unit in *phonology.* (In English, the sounds [t] and [d] represent separate *phonemes,* /t/ and /d/, because the degree of difference or contrast between the two sounds is capable of distinguishing one English *word* from another, as with [tæd], [dæd]; [dɑt], [tɑt].)

phonemic 1. having to do with the *phoneme.* 2. the type of *phonological* contrast that allows sounds to distinguish one *word* from another. (See the comments at *phonemic.*)

phonetic 1. having to do with speech sounds and, usually, their articulations. 2. having to do with the transcribing of speech sounds with a special alphabet.

phonetics the study and description of the individual sounds used in language and of individual languages. (*Phonetics* is more concerned with describing sounds than explaining how sounds function as a system. Like *phonology, phonetics* is never concerned with the spelling system of a language. Compare to *phonology.*)

phonological   having to do with the sound system of a language.

phonology   the study of sound systems, including *phonetics,* and the ways that sounds in language vary due to *grammatical* patterns; an explanation of the sound system of a language. (*Phonology* always refers to some representation of the sounds of a language other than the spelling system of the language. Compare to *morphology.*)

phrasal prepositional verb   a *verb phrase* that consists of a *phrasal verb* followed by a *prepositional phrase.* (The *verb* is said to *govern* an *adverb particle* and the subsequent *prepositional phrase.* Compare to *phrasal verb* and *prepositional verb.* Some writers treat *phrasal prepositional verbs* as *idioms* because the meaning of the *prepositional verb* is not the "sum" of the meanings of its *constituent* parts. In the examples, "|" separates the *verb, adverb particle,* and the *prepositional phrase* when required.) ☐ *We **ran | out | on them**.* ☐ *I didn't mean to put the whole job **off | on you**.* ☐ *I asked the babysitter to **look | in | on little John** at least once every half hour.* ☐ *In order to make ends meet, we will have to **cut | down | on expenses**.*

phrasal tense AND **compound tense**   a type of *tense* or *aspect* where the *tense* or *aspect* marking is found on a *verbal auxiliary* rather than on the *verb* itself. (It is "compound" only in the sense that it involves a *phrase* rather than a single *inflected verb.* The term covers *aspect* in English, as well as *tense.* In English, the only *tenses* that are not *phrasal tenses* are the *present tense* and the *past tense.* The *present tense* has no *inflection* except the *-s* or *-es* added to the verb when there is a *third person singular subject.* See *periphrastic conjugation.* The examples show *phrasal tenses* in bold print.) ☐ *She **would have gotten** there under her own steam.* ☐ *She **will have gone** by then.* ☐ *We **will leave** before noon.* ☐ *That poor broken vase really **ought not to have been standing** there by the door.*

phrasal verb AND **two-word verb, particle with verb**   a *verb phrase* that contains a *verb* followed by an *adverb particle;* a *lexeme* consisting of a *verb* followed by an *adverb particle.* (The *verb* is said to *govern* the *adverb particle*. The permissible list of *adverb particles* in this *construction* includes most of the *forms* that are recognized as *prepositions*. The *verb* may be *transitive* or *intransitive*. Compare to *prepositional verb* and *phrasal prepositional verb*. Some writers treat *phrasal verbs* as *idioms* because the meaning of the *phrasal verb* is not the same as the "sum" of its *constituents*. The examples show *phrasal verbs* in bold print.) □ *I knew I should have **called** her **up**.* □ *The inventor **thought up** a new way to process used newsprint.* □ *We would all be much happier if you didn't **put** things **off** until it's too late.* □ *What time do you think the thief **broke in**?* □ *By then, half the audience had **walked out**.*

phrase   a group of *words* functioning as a single *part of speech*. (Compared to *clause*, which is a *sentence* functioning as a single *part of speech*. Some *grammarians* use *phrase* to include *clause*. Others use *clause* as if it had this definition of *phrase*. The examples show a number of different kinds of *phrases* in bold print. See other entries containing *phrase* at *absolute phrase, adjective phrase, adverb(ial) phrase, appositive phrase, gerund phrase, infinitive phrase, locative phrase, noun phrase, participial phrase, participle phrase, periphrastic verb phrase, phrase-structure grammar, prepositional phrase, verb(al) phrase*.) □ ***Our being late*** *bothered us a great deal.* □ *I just know **how much it bothers each of you to be late**.* □ ***The old cow** lumbered into its stall.* □ *I am very tired **of all this**.* □ ***Flying planes for a living*** *is not as exciting as it may sound.* □ *Bill doesn't mind **coming out to the airport to pick you up**, do you, Bill?* □ *We each **should have been able to have gotten** a clean, fresh one.*

phrase-structure grammar   **1.** a simple *formal grammar*, capable only of producing or generating uncomplicated, basic *sentences*. **2.** a component of a *transformational-generative grammar* that produces basic *sentences* or *kernel sentences* that will be acted upon further by *transformational rules*.)

pluperfect (tense)   the *past perfect tense*. (See *past perfect (tense)* for definition and examples.)

plural   an indication of more than one in *nouns* and some *pronouns*. (The *plural* is indicated with *s, es* and with various *irregular* formations in English, and the *singular* is unmarked. See *grammatical number.* See also *count noun.* See *double plural, irregular plural, plural verb, regular plural, s-plural.* The examples show plurals in bold print.) ☐ *The birds have been eating our* **berries.** ☐ *Your pet* **foxes** *have trampled the* **vegetables.** ☐ *The* **geese** *are hopping around as if they had* **mice** *underfoot.* ☐ **We** *do not agree with* **their** *other* **ideas.**

plural verb a term used for *present tense verbs* marked with the *suffix -s* showing *agreement* with a *third person singular subject.* (This term refers to any *verb*, but only when the *verb* is in the *present tense* and the *subject* is *third person singular.* Such *verbs* display the *suffix -s,* which is erroneously classified as a *plural* by this expression. This is not *plural grammatical number;* the only *grammatical number* involved is *singular,* and that *number* is part of the *subject,* not the *verb.* This expression is used in the *grammatical rule* that says a "*singular subject* requires a *plural verb.*" See also *grammatical agreement, s-form.* The following examples illustrate *agreement* between a *third person singular subject* and a *present tense verb.*) ☐ *I swim on Mondays, and she swims on Tuesdays.* ☐ *The water runs and runs if you do not turn off the faucet tightly.* ☐ *The child seldom walks anywhere.* ☐ *This machine types as well as any other.*

point-action aspect a type of *aspect* of the *verb* that is centered on a particular point in time. (See *ingressive aspect* and *effective aspect.*)

polysemic exhibiting *polysemy.*

polysemy the coexistence of two or more distinct meanings, shades of meaning, or nuances in a single *word.* (Many *words* occur in two or more different *parts of speech*—such as *a hammer* and *to hammer*—and many more exhibit *polysemy.* This means that they may have different *semantic* and *syntactic* potentials when occurring in different contexts. In a dictionary, the *words* having numbered senses exhibit *polysemy.* The examples illustrate *polysemic words.*) ☐ *I sat down on the* **bank** *and baited my hook. I entered the* *bank and walked to the teller. The electrician killed the lights one* **bank** *at a time.* □ *John is* **head** *of the whole organization. I struck my* **head** *on the beam. Angela hit the nail on the* **head**. □ *Ted pushed the* **hammer** *to the floor. I squashed my finger with the* **hammer**.

positive (aspect) See *affirmative (aspect)*.

positive comparison See the following entry.

positive (degree) AND **positive comparison** the lowest *degree* of *comparison* in *adjectives* or *adverbs*. (Refers to a *degree* of "intensity" greater than none, but less than the maximum. Does not refer only to *semantically* positive *adjectives* or *adverbs*. There is no "negative degree" or "negative comparison." See also *comparative degree, superlative degree*. The examples show *adjectives* in the *positive degree* in bold print.) □ *That is a* **big** *piece of cake.* □ *This has been a* **good** *day.* □ *Maybe tomorrow will be a* **fine** *day.* □ *I hope never to see a* **bad** *day.*

possessive 1. the *grammatical relationship* between an owner and the entity owned. (When the owner is expressed as a *noun*, it is marked with a *possessive marker* in English. When the owner is expressed as a *pronoun*, a *possessive pronoun* is used. The *possessive* is essentially the major type of *genitive (case)* in English. The term *possessive* is preferred by some to escape the implications of the *word case* in *genitive case*. See also *genitive (case)* for further discussion of the *semantic* subtypes of the *genitive case*. The term *possessive genitive* is used in contrast with the other subtypes of the *genitive case*. See also *absolute possessive, determinative possessive pronoun, double possessive, independent possessive (pronoun), object of a possessive, possessive adjective, possessive case, possessive genitive, possessive marker, possessive pronoun*. The examples show *possessives* in bold print.) □ **My** *hat remains at home, hanging in* **my brother's** *closet.* □ *The* **boy's** *gloves were on the wrong hands.* □ *That painting* **of his** *is not good.* □ *The eyes* **of the boy** *looked downward.* 2. a noun or pronoun in the *possessive case*.

possessive adjective See *determinative possessive pronoun*.

possessive case   See *genitive (case)*.

possessive genitive   a use of the *genitive case* to show ownership of someone or something. (This term is used in contrast with the other types of *genitive*. The examples for this sense are found under the more general term *possessive,* which is not used contrastively.)

possessive marker   in speech, the *morpheme* that represents the *genitive (case);* in writing, the -*'s* and its spelling variants that indicate the *genitive (case)*. (See examples at *possessive*.)

possessive pronoun   a *pronoun* showing possession. There are thirteen such *forms* in English: *my, mine, his, her, hers, its, our, ours, your, yours, their, theirs,* and *whose*. (The examples show *possessive pronouns* in bold print.) □ ***Whose** is it?* □ *It's **ours**.* □ *No, it is **mine**.* □ ***Our** house is **your** house.*

postmodifier   a *modifier* or *quantifier* that follows the *constituent* it modifies. (Compare to *premodifier*. The examples show *postmodifiers* in bold print.) □ *The child **with the thick glasses** read voraciously.* □ *A boy **with mismatched socks** tried to sneak out of the room unnoticed.* □ *They were able to locate a few more packages **in a small shop on the other side of town**.* □ *The little house **on the corner** was the site of the celebration.*

postponed subject   the *subject* of a *sentence* that has been displaced by *it* through the process of *extrapolation;* the *subject* of a *sentence* that has been moved from the beginning of the *sentence* to the end. (In the examples, the first *sentence* is the normal or expected version, and the second has undergone *extrapolation*. See also *anticipatory subject*. The *postponed subject* is shown in bold print.) □ *Running a railroad can be troublesome. / It can be troublesome **running a railroad**.* □ *Having a day off from work is nice. / It is nice **having a day off from work**.* □ *The benevolent priest was the one who paid the call, as usual. / As usual, it was **the benevolent priest** who paid the call.* □ *The intrepid mail carrier walked through snow and sleet. / Through snow and sleet walked **the intrepid mail carrier**.*

postposition a *word* or *affix* that follows a *nominal* and indicates spacial relations, such as location or direction, or other *grammatical relationships;* a *word* or *affix* that follows a *nominal* and has the same function as a *preposition.* (The Finnish language uses *postpositions* extensively. An instance of a *postposition* in English is found in an *idiom,* and is shown in bold print in the examples.) ☐ *You can depend on it. I will be there, the weather* **notwithstanding.** ☐ *My complaints* **notwithstanding,** *the incinerator was located practically in my backyard.* ☐ *The law* **notwithstanding,** *I am going to have to remove this from the premises.*

predeterminer in English, a *word* that may occur before a *determiner.* (Typically: *all, both, half, twice.* The examples show *predeterminers* in bold print.) ☐ *We need* **all** *the help we can get.* ☐ *Now, take* **both** *the round one and the square one and place them in the small container provided.* ☐ *Tom deserved only* **half** *the amount he was given.* ☐ *Francine got* **twice** *the chocolate sauce that anyone else got.*

[predicate] See *bare* predicate, (complete) predicate, *compound* predicate, *predicate adjective,* predicate gerund, *predicate nominative, predicate noun, predicate object(ive), predicate verb, predicating verb, predication, simple predicate.*

predicate adjective an *adjective* in the *predicate* that describes the *subject;* a *complement* that follows a *linking verb.* (Compare to *attributive adjective.* Some *adjectives* can be used both attributively and in the *predicate.* The examples show *predicate adjectives* in bold print.) ☐ *The judgment is* **unfair.** ☐ *The judgment does not seem* **unfair** *to me.* ☐ *The barn is* **red.** ☐ *Three of the lovely cakes with the thick icing ought to be* **enough.**

predicate genitive a *complement* in the form of a genitive following a *linking verb.* (Not widely used. It is not always possible to see the *genitiveness* of some of these *constructions.* The examples show *predicate genitives* in bold print.) ☐ *The house is* **of stone.** ☐ *Bob's shirt is cleaner than is* **Frank's.** ☐ *She was not* **of that type.** ☐ *The two boys are* **of the same height.**

predicate gerund a *predicate nominative* in the *form* of a *gerund.* (The examples show *predicate gerunds* in bold print.) ☐ *Stand-*

*ing like that and winking is just **teasing**.* □ *Building your house now is **building for the future**.* □ *Your constant bickering is **annoying**.*

predicate infinitive   a *predicate nominative* derived from an *infinitive*. (Occurs after a *linking verb*. The examples show *predicate infinitives* in bold print.) □ *To work is **to pray**.* □ *To be happy at one's work is **to thrive**.* □ *His goal is **to become well**.* □ *To build here is **to build** on solid rock.*

predicate nominative AND **predicate noun, subject(ive) complement**   a *nominal* that renames or identifies the *subject*. (A type of *complement* that follows a *linking verb*. A *predicate noun* usually refers to a single *noun*, while a *predicate nominative* can refer to a single *noun* or a *noun phrase*. This is the same as *subjective complement*. The *subject* is the same entity as the *predicate nominative*, and is unchanged by the *action of the verb*. The examples show *predicate nominatives* in bold print.) □ *She became **vice president**.* □ *John is now **the postmaster**.* □ *The cow is **a quadruped**.* □ *Fred is **the boss**.*

predicate noun   See the previous entry.

predicate object(ive) AND **factitive object, resultant object, second object**   the *second object* of a *factitive verb;* the name, office, or designation given to a human or nonhuman *direct object* by means of a *factitive verb*. (The examples show *predicate objectives* in bold print.) □ *We elected her **our representative**.* □ *The entire city council appointed Sally **mayor**.* □ *We called Jane **Babs** just to irritate her.* □ *Bob and Bill chose Bill's brother **their representative**.*

predicate verb AND **predicating verb**   a *verb* that expresses the "action" that the *subject* of a *clause* is said to initiate; a *verb* that is not a *linking verb, modal verb,* or *auxiliary verb*. (The examples show *predicate verbs* in bold print.) □ *The birds **sang** sweetly.* □ *All men must **die**.* □ *Please **call** me a cab immediately.* □ *I cannot seem to **find** the tie that **goes** best with this suit.*

predicating verb   See the previous entry.

predication The part of a *proposition* that makes an assertion about or discusses the main focus or *argument* of the *proposition*. (See *argument* and *proposition*. The *predication* is shown in bold print.) □ *My stereo **is brand-new and works like a charm**.* □ *Four young girls **are entering the room**.* □ *Paris **is the capital of France**.* □ *The path ahead **is fraught with peril**.*

prefix an *affix* that comes before another *form;* a *particle* or *morpheme* that is placed before a *stem, root,* or *word.* (*Prefixes* cannot stand alone. They are *bound forms.* Compare to *infix* and *suffix.* The examples show *prefixes* in bold print.) □ *How very **un**interesting.* □ *We are most **dis**pleased.* □ *This is a **non**profit organization.* □ *I would not want anyone to think I am **il**literate.*

premodifier a *modifier* or *quantifier* that precedes the thing it modifies. (Compare to *postmodifier.* See also *attributive adjective.* The examples show *premodifiers* in bold print.) □ *Please take off that **silly** hat!* □ *We were able to locate a **few more** packages in a **small, out-of-the-way** shop near the highway.* □ *You would look much better with a **fresh** shave.* □ *I simply must have the **red** one.*

premodify [for a *modifier*] to stand before the *constituent* it modifies. (*Attributive adjectives* and *noun adjuncts* premodify the *nouns* that follow them. In the examples, the elements in bold print *premodify* the *words* that follow them. See *premodifier.*) □ *There were dirty dishes in the **kitchen** sink.* □ *The **police** car sped away.* □ *Who left the **corn**cob on the floor?* □ *Please put the **hair**brush back where you got it.*

preposition a *word* indicating a spacial or *grammatical relationship.* (A *function word* placed before some other *word,* typically: *aboard, about, above, across, after, against, along, amid, amidst, among, around, at, before, behind, below, beneath, beside, besides, between, beyond, but, by, concerning, down, during, except, for, from, in, into, like, near, of, off, on, out, over, past, since, through, throughout, to, toward, towards, under, underneath, until, unto, up, upon, with, within, without,* etc. See also *complex preposition, final preposition, object of a preposition, phrasal prepositional verb, prepositional ad-*

verb, prepositional complement, prepositional object, prepositional phrase, prepositional verb, verbal preposition. The examples show a sampling of different *prepositions*.) □ *Put this **under** your tongue.* □ *This is **for** keeps.* □ *She was talking **to** you.* □ ***In spite of** everything, I still detest sweet potatoes.* □ *Place your books **beneath** your chair.* □ *I am **in** this **over** my head.*

prepositional adverb   See *adverb particle.*

prepositional complement   See *object of a preposition.*

prepositional object   See *object of a preposition.*

prepositional phrase   a *phrase* formed of a *preposition* and a following *nominal* that is the *object of the preposition.* (The examples show *prepositional phrases* in bold print.) □ *We put the collar **on the cat.*** □ *We drove **under the bridge.*** □ *Try to keep **on the straight and narrow pathway.*** □ *The small child **with the rosy red cheeks** grabbed my wallet and fled **into the crowd.***

prepositional verb   a *verb structure* that contains a *verb* followed by a *prepositional phrase;* a *lexeme* consisting of a *verb* followed by a *prepositional phrase.* (The *verb* is said to *govern* a *prepositional phrase.* Compare to *phrasal verb.* Some writers treat *prepositional verbs* as *idioms* because the meaning of the *prepositional verb* is not the "sum" of the meanings of its *constituents.* The examples show the *prepositional verb,* its required *preposition,* and the *object of the preposition.* In the examples, "|" separates the *verb* from the *prepositional phrase* when they are adjacent.) □ *Please **look | after this.*** □ *Sometimes I **wonder | about you.*** □ *I want you to **think** carefully **about what you are going to do next.*** □ *Excuse me. I need to **speak | with you or someone else | about the schedule.***

prescriptive grammar   a type of *grammar* that attempts to specify a preferred form of a language. (As opposed to the way the language is actually used. See also *proscriptive grammar* and *pedagogical grammar. Prescriptive grammars* are always traditional and are often based on evidence drawn from Latin *grammar* or logic rather than drawing upon direct observation of language use. The term was devised by *descriptivists* primarily for use as a criticism. In fact, most of the *grammar rules* that people are familiar with are from *prescriptive grammar* or *proscriptive grammar.* It has been pointed out that even a *descriptive grammar* becomes a *prescriptive grammar* when it is regarded as the only true and possible *grammar,* even in the face of counterevidence. See *prescriptivist.*)

prescriptivism   an attitude or philosophy about language that holds that language will decay unless the language people use is monitored and corrected. (*Prescriptivism* is closely linked with fixed rules of usage, the rule of logic in language use and *sentence construction,* and a tendency to favor Latin *grammar* as a model for English. The attitude or philosophy is held in contempt by *descriptivists,* who coined the term *prescriptivist.* See *prescriptivist.* See Fowler in the bibliography for an example of a study exhibiting *prescriptivism.*)

prescriptivist   a person who advocates or practices *prescriptivism.* (From the point of view of *linguists,* anyone who tries to tamper with human language—monitoring and correcting people— consciously attempting to maintain or improve the state of a particular language is said to be a *prescriptivist. Prescriptivists* are said to believe that without intensive normative efforts, a language would degenerate in some fashion. They are viewed as elitist authoritarians by some *descriptivists,* who created the term. In general, *prescriptivists* have far more influence and a greater following than *descriptivists.* In fact, it is not clear what would happen to a modern standardized language—and the culture speaking it—if there were no attempts to maintain such a language and encourage the spread of a single variety of it by means of an education system.)

[present]   See *historical present, present continuous (aspect), present emphatic, present indicative, present infinitive, present participle, present perfect aspect, present perfect continuous (aspect), present perfect infinitive, present perfect progressive (aspect), present perfect (tense), present progressive (aspect), present (tense), simple present (tense).*

present continuous (aspect)　See *present progressive (aspect).*

present emphatic　See *emphatic mood.*

present indicative　having to do with a *sentence* in the *present tense* and the *indicative (mood).* (See *past indicative.* The examples show *verbs* in the *present indicative* in bold print.)　□ *John **keeps** rabbits as pets.*　□ *Sally **is** very pleased with her new computer.*　□ *We **keep** trying, no matter what.*　□ *Everyone **needs** a little vacation now and then.*

present infinitive　the normal *form* of an *infinitive phrase* used to indicate an action happening at the same time or later than the action of the *main verb.* (Compare to *present perfect infinitive. Infinitives* are not marked for *tense* or any other *grammatical category.* See *infinitive.* The examples show *present infinitives* in bold print.)　□ *I want **to do** it.*　□ *I need **to fix** it now.*　□ *Bob has made plans **to take** a little time off.*　□ *I cannot seem to manage **to lift** this.*

present participle　a *form* made by adding the *suffix -ing* to the *present tense form* of the *verb.* (This *form* can function as part of the *verb phrase* or as an *adjective.* See a special *adjective* use at *appositive adjective.* The examples show *present participles* in bold print.)　□ *The cat is **clawing** the furniture to shreds.*　□ *We are **sending** the cat to obedience school.*　□ *The **laughing** clowns failed to cheer her up.*　□ ***Finding** something to eat was our highest priority.*

present perfect aspect　See *present perfect (tense).*

present perfect continuous (aspect)　See *present perfect progressive (aspect).*

present perfect infinitive　an *infinitive phrase* with the *perfect auxiliary have* used to indicate an action happening before the action of the *main verb.* (Compare to *present infinitive.* The expression is virtually a contradiction in terms. See *infinitive.* The examples show *present perfect infinitives* in bold print.)　□ *I wanted her **to have completed** it by noon.*　□ *They could have been able **to have done***

it on time had they arranged to have the correct instruments in stock. □ *They ought* **to have been** *here by now.* □ *The family planned* **to have cleaned** *the place up before anyone arrived.*

present perfect progressive (aspect) AND **present perfect continuous (aspect)** an *aspect* of the *verb* indicating that an activity that began in the past is still progressing and has not terminated. (This aspect is formed with *have* in the *present tense* followed by the *past participle* of *be,* followed by a *verb* with an *-ing suffix.* See comments on naming *aspects* at the entry for *aspect.* The examples show *verbs* in the *present perfect progressive aspect* in bold print.) □ *I* **have been looking** *for you all day.* □ *They* **have been riding** *their bikes since sunrise.* □ *The frogs* **have been croaking** *since the rain.* □ *Our weeds* **have been growing** *like wildfire for a week now.*

present perfect (tense) AND **present perfect aspect** an *aspect* of the *verb* indicating that the *action of the verb* is completed at the time of the utterance. (It is formed from the *present tense* of *have* plus the *past participle* of another *verb.* See comments on naming *aspects* at the entry for *aspect.* The examples show *verbs* in the *present perfect tense* in bold print.) □ *I* **have asked** *you to witness the signing.* □ *We* **have come** *a great distance to examine your records.* □ *She* **has brought** *us some very sad news.* □ *I* **have** *never* **seen** *such a mess.*

present progressive (aspect) AND **present continuous (aspect)** an *aspect* of the *verb* indicating that an activity or action is taking place at the present time. (It is formed with the *present tense* of *be* plus the *present participle* of another *verb.* See comments on naming *aspects* at the entry for *aspect.* The examples show *verbs* in the *present progressive aspect* in bold print.) □ *He* **is running** *as fast as he can.* □ *They* **are not keeping** *track well.* □ *We* **are doing** *the best that we can do.* □ *Mary* **is buying** *shoes for the children at the mall.*

present (tense) a *verb tense* indicating a current action or condition. (See also *historical present.* The examples show *verbs* in the *present tense* in bold print.) □ *I* **see** *you.* □ *The cows* **are coming** *home.* □ *I* **am** *very pleased to meet you.* □ *She* **keeps** *singing the same song over and over.*

preterit See *simple past (tense), dental preterit.*

preverb adverb an *adverb* that occurs before the *verb.* (Such *adverbs* may also occur in other positions. The examples show *preverb adverbs* in bold print.) □ *She **seldom** drives the car to work.* □ *I **certainly** do.* □ *She **usually** works on Mondays.* □ *Jane **always** cooks too much food.*

principal clause See *main clause.*

principal parts (of a verb) three specific *forms* of each *verb*: *present tense, past tense, past participle.* (The principal parts of the *verb begin* are *begin, began, begun.* Some *irregular verbs*—such as *come*—have only two different principal parts: *come* and *came*, but they are recited as three: *come, came, come.* Some, like *cost, cost, cost*, have only one form.)

pro-form a *form* that can stand for some other *form* in a *sentence.* (This is generic for *pronoun, pro-verb*, and a few other *forms.* Each example consists of two *sentences.* The first *sentence* is a *statement*, and the second *sentence* uses a *pro-form.* The *proform* and the *structure* functioning as its *antecedent* are in bold print.) □ *I want to go to **the zoo**. I want to go **there**.* □ *Angela **spills her coffee every morning**. John **does that** too.* □ *I will **hurry with all due haste**. I too will do **so**.*

progressive a shortened *form* of *progressive (aspect).* (The term has nothing to do with "advanced" or "liberal." It *conveys* the notion "in progress." See *future perfect progressive (aspect), future progressive (aspect), passive progressive perfect infinitive, past perfect progressive (aspect), past progressive (aspect), present perfect progressive (aspect), present progressive (aspect), progressive (aspect), progressive auxiliary, progressive perfect infinitive, progressive tense, progressive verb.*)

progressive (aspect) AND **continuous (aspect), progressive tense** an *aspect* of the *verb* indicating that the *action of the verb* is "progressing" or "continuing" and has not yet concluded. (Some verbs, such as *know, feel, believe, see, hear, doubt,* are thought by some not to occur in the *progressive aspect.* There is ample evidence that they do, especially in spoken English. The *progressive aspect* consists of the conjugated *form* of *be* followed by a *verb* with the *-ing suffix.* The *auxiliary be* may exhibit various *tense* and *aspect* inflections. In the term *progressive aspect,* the focus is on the continuity of the *action of the verb.* In the term *imperfect(ive) (aspect),* the focus is on the fact that at a given point in time, the *action of the verb* is not completed or terminated. Terms for the various *progressive aspects* are *future continuous (aspect), future perfect continuous (aspect), future perfect progressive (aspect), future progressive (aspect), past continuous (aspect), past perfect continuous (aspect), past perfect progressive (aspect), past progressive (aspect), present continuous (aspect), present perfect continuous (aspect), present perfect progressive (aspect), present progressive (aspect).* See comments on naming *aspects* at the entry for *aspect.* The examples show the various uses of the *progressive aspect.*) ☐ *Mary is selling pet rocks at the fair.* ☐ *Bill will be sweeping the floor for another hour.* ☐ *Rain was falling during the entire production.* ☐ *The frogs had been booming for over an hour when the hunters came.*

progressive auxiliary   a *form* of the *verb be* and the *suffix -ing* on the *verb,* as required in the formation of the *progressive aspect.* (The examples show *progressive auxiliaries* in bold print.) ☐ *He is just running wild.* ☐ *They will be fixing this pothole soon.* ☐ *You just cannot have been trying to do what it looked like.* ☐ *Bill won't be coming here anymore.*

progressive perfect infinitive   a *construction* consisting of *to* followed by *have been* followed by the *present participle* of a *verb.* (See also *perfect infinitive, passive perfect infinitive, passive progressive perfect infinitive.* The term is not in wide use, but if one encountered this *construction* and were obliged to name it, this term is appropriate. The examples show *progressive perfect infinitives* in bold print.) ☐ ***To have been loving** the same man for so long took a lot of courage.* ☐ ***To have been thieving** for so many years must have turned you into an expert.* ☐ ***To have been transporting** booze across the state* *line like that was really dangerous.* □ ***To have been coughing*** *like that for days is a sign of serious illness.*

progressive tense See *progressive (aspect)*. (Assuming that there are only two *tenses* in English, the *present tense* and the *past tense,* all the other temporal dimensions of the *verb* are considered to be part of the *aspectual* system. Nonetheless, it is traditional to refer to some of the combinations of *tense* and *aspect* as "*tenses*.")

progressive verb a *verb* with the *-ing suffix,* as used in a *progressive (aspect)*. (The examples show *progressive verbs* in bold print.) □ *How long has she been **breathing** like that?* □ *They ought not to be **gawking** like that.* □ *Are you **keeping** busy?* □ *All of them were **sneezing** and **coughing**.*

pronominal adjective a *pronoun* that functions as an *adjective;* a member of a group of *pronouns* that function as *adjectives.* (The latter consist of the *possessive pronouns* and *any, all, both,* and *some.* The examples show *pronominal adjectives* in bold print.) □ ***Any*** *question like that has to be answered by **my** father.* □ ***Our*** *whole means of support is the store.* □ ***Both*** *Jane and **my** brother found **your** visit amusing.* □ ***All*** *this nonsense must come to an end.*

pronoun AND **noun substitute** a *form* that takes the place of a *noun* or a *nominal.* (Many *pronouns* also have additional *grammatical functions.* See the related entries: *anaphoric pronoun, collective pronoun, conjunctive pronoun, demonstrative (pronoun), determinative possessive pronoun, emphatic pronoun, exclusive pronoun, impersonal pronoun, indefinite pronoun, independent possessive (pronoun), intensive (personal) pronoun, interrogative (pronoun), negative pronoun, objective pronoun, personal pronoun, possessive pronoun, reciprocal pronoun, reflexive pronoun, relative pronoun, subjective pronoun.* The examples show a wide variety of *pronouns.*) □ ***She*** *sails!* □ *Give **them their** due.* □ ***That*** *is too much. Jane wanted Mark to have lunch with **her**, but **that** was impossible.* □ *Keep **these** always.* □ ***Who*** *do **you** think **you** are?*

proper adjective an *adjective* formed from a *proper noun.* (These *adjectives,* like the *nouns* they are derived from, are capitalized. The examples show *proper adjectives* in bold print.) □ *We bought* *a lot of **Indian** silks in India.* ☐ *The **Martian** landscape is bleak indeed.* ☐ ***French** organ music of the early 1900s is among the best ever written.* ☐ *I have never understood **Australian** humor.*

proper noun any one of a large group of *nouns* referring to personal names, place names, organizations, institutions, historical periods, members of national groups, racial groups, religions, religious groups, social groups, athletic groups, calendar matters, and deifications. (The *proper* in this term is from the Latin word *proprius* meaning "one's own." This *proper* has nothing do with appropriateness. There are some *grammatical* distinctions based on personal names and *pronouns*, but *proper nouns* are unique primarily because the first or only letter must be capitalized. *Proper nouns* are preceded by a determiner only in special circumstances, such as in "The William you met at the party, not just any William...." The examples show *proper nouns* in bold print.) ☐ *My hat is in **Sweden**.* ☐ ***Mr. Brown** is an expert on the **Italian** Renaissance.* ☐ *Is this **March** or **April**?* ☐ *She works for **Walton Laboratories**.* ☐ *The **Socialist Party** won again.* ☐ *Is she a **Methodist** or a **Presbyterian**?* ☐ *They spent a week in **Hungary**.*

proposition the basic meaning of a *sentence* or *statement;* the information that a *sentence* is meant to *convey.* (A term from logic. The elements of a *proposition* are *argument* and *predication.* A single *sentence* or *statement* may actually contain a number of *propositions.*)

prop word See under *expletive.*

proscriptive grammar a set of statements about correct and incorrect *forms* in a language; a statement of *linguistic* etiquette. (Essentially directions about how to avoid errors when speaking or writing English. Many of these statements are at odds with the practices of skilled writers, and some are borrowed from Latin *grammar.* This type of *grammar* cannot and does not purport to describe a language or to advance our knowledge about language in general. See comments at *prescriptivist.* See Callihan in the bibliography for an example of a guide to how to avoid errors in writing English.) For subjects that are of typical concern in a *pro-scriptive grammar,* see *cleft infinitive, comma fault, comma splice, dangling modifier, dangling participle, divided infinitive, double adverb, double comparative, double superlative, double passive, double plural, final preposition, fused sentence, hanging participle, misplaced modifier, run-on sentence, split infinitive, split verb,* and *subordinate clause fragment.*)

pro-verb   a *verbal construction* using some *form* of the *verb do* to stand for a full *verb phrase.* (Parallel to *pronoun.* Usually spelled with the hyphen to avoid confusion with *proverb,* "a saying." The examples show *pro-verbs* in bold print.)   □   *I just love to go to the country on weekends. They **do** too.*   □   *I asked you to take out the garbage. **Did** you **do** it?*   □   *Can you believe it? Fred and Margo took all their money out of the bank and put it into a money-market account with one of those mutual fund companies. Yes, they **did!**️*   □   *I hope I can earn as much as he **does.***

pseudo-cleft sentence   a *sentence* with a wh-*clause* as a *subject* or *complement.* (See the explanation at *cleft sentence.* The examples have the wh-*clause* of a *pseudo-cleft sentence* in bold print.)   □   ***What the child uttered*** *was shocking indeed.*   □   ***Whom I like or dislike*** *is none of your business.*   □   ***Why the experiment failed*** *I don't know.*   □   *I am **what you expected,** am I not?*

Q

qualifier See *modifier*.

qualifying adjective See *descriptive adjective*.

quantifier See *(indefinite) quantifier*.

(question) tag a question *phrase* attached to the end of a *declarative sentence*, making the *sentence* a *tag question*. (See also *tag*. Typically in conversation where an answer is expected or demanded. Additionally, the tone of voice may suggest disbelief, reprimand, or reassurance. The examples show *question tags* in bold print.)
□ *You really aren't serious,* **are you?** □ *You left the computer running again,* **didn't you?** □ *Oh, dear! I seem to have made quite a fool of myself,* **haven't I?** □ *This place is quite a mess,* **huh?**

question word See *interrogative word*.

R

radical   See *root*.

reciprocal pronoun   a *pronoun* expression that refers to some sort of mutual interaction—as specified by the *verb*—between two or more entities. (There are two such expressions in English: *each other* and *one another*. The examples show *reciprocal pronouns* in bold print.) ☐ *They soon learned to like* **one another** *and also began to see themselves in a new light.* ☐ *The boxers struck* **each other** *until the bell rang.* ☐ *Try to help* **each other** *so that life will be more pleasant.* ☐ *The monkeys spent the afternoon grooming* **one another.** ☐ *They cannot even stand the sight of* **one another** *any longer.*

reciprocal verb   a *verb* whose meaning implies that the persons or things represented by the *subject* are acting on one another reciprocally. (The *subject* may be recapitulated by *reciprocal pronouns.* This is shown in parentheses in the examples. The examples show *reciprocal verbs* in bold print.) ☐ *Fred and Sam were* **arguing** *(with one another).* ☐ *The two little boys spent the entire afternoon* **fighting** *(with each other).* ☐ *The bunnies* **cuddled** *close together to keep warm.* ☐ *Bob and John* **greeted** *each other profusely.*

reduction   the process that results in *ellipsis;* the deletion of *constituents* or parts of *constituents* as with *ellipsis.* (See also *function verb.*)

redundant comparative   See *double comparative.*

redundant superlative   See *double superlative.*

reduplication   the doubling of a *word* or *inflection* for purposes of intensification. (This is a normal productive pattern in many languages, but only used informally or in slang in English— occasionally to indicate authenticity. Such uses could be considered idiomatic. Not all *reduplication* in English involves exact duplication. The elements exhibiting *reduplication* are in bold print.) □ *For a short period, we had a butler who spoke* **English English.** □ *It was fun. Not* **fun fun,** *just sort of diverting.* □ *They lived in a* **big big** *house on Maple Street.* □ *Don't be so* **wishy-washy!** □ *Stop your silly* **sing-song** *speech!*

reference grammar   a type of *descriptive grammar* that is presented in the form of a reference book, organizing the grammatical facts of a language into separate articles or topics. (See Quirk et al, 1985, in the bibliography for an example.)

referent   the entity or concept referred to by a *nominal.* (See also *antecedent*, which is a *referent* of a *pronoun.* In the examples, both the *referent* and the "referring" *nominal* are in bold print.) □ **John** *keeps all* **his** *compact discs under* **his** *bed.* □ **Sally** *is in big trouble, and I do not know what is going to happen to* **her.** □ *Will* **you** *please pick up* **your** *stuff and get out of here?* □ **She** *put* **her** *coat on his chair.*

reflexive pronoun   a *form* of the *personal pronouns* used to repeat a reference to the same *grammatical person* previously mentioned in the *sentence.* (These pronouns are limited to *myself, yourself, himself, herself, itself, ourselves, yourselves, themselves.* See also *intensive (personal) pronoun.* The examples show *reflexive pronouns* in bold print.) □ *I am going to sit right down and write* **myself** *a letter.* □ *Give* **yourself** *a break.* □ *They just couldn't help* **themselves.** □ *So, I sat down and asked* **myself** *what Abraham Lincoln would do in a situation like this.*

reflexive verb   a *verb* that takes a *subject* and *object* representing the same entity. (The examples show *reflexive verbs* in bold print.) □ *Don't* **kid** *yourself.* □ *John* **asked** *himself what he ought to do next.*

☐ *Don't **work** yourself into a frenzy.* ☐ *I **wash** myself every day.* ☐ *He **kept** himself out of trouble.* ☐ *I **pride** myself on my ability to keep things under control.*

reflexive voice   See *middle voice.*

regular   pertaining to a *form* that exhibits the typical, general, or normal behavior one expects of the other *forms* in its *form class.* (Compare to *irregular.* The examples show *regular* members of the *form class noun* in bold print.) ☐ *The **cat** needs to be trained better.* ☐ *Please put all these **things** in the **refrigerator**.* ☐ *This **piano** will be tuned very soon.*

regular plural   a *noun plural form* made by adding an s-*plural* (spelling -*s* or -*es*) rather than by changing the spelling of the *word.* (See also *irregular plural.* The *nouns* in bold print exhibit the *regular plural.*) ☐ ***Cats** are not always welcome here.* ☐ ***Roses** are welcome almost anywhere.* ☐ *We were given three **ducks** and two sheep.* ☐ *It made four big **stacks** of data.*

regular verb AND **weak verb**   a *verb* that *forms* its *past tense* and *past participle* by adding -*ed, -d, or -t* (in spelling). (The second entry term is the opposite of *strong verb*, which refers to the surviving Old English *strong verbs* in Modern English. In *weak verbs*, the spelling of the *verb stem* remains the same. *Regular verb* is the opposite of *irregular verb.* See also *dental preterit.* The examples show *regular verbs* in bold print.) ☐ *We **walked** all the way home.* ☐ *I have **fixed** all that was in need of repair.* ☐ *He **bottled** up all his emotions.* ☐ *Their house **burnt** to the ground.*

relating word   See *function word.*

relative adverb   an *adverb* that *introduces* a *relative clause.* (The most typical *relative adverbs* are *before, after, since, where, when, why.* The same *words* can be considered *conjunctions*, in which case they are termed *subordinating conjunctions.* The examples show *relative adverbs* in bold print.) ☐ *I will tell you the time **when** you should leave for the station.* ☐ *I need to know the name of the town **where***

you were born. □ *He could not tell me **why** the dog ran away.* □ *I have been unable to walk correctly **since** the car struck me.*

relative clause a *dependent clause introduced* by a *relative pronoun* and *modifying* some element in the *main clause.* (The examples show *relative clauses* in bold print.) □ *The man **whom we all met last week** lost all his money in the stock market crash.* □ *He **who hesitates** is lost.* □ *The fruit **that you see in the store these days** is not too fresh.* □ *Keeping up a house **that you really love** is no real problem.*

relative pronoun AND **relativizer** a *pronoun that introduces* a *subordinate clause* and acts as one of the *grammatical* elements in this *clause.* (For instance, in the first example, the *relative pronoun who* is also the *subject complement* in the *clause.* The examples show *relative pronouns* in bold print.) □ *I know **who** you are.* □ *We saw the car **that** had been wrecked.* □ *I had no way of telling **what** you wanted.* □ *He **who** hesitates is lost.*

relativizer See *relative pronoun.*

remoter object See *indirect object.*

reported speech See *indirect discourse.*

restrictive clause See *restrictive (relative) clause.*

restrictive modifier a *modifier* that restricts the range or scope of a *noun* so as to specify a smaller *subclass* of representatives. (The examples show *restrictive modifiers* in bold print.) □ *The man **we saw on Monday** matches your description perfectly.* □ *Children **with braces** don't eat peanut butter more than once.* □ *The **red** one is the one **we want**.* □ *The man **whom we all met last week** lost all his money in the stock market crash.*

restrictive (relative) clause AND **defining relative clause, determinative clause, essential clause** a *clause* that helps make specific the meaning of a *nominal;* a *clause* having the same specifying and selecting function as the *specific determiner.* (These *clauses* usually begin with *who, whose, whom, which,* or *that.* The *restrictive relative clause* contrasts with the *nonrestrictive clause* in that the former gives information that helps identify a specific *referent* for the *nominal* to which the *restrictive relative clause* is linked. A *nonrestrictive clause* makes a general or parenthetical comment that can apply to any *referent* for the *nominal* in question. In writing, the *restrictive relative clause* is not set off from the rest of the *sentence* by commas, and the *nonrestrictive clause* is set off by commas. *Restrictive relative clause* is the most familiar term, but *defining relative clause* is more descriptive of the function of this *clause.* The examples show *restrictive relative clauses* in bold print.) □ *The mail carrier **whom the dog bit** is recuperating nicely.* □ *The shopping cart **that had been stolen** was returned unharmed to the supermarket.* □ *All the people **who arrived at the concert late** were made to stand in the foyer until intermission.* □ *The cow **that was to give birth** had not yet come in from the pasture.* □ *People **who try** will succeed.* □ *The dog **that had rabies** died.* □ *The hotel **that we stayed in** was enormous.*

resultant object   See *predicate object(ive).*

result(ative) case   See *factitive case.*

root AND **radical**   the basic, indivisible, and unchanging component of a *word;* the *monomorphemic stem* of a *word;* a *content word* that is *simple* and *uninflected.* (All *roots* are *morphemes,* but not all *morphemes* are *roots.* These terms are more relevant to *philology* than *grammar.* See also *stem.* The examples show the *word roots* in bold print. The "|" separates *roots* in a sequence in these examples.) □ *The **black|birds chattered** endlessly.* □ *She **keeps trying.*** □ *They **rented** a **house|boat** for a **week.*** □ *They have a large **photo|graph collect|**ion.*

rule   **1.** [in *traditional grammar*] a precept that refers to the terminology of *traditional grammar* and advises what to do and what not to do. **2.** a statement of a *linguistic* relationship; part of a description of a *well-formed utterance.* (Such *rules* in modern *grammar* are often stated formulaically with symbols that are defined only within the set of *rules.*)

run-on sentence   **1.** [in written English] a type of error in which two or more *independent clauses* are connected by commas rather than the appropriate *conjunctions*. (This kind of connecting is quite common in spoken English where commas are irrelevant. The cause of a *run-on sentence* is a *comma splice*. Each example is a *run-on sentence* and is marked as a *starred form*.) □ *Ingrid was from Germany, she spoke with an accent.* □ *Fred was busy, he found time to go to the movie, though.* □ *Tony took twenty minutes, she cleaned behind the radiator, she put fresh flowers in the vases, she left her bill on the hall table.* □ *I am tired of all this, I am going home.* **2.** [in written English] a type of error in which two or more *independent clauses* are connected by *coordinating conjunctions* without the required commas. (Not all style sheets agree on where the commas are required, however. Each example is a *run-on sentence* and is marked as a *starred form*.) □ *Tom went to the zoo and he fed the monkeys peanuts.* □ *Bob drove a Buick and Fred drove a Ford and Tom carried two gas cans to the picnic.* □ *They put all four of them aside and the boys did not touch them again for a week.*

S

Saxon genitive   See s-*genitive.*

school English   See *edited English.*

secondary object   See *indirect object.*

second object   See *predicate object(ive).*

second person   a *grammatical person* indicating the entity spoken or written to, rather than the person doing the speaking or writing, or the entity spoken or written about. (This is evident in the *personal pronoun forms.* See also *first person, third person.* The examples show *pronouns* in the *second person* in bold print.)   □ *Please take off your hat indoors.*   □ *Do you know anyone who wears a hat?*   □ *Do any of you wish to wash your hands?*   □ *This is your problem, not mine.*

semantic   having to do with meaning; having to do with *semantics.*

semantics   the study of meaning; the specification or explanation of meaning.

semantic subclass   a grouping of *constituents* of similar meaning, usually with similar, and sometimes subtle, *grammatical* behavior. (*Semantic subclasses* usually can be identified or confirmed satisfactorily by meaning. Compare to *grammatical subclass.*)

sentence **1.** a group of *words* expressing a complete thought. (This is the traditional definition of a *sentence*. Some language scholars claim this definition is not useful because it assumes that there is agreement or common knowledge as to what constitutes a complete thought. The effectiveness of distinguishing real *sentences* from *sentence fragments* depends not on identifying complete thoughts, but on a *linguistic* intuition that can distinguish a *well-formed sentence* from one that is not *well-formed*. See also *cataphoric sentence, cleft sentence, comparative sentence, complete sentence, complex sentence, compound-complex sentence, compound sentence, conditional sentence, coordinate sentence, declarative sentence, embedded sentence, equative (sentence), exclamatory sentence, existential sentence, fragmentary sentence, fused sentence, imperative sentence, indicative sentence, interrogative sentence, kernel sentence, pseudo-cleft sentence, run-on sentence, sentence adverb, (sentence) connector, (sentence) diagram, sentence fragment, sentence modifier, sentence pattern, simple sentence.*) **2.** a *grammatically well-formed utterance.* (This definition relies on the same *linguistic* intuition as sense 1 but is more specific as to the actual kind of knowledge being referred to. See also *grammatically well-formed.*)

sentence adverb AND **sentence modifier** an *adverb* that *modifies* or enhances an entire *sentence*. (The definition covers almost all *adverbs* that do not *modify adjectives* or other *adverbs*. These forms are to be found at the beginning or end of a *sentence*, or within the *verb phrase*. The term seems to be vague and covers an extensive variety of *constructions*. See *absolute phrase* for another construction that *modifies* whole *sentences*. Compare to *sentential adverb*. The examples show *sentence adverbs* in bold print.) ☐ *Slowly, he turned to face his attacker.* ☐ *Anyway, all of this will be settled soon.* ☐ *In the first place, we were not in a position to call in the full forces.* ☐ *After all was said and done, everything worked out.*

(sentence) connector See *conjunctive (adverb)*.

(sentence) diagram a diagram showing the result of the *parsing* of a *sentence*. (This drawing and the procedures of *parsing* are an important application of *pedagogical grammar.* Compare to *tree diagram* and *immediate constituents.*)

sentence fragment AND **fragmentary sentence**   a group of *words* that does not qualify as a *sentence;* a group of *words* that does not "express a complete thought"; a *string* of *constituents* that is not *grammatically well-formed.* (A *sentence fragment* is a traditional error in written English. See comments on the notion of "complete thought" at *sentence.* It should be noted that *sentence fragments* usually lack specific *constituents* or *grammatical constructions.* They are not usually randomly chosen *strings* of *words. Sentence fragments* are usually flawed attempts at producing *grammatically well-formed utterances* or represent erroneous pronunciation. Of course, in spoken English, the examples given here are typical of everyday communication. All the examples would appear as written English in *direct quotations.* Each example is a *sentence fragment* in *edited English* and is shown as a *starred form.*)   ☐   **Because we were late for the movie.*   ☐   **Three girls sitting in the sand, wiggling their toes down into the stuff to keep them cool.*   ☐   **Keeping busy.*   ☐   **Wonder why.*

sentence modifier   See *sentence adverb.*

sentence pattern   the *order* of the elements of a *sentence.* (More of a general expression than a specific *grammar* term. Refers to the various *sentence* types, or to typical *sentence structures* in specific languages. In English, *declarative sentences, imperative sentences, interrogatory sentences,* and *exclamatory sentences* each have specific *sentence patterns.* The examples show these four *sentence patterns.*)   ☐   *The dogs barked all night long.*   ☐   *Make those children be quiet!*   ☐   *Was that the howling of wind that kept me awake?*   ☐   *This cake is out of this world!*

sentential adverb   See *disjunct, sentence adverb.*

sentential ambiguity   the property of a *sentence* that has two or more distinct meanings. (*Sentential ambiguity* can be caused by *lexical ambiguity* or *grammatical ambiguity.* The following sentences exhibit *sentential ambiguity.*) ☐ *Falls like that can be dangerous.* ☐ *She sat out drinking in the moonlight.* ☐ *The turkey is ready to eat.* ☐ *Spending money pleases me.*

sentential meaning   the meanings of *sentences.* (Compare to *lexical meaning.*)

separative pronoun   a *pronoun* that stands for an individual entity or for one or more individual entities within a group. (Compare to *collective pronoun.* These *pronouns* are *each, each one, either, every, everybody, everyone, everything, neither, several.* The examples show *separative pronouns* in bold print.) ☐ ***Everybody*** *remained in the theater.* ☐ *Please put* ***everything*** *back where you got it.* ☐ ***Each one*** *was given a large piece of cake.* ☐ ***Each*** *should try as hard as possible.*

s-form   the *form* of the English *verb* that is used in the *present tense* with a *third person singular subject.* (See remarks at *plural verb.*)

s-genitive AND **Saxon genitive**   the *marker* of the *genitive case* that is spelled *'s,* or *-s* in the word *its.* (This is the historical *form* of the *genitive (case)* that came down from Anglo-Saxon (Old English). Compare to *Norman genitive, of-genitive.* The examples show *s-genitives* in bold print.) ☐ *This is* ***Tom's*** *house? It's horrible!* ☐ *The lion was favoring one of* ***its*** *paws.* ☐ *I had a brief discussion with the* ***newspaper's*** *editor.* ☐ ***Jane's*** *idea is the best of all.*

sign of the infinitive   See *infinitive marker.*

simple   the shortest, least complex, or least encumbered *form* of a *constituent.* (This has nothing to do with "easiness.")

simple form (of the verb)   See *simple verb.*

simple futurity   in English, *will* and sometimes *shall* followed by a *verb* used to show *future time.* (The examples show the *verbs* that convey *simple futurity* in bold print.) ☐ *I* ***will go*** *there all in good time.* ☐ *Jane knows what she* ***will do*** *when she gets there.* ☐ *I promise I* ***will bring*** *you something from Alaska.* ☐ *John* ***will pay*** *his bills late this month.*

simple past (tense) AND **preterit**   the *form* of the *verb* used to show that the state or act expressed by the *verb* occurred before the present time. (As opposed to the *verbal aspects* where the *verbal auxiliaries* bear the *inflection*. The examples show *verbs* in the *simple past tense* in bold print.) □ *Jane **left** for Cancun yesterday.* □ *The small kitten **lay** sprawled on the mat.* □ *The car **pulled** into my lane without signaling.* □ *They **walked** and **walked** for a great distance, and finally they **came** to a village.*

simple predicate AND **bare predicate** the *verb* and its *auxiliaries* without any *complements* or *modifiers*. (Compare to *complete predicate*. The examples show the *simple predicates* in bold print.) □ *Johnny **had run** too far.* □ *The car **ought** not **to have pulled** into my lane without signaling.* □ *She **will have been doing** calculations for an hour.* □ *By noon, John **will have been talked** to for over an hour.*

simple present (tense) The *present tense* alone with no *modifiers* and no *aspect* shown, usually indicating habitual or customary activity. Usually, present time is indicated by the *present progressive*. See also *historical present*. The examples show *verbs* in the *simple present tense* in bold print.) □ *I **do** it, I don't know why, but I **do** it.* □ *I **run** a small deli on North Main Street.* □ *I **speak** very slowly, so you can understand me.* □ *He **comes** here often.*

simple sentence a *sentence* consisting of only a single *independent clause*. (Compare to *compound sentence, complex sentence,* and *compound-complex sentence*. This has nothing to do with the simplicity or complexity of the meaning of the *sentence*. The examples are all *simple sentences*.) □ *The boys ran from the barn.* □ *The plethora of disparate results achieved by the seventy or so researchers in the lab set the entire project back at least a decade.* □ *The vase broke.* □ *I fell.*

simple subject the *headword* of a *noun phrase* serving as the *subject* of a *sentence*. (Compare to *complete subject*. The examples show *simple subjects* in bold print.) □ *The elderly **couple** kept their appointment, although no one else did.* □ *The silly **creature** with the purple stripes and enormous smile slowly faded away.* □ *Pet **dogs** can be annoy-*

ing if you are not used to them. □ ***Walls** are meant to be strong.* □ *The latest, new, chart-busting, trend-setting **album** from Domino and the Derricks, this year's hottest young herd of hopefuls, is setting sales records around the country.* □ ***I** spy.*

simple tense   one of two *tenses*, the *past tense* or *present tense* without an *aspect* indicated. (See also *simple past (tense)* and *simple present (tense)*. The examples show *verbs* in the *simple tenses* in bold print.) □ *I **saw** the movie you mentioned.* □ *Let's **see** another movie tonight.* □ *Here I **go**. Good-bye.* □ ***I** spy.*

simple verb AND **simple form (of the verb)**   1. the *form* of the *verb* found in an *infinitive* without the *to;* an unconjugated *verb*. (The basic *form* of an English *verb*. The examples show *simple verbs* in bold print.) □ *Please try to **do** it correctly this time.* □ *Didn't I ask you to **help** me?* □ *No one wants to **travel** on weekends.* **2.** the opposite of *compound verb*. (A single *verb* rather than two as in *read and write*. Also simple in the sense that the *verb* has no other *parts of speech* prefixed as with *double-cross* or *overhang*. See the examples for the previous sense.)

singular   the indication of "just one" in English. (The *singular* is unmarked in English. See also *grammatical number* and *plural*. The examples show *nominals* in the *singular* in bold print.) □ *Give **me** a **kiss**.* □ ***He** left early to buy a **cake** for the **party**.* □ ***She** put two cakes on the **table**.* □ ***She** picked out just **one** special **grain** from all those on the **table**.*

slot and filler grammar   a type of *grammar* or an approach to *grammar* wherein a *sentence pattern* is used to determine *word classes*. (A test *frame* based on a given *sentence pattern* is established by constructing a very general *sentence* following the *sentence pattern* but with a blank or "slot" left empty where one of the *forms* has been purposely omitted. All the *words* that can fill the slot and result in a *well-formed utterance* are said to belong to the same *word class*. This is a type of *descriptive grammar*. The examples show first the *frame* with the empty slot, followed by a list of the *words* that can serve as filler, followed by a list of *starred forms* that cannot serve as filler. The third example does not demonstrate anything conclusive. A great deal of ingenuity and intuition has to go into constructing the test frames. Other kinds of *grammar* are interested in explaining that intuition. Nonetheless, the *slot and filler grammar* is a useful pedagogical device for demonstrating the notion of *word class*.) ☐ *Please _____ it now.* ***do, kill, wash, paint, feel, eat;** *wonder, *wander, *go, *die, *cow, *the.* ☐ *What a lovely _____ hat!* ***old, straw, rubber, red, paper;** *shoe, *my, *the, *what.* ☐ *Please put it _____.* ***right, there, here, away, aside, up, down;** *some, *red, *forever, *symbolic.*

specific determiner   a *pronoun* or *particle* that points out or indicates exactly "which one(s)." (Compare to *definite article*, which is limited only to those *particles* identified as *articles*. The examples show *specific determiners* in bold print.) ☐ ***That** cat is mine.* ☐ *None of **those** cats could be mine.* ☐ ***My** book is the one with the red cover.* ☐ *We put **their** coats in the closet.*

split infinitive AND **cleft infinitive, divided infinitive**   [in English] an infinitive separated by an adverb. (An error in *edited English*. Frequently used in everyday speech. Its use is an attempt to place the *adverb* in a location that will allow an unambiguous interpretation. The examples are *starred forms* followed by correct versions. The *split infinitive* is in bold print.) ☐ **They all wanted to quickly bring** *the matter to an end. / They all wanted to bring the matter to an end quickly.* ☐ **Do you intend to just stand** *there and do nothing while the entire project collapses? / Do you intend just to stand there and do nothing while the entire project collapses?* ☐ **The cat tried to warily creep** *up to the place where the birds were, but was spotted by one alert finch. / The cat tried to creep up warily to the place where the birds were, but was spotted by one alert finch.* ☐ **I would just love to peacefully go** *to the concert. / I would just love to go to the concert peacefully.*

split verb   a *verb phrase* where an *adverb* occurs between the *verbal auxiliary* and the *main verb*. (Once viewed as an error, parallel to *split infinitive*. It is historically normal and natural English. See *proscriptive grammar*. The examples show *split verbs* in bold print.) □ *We **have** almost never **paid** cash for a car.* □ *We **had** seldom **thought** of her after that.* □ *But you **have** always **been** my friend.* □ *Fred **has** never **been** one to do that sort of thing.*

s-plural the basic formation of the English *plural*. (In spelling, the addition of -*s* or -*es* as appropriate. As opposed to *irregular* formations of the *plural*, such as *goose* > *geese, ox* > *oxen, child* > *children, octopus* > *octopodes* (or *octopuses, octopi*), and *datum* > *data*. The examples contain *nouns* exhibiting the s-*plural*.) □ *Seven cats scurried after three little mice and two rats.* □ *Trees are now growing in all the yards.* □ *Coats and hats hung neatly in their places.* □ *Our cars both need repairs.*

standard English widespread, acceptable English. (The opposite of *nonstandard English*. See *edited English*.)

starred form 1. a hypothetical *form* of a *word, sentence*, or other expression, usually marked with an asterisk. (Used in particular in citing *forms* or *morphemes* hypothesized in the historical reconstruction of a language.) 2. an incorrect or non-*well-formed linguistic structure*; an *ungrammatical form*, usually marked with an asterisk. (The examples show first the *starred forms*, followed by the *well-formed* versions.) □ **The old three men. . ./ The three old men. . .* □ **We kept trying to do it on. / We kept on trying to do it.* □ **We ought to been there sooner. / We ought to have been there sooner.*

statement See *declarative sentence*.

state verb See *stative verb*.

static verb See the following entry.

stative verb AND **state verb, static verb** a *verb* that indicates the existence of a state of being or enduring rather than indicating an action. (These include *be* and *have; verbs* that indicate an involuntary response of the senses: *see, hear, feel;* states of the mind: *believe, know, sense, feel*. Compare to *active verb*. The examples show *stative verbs* in bold print.) □ *I **know** just how you **feel**.* □ *He **saw***

what you meant. □ *We **are** tired.* □ *I can just **feel** the burning envy she radiates.*

stem AND **kernel** **1.** the part of a *word, root, base,* etc. to which an *affix* is added. (A *stem* may include one or more *roots* and other *affixes.* A *root* contains no *affixes.* The examples show *stems* in bold print.) □ *Please be **careful!*** □ ***Careful**ness is a virtue that is important in this job.* □ *We **walk**ed all the way.* □ *The professor glowered **dark**ly at the **help**less freshman.* **2.** In English, the *verb* in an *infinitive;* the *bare infinitive.* (That is, the *infinitive* without the *to.* The examples show *stems* in bold print.) □ *I just **wanted** to **cry.*** □ *We **intend** to **go** to the party.* □ *It's too late to **do** anything about it.* □ *Will we **get** cold in Alaska?*

string a sequence of *linguistic* units. (Can be sounds, *morphemes, words,* or *clauses.* Part of the *metalanguage* of *linguistics* and, sometimes, *grammar.*)

strong past tense the *form* of the *past tense* of a *strong verb.*

strong verb See *irregular verb.*

structural linguistics a type of *linguistics* popular in the United States in the mid-1900s that concentrated on describing the *linguistic structures* of languages, primarily the sound systems and patterns of *word formation.*

structural meaning the meaning associated with a particular *linguistic structure,* such as a *sentence* or a *phrase.* (This goes beyond the meanings of the individual *words* and has to do with how the entire *sentence conveys* meaning. Each of the examples has a *structural meaning* of one entity operating on or having some effect on some other entity.) □ *The dog bit the man.* □ *Tom baked a cake.* □ *I will read this book soon.*

structural word a *word* or *particle* used to show *grammatical structure.* (As opposed to a *content word* such as a *noun* or a *verb.* See the comments and list of near synonyms at *function word.*)

structure   **1.** pattern; design; arrangement. (See *constituent structure, deep structure, phrase-structure grammar, surface structure, underlying structure.*) **2.** a particular type of pattern; a *constituent;* a particular sequence of *parts of speech, phrases, complements,* etc.; a *construction.*

subclass   a subdivision of one of the *parts of speech* or *form classes.* (All members of a *subclass* exhibit the same kind of *grammatical* or *syntactic* behavior. See *grammatical subclass* and *semantic subclass.*)

subdisjunctive (conjunction)   the *conjunction or* used to *introduce* a *word* or *phrase* that renames or restates a preceding *nominal.* (The examples show *subdisjunctive conjunctions* in bold print.) ☐ *Grains,* **or** *kernels, of corn make good cattle feed.* ☐ *Mr. Tucker,* **or** *Bubba to his friends, grows peanuts back in the hills.* ☐ *The s-genitive,* **or** *Saxon genitive, is the most common form of the genitive.* ☐ *We always keep some pop,* **or** *soda if you're from the East, in the refrigerator.*

subject   [in a sentence] the *noun* or *nominal* that is the *author* of the action of the verb; the *agent.* (Compare *grammatical subject* with *logical subject.* See also *anticipatory subject, apparent subject, complete subject, compound subject, dummy subject, grammatical subject, logical subject, postponed subject, simple subject, subject complement, subjective, subject(ive) case, subject(ive) complement, subjective genitive, subjective pronoun, subject of an infinitive.* The examples show *subjects* in bold print.) ☐ ***Sunshine*** *makes me happy.* ☐ ***Fred*** *drives a hard bargain.* ☐ ***Some good hot coffee*** *is what I need.* ☐ *Will* ***you*** *please hurry up?*

subject complement   See *subject(ive) complement* at *predicate nominative.*

subjective   having to do with the *grammatical subject* of a *sentence.* (Has nothing to do with personal judgments or biases.)

subject(ive) case   See *nominative (case).*

subject(ive) complement   See *predicate nominative.*

subjective genitive   a *semantic subclass* of the *genitive case* used to describe a *construction* wherein something that is possessed serves as the *subject* of a *sentence*. (Compare to *objective genitive*. The examples show *subjective genitives* in bold print.) ☐ *The **child's playmate** was injured in the bus accident.* ☐ *The **playmate of the child** was injured in the bus accident.* ☐ ***My application for employment** was turned down.* ☐ ***Jane's aunt** was arrested for speeding.*

subjective pronoun   one of the set of *personal pronouns* that serves as a *subject*. (They are *I, you, he, she, it, we,* and *they.* Compare to *objective pronoun*. The *personal pronoun you* is the same whether it is a *subjective pronoun* or an *objective pronoun*. The examples show *subjective pronouns* in bold print.) ☐ *Hurry, **I** need the scissors after you.* ☐ ***We** are leaving this place at once.* ☐ ***They** cannot possibly mean that!* ☐ ***I** spy.*

subject of an infinitive   the *subject* of a *verb* in an *infinitive clause*. (See remarks at *infinitive clause*. If this "*subject*" is a *personal pronoun*, it is an *objective pronoun*.) ☐ *Do you really want **me** to do all that?* ☐ *I must go right now and call **someone** to fix that.* ☐ *The president wanted **him** to visit a number of Asian countries.* ☐ *Sorry, we need **him** to help us with our planning for the future course of the company.*

subjunctive construction   a term focusing on the *formal* nature of the *subjunctive mood* in English.

subjunctive mode   See the following entry.

subjunctive (mood) AND **subjunctive mode**   a *semantic* categorization of a use of a *verb* to express doubt, wish, regret, concession, possibility, supposition, hypothesis, or a *condition contrary to fact,* rather than matters of fact. (Currently, the use of a special *verb form* for the *subjunctive* in English is limited to the use of *were* rather than *was* to express various aspects of *conditions contrary to fact,* and is almost always found in a *clause* that is introduced by *if*. This special *form* is not widely used, the *conditional* handling everything previously handled by the *subjunctive*. The indicator of the *subjunctive mood* is in bold print.) ☐ *If I **were** king, things would be different.* ☐ *I moved that the meeting **be** postponed.*

□ *If I **were** you, I would avoid being pedantic.* □ *He ordered that she **go** to the scene of the crime.*

subordinate clause   See *dependent clause.*

subordinate clause fragment   A *dependent clause* that stands alone in error or in *ellipsis.* (These *clauses* cannot stand alone and must be attached to an *independent clause.* A *subordinate clause fragment* is a *grammatical* error in *edited English.* See other *grammatical* errors under *proscriptive grammar.* The examples are presented as *starred forms* since they are not *grammatically well-formed.* They would be considered *well-formed* if they were *elliptical* answers to questions. Each example is a *subordinate clause fragment.*) □ **When the rain fell hard.* □ **After the plains flooded.* □ **If she thought I actually owned a car.* □ **Because I keep to the right when I walk.*

subordinating conjunction AND **subordinator**   a *word* or *phrase* that *introduces* a *subordinate clause.* (This *form* serves to connect a *subordinate clause* to a *main clause.* Note that in many cases, the *subordinating conjunction* is a *preposition* functioning as a *conjunction.* Typical *subordinating conjunctions* are *after, although, as, as if, as much as, assuming, as though, because, before, even if, excepting, for, given, how, if, inasmuch as, in case, in order that, in that, lest, provided, since, so that, such that, than, that, then, though, unless, until, what, when, whenever, where, whereas, while, who, whoever, whom, whomever.* Most of these *words* can also be considered *adverbs,* in which case they are *relative adverbs.* The examples show *subordinating conjunctions* in bold print.) □ *We profited **because** we invested wisely.* □ ***Although** we invested almost nothing, we profited handsomely.* □ *She left **so that** we could take her place.* □ *Tom always knew **when** Jane was on vacation.* □ *I will gladly do it **unless** you want to.* □ *Harriet goes fishing every Saturday **unless** the Cubs are playing at home.*

subordination   the process of combining related *simple sentences* into a larger *complex sentence* expressing the same information.

subordinator   See *subordinating conjunction.*

substandard English   a variety of English considered to represent a lack of education on the part of its speakers. (Some language scholars object to this term and prefer *nonstandard English*. Not everyone has sufficient knowledge or understanding of the different varieties of English to determine whether a given variety of English represents normal dialect variation or *substandard English*.)

substantive   a *word* or *phrase* serving as a *noun* or *nominal*. (The elements in bold print in the examples are *substantives*.)   □ *Finding something to eat was **the first task of business**.*   □ ***Fred** kept his **promise** just as we knew he would.*   □ *The **authors** met together for the first **time** with the reading study **group**.*   □ *Please do whatever is necessary to keep the **ants** from coming into the **house**.*   □ *The **poor** will always be with us.*

suffix   an *affix* that is placed at the end of a *word*; a *morpheme* that is attached to the end of another *morpheme*. (The second member of a *(noun) compound* is not properly called an *affix*. *Suffixes* are *bound forms*. See also *infix* and *prefix*. The examples show *suffixes* in bold print.)   □ *I have a musical **clock**.*   □ *Her uncommon**ness** attracted me.*   □ *The attend**ant** politely said hello to everyone.*   □ *The lumberjack fell**ed** the trees.*

suffixation   the adding of a *suffix* to a *stem*; the use of *suffixes* as *inflection*.

superlative   an *adjective* or *adverb* displaying the *superlative degree*. (See *superlative (degree)*. Compare to *comparative (degree)* and *positive (degree)*. See also *redundant superlative, double superlative*. The examples show *superlatives* in bold print.)   □ *That dog is the **smallest** dog of all.*   □ *He drove **fastest** in our heat.*   □ *It depends on which of the three is **quickest**.*   □ *The one that is the **most expensive** attracts my attention every time.*

superlative comparison   See the following entry.

superlative (degree) AND **absolute degree, superlative comparison**   **1.** the extreme *degree* of comparison; a type of comparison referring to the maximum amount of the quality named by an *adjective*. (Formed with *-est* or *most* as in the examples. Compare to *positive degree, comparative (degree).* The *constituents* in bold print are in the *superlative degree.*) ☐ *We are **most pleased** with the results.* ☐ *It was the **worst** fire I have ever seen.* ☐ *I've seen foggy days, but this is the **foggiest** it has ever been around here.* ☐ *Give Wallace the **biggest** piece of cake, please.* **2.** See the previous entry for *superlative.*

superordinate clause   the *independent clause* in a *complex sentence.* (Compare to *subordinate clause* at *dependent clause.* The examples show *superordinate clauses* in bold print.) ☐ ***I went home** after I finished jogging.* ☐ ***I played the fiddle** while dinner burned.* ☐ ***She threatened to jump out the window** unless I agreed to the plan.* ☐ ***We danced awhile** before we all got to go home.*

supine   the English *infinitive construction; to* plus a *verb.* (The term is borrowed from Latin. See *infinitive.* Each example shows the *supine* in bold print.) ☐ *They wanted **to go** very badly.* ☐ *What on earth are you trying **to do**?* ☐ *You are free **to spend** whatever amount you want **to spend**.* ☐ *Wallace sought **to have** the company pay for the medical treatment.*

surface structure   **1.** the structural relationships of *constituents* of a *construction* observable in the very *words* or *morphemes* of the *construction.* (Compare to *deep structure.*) **2.** a representation of a particular *deep structure* by the associated *surface structure.* (See *deep structure.*)

syntactic   the *adjective form* of *syntax.*

syntagm(a)   any two or more *words* or *morphemes* combined according to the *rules* or patterns of a particular language. (The mark "|" shows the boundaries between the elements of the *syntagma.* The mark "‖" separates each *syntagma* in the examples.) ☐ *dis|tress* ☐ *un|happi|ness* ☐ *re|veal* ☐ *Two | road|s | di|verge|d | in | a | dense | forest.*

syntagmatic   having to do with the sequential relationships of *linguistic* units; having to do with the relationship between the individual elements of a *syntagma.*

syntax   the analysis, study, or statement of the arrangements and interrelationships exhibited by *words, phrases,* and *clauses* in *sentences.* (See also *word order.*)

T

tag   See *tag question* and *question tag*.

tagmeme   the basic *grammatical* unit of *tagmemics*. (Parallel to the *morpheme* in *morphology* and the *phoneme* in *phonology*.)

tagmemics   a type of *descriptive grammar* whose goal is the specification of *sentence structures* by stating which elements can occupy which positions in a *sentence; slot and filler grammar.*

tag question   a question formed from a *declarative sentence* by the addition of a *question tag*, often a short *clause* with the *verb* before the *subject* or some other *word*. (Each example is a *tag question*.)   □ *You certainly aren't serious, are you?*   □ *You left the television running again, didn't you?*   □ *I seem to have made quite a fool of myself, haven't I?*   □ *This room is quite a mess, eh?*

telic verb   a *verb* whose *action* has a clear terminal point or "expiration." (For instance, *hit, kick, kill, strike, stop, cease*, etc. Compare to *atelic verb*. The examples show *telic verbs* used in *sentences*.)   □ *Polly **kicked** the ball hard.*   □ *When is he **stopping**?*   □ *You are getting ready to **hit** me, I think.*   □ *Tom **killed** the helpless cicada.*

temporal adverb   See *adverb of time.*

temporality   *tense* and *aspect;* time as expressed by *tense, aspect,* and *adverbs of time.*

tense   the quality of the *verb* expressing the time of action. (See *present (tense), past tense, future (tense)*. See also *compound tense, durative (tense), emphatic tense, future perfect (tense), imperfect(ive) (tense), nonpast (tense), past perfect (tense), perfect (tense), periphrastic future tense, periphrastic tense, phrasal tense, pluperfect (tense), present perfect (tense), progressive tense, simple past (tense), simple present (tense), simple tense, strong past tense, tense shift, weak past tense*.)

tense shift   in *formal*, sense 2, literary English, the changing of *tense* on the part of one *verb* to accommodate the *tense* or *aspect* of a *verb* in another part of the *sentence*. (Generally, in a *sentence* that has a *dependent clause* as an *object* of its *verb*, and the *verb* in the *dependent clause* is in the *indicative mood*, the *verb* in the *dependent clause* is said to "shift" to conform to the *tense* of the *verb* in the *main clause*. The examples show the "unshifted" followed by the "shifted" version, followed by a *starred form* showing the same *sentence* without the *tense shift*.) □ *We know how he **does** it. We knew how he **did** it. *We knew how he does it.* □ *They know that we **are** happy. They knew that we **were** happy. *They knew that we are happy.* □ *This shows what we **knew** all along. This showed what we **had known** all along. *This showed what we knew all along.*

terminate aspect   an *aspect* of the *verb* encompassing the beginning and ending of an act; an *aspect* covering a single action, both the starting and ending. (This can be used with both *simple verbs* and *compound verbs*. See comments on naming *aspects* at the entry for *aspect*. The *verb* in bold print can be said to be in the *terminative aspect*.) □ *They **handed out** the papers.* □ *Max **stumbled and fell**.* □ *Sally **decided** to buy a lot of new clothes.* □ *The car **flipped over**.*

T.G.   See *transformational-generative grammar.*

third person   an indication, in some *pronouns* and one *verb* form, of the entities spoken or written about, rather than the entities spoken or written to, or the speaker. (The *third person pronouns* are *he, she, it, they, him, her, them, his, its,* and *their*. Verbs (except *be*

and *have*) with a *third person singular subject* bear the *marker -s* when in the *present tense*. See also *first person, second person*. The examples show *nominals* in the *third person* in bold print.)
☐ *The game wardens were obliged to dispatch* **the excess elephant population.** ☐ **He** *speaks well.* ☐ *Bob spoke well of* **Jane** *and* **Andrew.**
☐ *Give* **them their** *money back.* ☐ **They** *detest all this attention, of course.*

time adverb See *adverb of time*.

to-infinitive a *verb* preceded by *to.* (As opposed to a *bare infinitive*.)
☐ *I really wanted* **to go.** ☐ *You never would have been able* **to do** *that in the past.* ☐ *I wouldn't want* **to do** *it if you had been kinder early on.* ☐ *Can't someone try* **to fix** *this for me?*

traditional grammar a typical *pedagogical grammar* that concentrates on *parsing* and naming *constituents*. (Such *grammars* are nearly always aimed at an understanding of *grammar* sufficient to permit and encourage literacy or better writing. Most *pedagogical grammar* is also *traditional grammar*. See *grammar*, sense 3. See Friend, J. A. in the bibliography for more information on *traditional grammar*.)

transformational-generative grammar AND **generative-transformational grammar, T.G., transformational grammar** a type of *grammar* that produces or creates *sentences* by way of a sequence of *rules* and in doing so assigns a *syntactic* description to each *sentence*, and derives the *surface structure* of each *sentence* from one or more *deep structures* through a set of *transformational rules*. (This refers to the form of the *grammar*, rather than to a specific *grammar*. *Transformational-generative grammars* are of theoretical value, but are not practical as *pedagogical grammars*.)

transformational grammar See *transformational-generative grammar*.

transformation(al) rule in a *transformational-generative grammar*, a *rule* that acts on a *kernel sentence* or another *string* derived from one or more *kernel sentences* to produce additional, and often, more complex *sentences*. (See *phrase-structure grammar, deep structure, surface structure,* and *underlying structure.*)

[**transitive**]   See *complex transitive verb, ditransitive verb, intransitive verb, monotransitive verb, transitive (verb).*

transitive (verb)   a *verb* having a *direct object*; a *verb* carrying its "action" from a *subject* to a *direct object*. (See also *active voice, passive voice.* Compare to *intransitive verb.* Some *verbs,* such as *eat,* can be used both as *transitive verbs* and *intransitive verbs,* but not at the same time. "I am eating" contains an *intransitive verb.* "I am eating a sandwich" contains a *transitive verb.* The examples show *transitive verbs* in bold print.)   □   *The dog **bit** the man.*   □   *We **love** white cake with white icing.*   □   *The carpenter **shaved** a bit off the bottom of the door.*   □   *I **typed** the whole thing in less than an hour.*

tree diagram   a drawing of the *structure* of a *sentence* or part of a *sentence.* (This diagram looks like the branching root system of a tree. The *tree diagram* is associated with *transformational-generative grammar.* Compare to *sentence diagram.*)

two-object verb   a *verb* that can take both a *direct object* and an *indirect object* in the same *sentence.* (These *verbs* may also function as *transitive verbs* without a second *object.* See also *ditransitive verb.* In the examples, the two *objects* are in bold print separated by "|.")   □   *I bought **the little boy** | **the toy.**   □   They gave **us** | **a very bad time.**   □   I lent **her** | **one.**   □   You must give **me** | **whatever I deserve.***

two-word verb   See *phrasal verb.*

U

ultimate constituent   the lowest level *constituent*; a *grammatical construction* that has no *immediate constituents*. (See *immediate constituent*. *Ultimate constituents* cannot be further divided into *constituents*.)

uncountable noun   See *noncount noun*.

underlying structure   the *deep structure* that gives rise to (a) *surface structure*; any level of *structure* beneath the *surface structure*. (See both senses of *surface structure*.)

understood   pertaining to an element of a *sentence* that must be assumed to exist even when it is not present. (The *subject* of an *imperative sentence* is *understood you*. Otherwise the *imperative sentence* would not be a *sentence* because it would lack a *subject*. It should be noted that there is an inherent conflict between the concepts of *understood* and *complete*. Structures termed *complements* are said to make *complete* an *utterance* that would be detectably "incomplete" without the *complement* and, therefore, wrong. On the other hand, *structures* that are otherwise obviously "incomplete" in that they lack major *grammatical* elements, such as a *subject* that can be said to be *understood*, are considered to be correct. In the following examples, the *understood you* is shown in brackets. See also *ellipsis*.)   ☐ *Don't [you] make fun of grammar rules!*   ☐ *[You] come here!*   ☐ *[You] give him time to finish!*   ☐ *[You] please stop doing that!*

ungrammatical   not in keeping with *grammar rules;* not accounted for by a *grammar* or by the intuition of a competent speaker of the language being examined. (This is the *linguistic* equivalent of "wrong." In part the term is a reaction against the notion of fixed right and wrong in language. It is also used to label errors other than spelling, style, or word choice. Each of the example *sentences* is *ungrammatical* for various reasons and is shown as a *starred form.*)   □   *Four man entered the room smiling.*   □   *She have been there many times before.*   □   *Fred kept singing, besides Mary fainted.*   □   *Having bought our ticket, the train left the station.*

uninflected   without *inflection.* (See also *unmarked.*)

unmarked   lacking a *grammatical marker* of some kind; *uninflected.*

utterance   any minimal, free-standing specimen of language, spoken or written; roughly, a *sentence.* (There is an assumption that *utterances* are spoken and that written language is just spoken language written down. Linguists use the term to avoid "*sentence*," which implies an initial judgment of *grammaticality* or *complete*ness. Linguists require a term for *strings* of *words* that may or may not be *grammatical* or may be *grammatical* only to some degree. Each of the following examples constitutes an *utterance* although each is not necessarily a *well-formed* or *grammatical sentence.*)   □   *Come on, now!*   □   *There are wasps!*   □   *Walk over to. . . .*   □   *Now, if you could just. . . .*   □   *Tally ho!*   □   *Huh?*

V

variable word a word subject to *formal* changes. (This includes words subject to *inflection* and *irregular forms*. Compare to *invariable word* at *indeclinable word*. The variable words are in bold print in the examples.) ☐ **We profited** *because we invested wisely.* ☐ *Although we* **invested** *nothing, we* **profited** *handsomely.* ☐ **She left** *so that we* **could take** *her place.* ☐ **Dorothy** *always* **knew** *when* **Mickey** *was on vacation.* ☐ **I will gladly do** *it unless you* **want** *to.*

verb a word conveying action or a state of being; the core of the predicate and, in modern *linguistics*, the core of the *sentence*. (See related subjects at: *action (of the verb)*, *active verb*, *atelic verb*, *auxiliary verb*, *causative verb*, *complete verb*, *complex transitive verb*, *compound verb*, *copular verb*, *copulative verb*, *defective verb*, *denominative verb*, *ditransitive verb*, *equational verb*, *factitive verb*, *factive verb*, *finite verb*, *flat verb*, *full verb*, *function verb*, *helping verb*, *inceptive verb*, *inchoative verb*, *intransitive verb*, *irregular verb*, *lexical verb*, *linking verb*, *main verb*, *modal verb*, *monotransitive verb*, *nonfinite verb*, *notional verb*, *particle with verb*, *periphrastic verb phrase*, *personal verb*, *phrasal prepositional verb*, *phrasal verb*, *plural verb*, *predicate verb*, *predicating verb*, *prepositional verb*, *principal parts (of a verb)*, *progressive verb*, *pro-verb*, *reciprocal verb*, *reflexive verb*, *regular verb*, *simple form (of the verb)*, *simple verb*, *split verb*, *state verb*, *static verb*, *stative verb*, *strong verb*, *telic verb*, *transitive (verb)*, *two-object verb*, *two-word verb*, *verbal*, *verbal adjective*, *verbal auxiliary*, *verb(al) group*, *verbal noun*, *verb(al) phrase*, *verbal preposition*, *verbid, verbless clause, verbless group, weak verb.* The examples show different types of English *verbs.*) □ *Dogs usually don't* **bite** *their masters.* □ **Run!** □ *She* **believes** *everything that she* **hears.** □ **Had** *she* **believed** *us, she would have* **felt** *more confident.* □ *I* **love** *the sound of* **running** *water.*

verbal **1.** pertaining to a *verb;* related to a *verb;* functioning as a *verb;* derived from a *verb.* (See *verbal adjective, verbal auxiliary, verb(al) group, verbal noun, verb(al) phrase,* and *verbal preposition.*) **2.** AND **verbid** a *noun, adjective,* or *adverb* derived from a *verb;* a *nonfinite verb.* (A *verbal* or *verbid* cannot serve as the *main verb* in a *clause* because it no longer functions as a *verb.* See *gerund, infinitive, nonfinite verb, participle,* and *verbal noun.* The examples show *verbals* in bold print.) □ **Running** *is an excellent form of exercise if you are in shape.* □ *I love the sound of* **running** *water.* □ **Running,** *I caught up to the group.* □ *My obsession in life has become* **to run** *every day.* **3.** having to do with speech, as in "verbal ability." (Not directly relevant to *grammar.* Should not be confused with the first two senses.)

verbal adjective an *adjectival form* derived from a *verb;* a *participle* functioning as an *adjective.* (The examples show *verbal adjectives* in bold print.) □ **Flying** *planes can be dangerous.* □ *I would like to have two* **calling** *birds for pets. The* **glistening** *rock felt cold in my* **shaking** *hands.* □ *It is best served with* **drawn** *butter.* □ *She slowly opened her raw and* **reddened** *hand.*

verbal auxiliary an *auxiliary* of the *verb;* a *class* including both the *modal (auxiliary)* and the *auxiliary verb.* (The *forms* of these *verbs* are *am, are, be, been, being, can, could, did, do, does, had, has, have, is, may, might, must, shall, should, was, were, will, would.* See *modal (auxiliary)* and *auxiliary verb* for additional definitions and examples. See also *auxiliary,* which is a more general term. The *verbal auxiliaries* appear in bold print in the examples.) □ *They* **will have** *gone by then.* □ *She* **ought to have** *finished by now.* □ *The car* **might have been** *damaged—I* **didn't** *notice.* □ *Bill* **would** *do it if he* **could.**

verb(al) group the *verb* and its *modals* and *auxiliaries.* (The definition usually excludes the *complements* of the *verb.* Compare to *verb(al) phrase.* The examples show *verbal groups* in bold print.) □ *Bill **should have been informed.*** □ *Sally **might have gone** on to the movies without us.* □ *We just **might have** one of those on a shelf in the back room.* □ *Certainly, we **ought to have given** more thought to the consequences.*

verbal noun a *nominal* derived from the *infinitive form* of a *verb* or the *present participle* of the *verb.* (The resultant *form* cannot exhibit *tense, aspect, number, person,* or *voice.* The examples show *verbal nouns* in bold print.) □ ***Running** is an excellent form of exercise if you are in shape.* □ *My obsession in life has become **to run** every day.* □ ***Seeing** is **believing.*** □ ***To work** is **to pray.*** □ *Please avoid **smoking** in the future.*

verb(al) phrase 1. a *phrase* consisting of a *verb* and its *auxiliaries;* a *phrase* having a *verb* as its *head.* (Refers only to those *constituents* that can be considered part of the *verb*—the "extended verb." This is important in English where so much of the *tense* and *aspect* marking is on the *verbal auxiliaries* rather than the *verb* itself.) □ *I **want to go there** tomorrow.* □ *I **spy.*** □ *My brother **seeks a better-paying job.*** □ *All the cakes and cookies **disappeared.*** 2. a *phrase* consisting of a *verb,* its *auxiliaries,* and *complements.* (There are two distinct uses of the term. In the context of modern *formal grammar* [such as some versions of *transformational-generative grammar*] the second sense is used exclusively. Abbreviated as *VP.*)

verbal preposition 1. a component of a *phrasal verb* that is recognizable as a *preposition* and is usually an indispensable part of the *verb form* and its meaning. (The examples show *verbal prepositions* in bold print.) □ *Call me **up** when you get a chance.* □ *She will get **over** it eventually.* 2. a *preposition* that combines with a *verb* to form new *nouns, adjectives,* or *verbs.* (The examples show *verbal prepositions* in bold print.) □ *They were injured in the hold**up.*** □ *Try to **up**hold your values.* □ *I hope the verdict is **up**held.* □ *Do not try to **under**cut my authority.*

verbid See *verbal,* sense 2.

verbless clause   a *clause* that, because of *ellipsis*, lacks a *verb*. (See *verbless group*. Since a *clause* is meant to have a *verb*, there is some preference for *verbless group*, rather than this term.)

verbless group   a *construction* that lacks a *verb* that would otherwise be present. (Often found after a *subordinating conjunction*. See also *comparative clause, elliptical construction,* and *function verb*. See also *verbless clause*. The "omitted *verbs*" and other omitted *constituents* are shown in square brackets in the examples. The *verbless group* is in bold print.) ☐ ***When [she was] angry,*** *she blushed.* ☐ *I am not as tall **as you [are tall]**.* ☐ ***Although [he was] horribly embarrassed,*** *he somehow got through the speech.* ☐ *The twins were always a handful,* ***especially when [they were] tired.***

vocabulary word   See *content word*.

voice   the relationship between the *subject* of a *verb* and the *action* expressed by the *verb*. (See *active voice,* where the *subject* is the *agent* of the *action of the verb*. See *middle voice* (or *reflexive voice*), where the *subject* initiates the *action of the verb* and also is the recipient of the *action of the verb*. See *passive voice,* where the *subject* is the recipient of the *action of the verb*.)

VP   a *predicate;* a *verb phrase,* sense 2. (This convenient abbreviation was introduced in early *transformational-generative grammar* writings and is now used in other discussions of *grammar*. In its earliest form, it was a single symbol with the vertical line of the P overlapped onto the right leg of the V. See also *NP*. The examples show various kinds of *VPs*. See *verb phrase* for further discussion.) ☐ *I **spy**.* ☐ *They **want to do the best that they can**.* ☐ *Bob **sought to keep all the money for himself**.* ☐ *Jane and her friends **go there often**.*

W

weak past tense   the *form* of the *past tense* of a *weak verb.*

weak verb   See *regular verb.*

well-formed   adhering to the accepted standards of structural *form;* correct; *grammatical.* (As with a *well-formed string* or a *well-formed utterance.* The opposite of *ill-formed.* See *grammatically well-formed.* Each of the examples shows a *syntagma* that is *well-formed* followed by an incorrect or non-*well-formed* version.) ☐ *The three old men. . . / *The old three men. . .* ☐ *We kept on trying to do it. / *We kept trying to do it on.* ☐ *We ought to have been there sooner. / *We ought to been there sooner.*

wh-clause   a *dependent clause* that begins with a wh-*word* or *how.* (The wh-*words* also mark the wh-*questions.* All the examples are clauses, not *sentences.*) ☐ *. . . what he wants. . .* ☐ *. . . how they can do it. . .* ☐ *. . . when she finally gets here. . .* ☐ *. . . which one she ends up choosing. . .*

wh-question   an English question that begins with *who, whom, when, what, why, where, which,* or *how.* (Of course, *how* does not begin with *wh,* but it is a member of this group nevertheless. Each example is a wh-*question.*) ☐ ***What** do you mean, expired?* ☐ ***How** can you say that?* ☐ ***Whom** did you say?* ☐ ***When** do you think it will be ready?* ☐ ***Why** weren't you there when you promised?*

wh-word   one of the set of *words* beginning with *wh* plus the *word* *how.* (The list is *who, whom, what, which, when, where, why,* and *how.* See the previous entries for various applications of this list.)

with the force of   See *force.*

word   the smallest unit of *grammar* that can stand alone as a *complete utterance;* [in speech] each *linguistic* unit that a speaker can utter individually; [in print] each item that is separated from other items by a space. (See *compound-complex word, compound word, content word, empty word, form word, function word, grammar word, grammatical word, head(word), indeclinable word, interrogative (word), invariable word, lexical word, naming word, notional word, orthographic word, prop word, question word, relating word, structural word, two-word verb, variable word, vocabulary word, wh-word, word building, word class, (word) ending, word formation, word order.*)

word building   See *word formation.*

word class   a group of *words* exhibiting the same *formal* behavior in specific contexts. (This is roughly equivalent to *part of speech,* but is more flexible. Compare to *form class.*)

(word) ending   an *inflection* that is a *suffix.*

word formation AND **word building**   the creating of *words* by creating sequences of *morphemes.*

word order   **1.** the order of the elements in a *sentence.* (The examples show the effect of different *word orders* in different *sentence* types.) □ *He does want to do it. / Does he want to do it?* □ *Bob cooked the turkey. / The turkey was cooked by Bob.* □ *Bill heated the lobster red. / Bill heated the red lobster.* □ *It was Oscar who stole the batteries. / Oscar stole the batteries.* **2.** the indication of *grammatical relationships* by the positioning of *words* and *phrases* in a *sentence* rather than by *inflection.* (This expresses a quality or character of a language. English is a language that relies on *word order* more than Latin does.)

Y

yes-no question   a question that calls for an answer including *yes* or *no.* (Each example is a yes-no question.)   □ *Are you all right?*   □ *Can you come here for a minute?*   □ *Has Jane arrived in the studio yet?*   □ *Are you the one who lives in San Francisco?*

Z

zero article the absence of an *article* where an *article* might be expected. (In the examples, the mark "|" indicates the position of the *zero article*.) □ | *Cats are sneakier than | dogs.* □ | *Glass can be used to make | intricate jewelry.* □ | *Money makes the world go round.* □ | *Curiosity killed the cat.*

Function Word Index

Each *function word* that is specifically discussed in an entry is indexed below to the *main entry head* within which the *function word* is discussed. Open ended classes, such as the *interjections,* and verbal subclasses, such as *stative verbs* and *telic verbs,* are not included. Words used in the examples are not indexed.

a   article, definitive (adjective), determiner, indefinite article
aboard   preposition
about   adverb of time, preposition
above   preposition
accompanying   comitative (case)
accordingly   conjunctive (adverb), illative conjunction
according to   complex preposition
across   preposition
after   preposition, relative adverb, subordinating conjunction
again   adverb of recurrence
against   preposition
all   collective pronoun, indefinite pronoun, nonspecific
   determiner, predeterminer, pronominal adjective
along   preposition
also   conjunctive (adverb), copulative (conjunction)
although   concessive conjunction, conditional conjunction,
   disjunctive (conjunction), subordinating conjunction
although—still   correlative (conjunction)
although—yet   correlative (conjunction)
always   adverb of frequency
am   personal ending, verbal auxiliary
amid   preposition
amidst   preposition
among   dual number, preposition
an   article, definitive (adjective), determiner, indefinite article
and   coordinating conjunction, copulative (conjunction)
and/or   coordinating conjunction, disconjunctive

any   definitive (adjective), determiner, indefinite pronoun,
  nonspecific determiner, pronominal adjective
anybody   indefinite pronoun
anyone   indefinite pronoun
anything   indefinite pronoun
are   personal ending, verbal auxiliary
around   preposition
as   clause of degree, clause of manner, clause of time, comparative
  clause, comparison of adverbs, conditional conjunction,
  conjunctive pronoun, subordinating conjunction
as a result   conjunctive (adverb)
as for   complex preposition
as if   clause of manner, subordinating conjunction
as long as   conditional conjunction
as much as   subordinating conjunction
assuming   subordinating conjunction
assuming (that)   conditional conjunction
as though   clause of manner, subordinating conjunction
as to   complex preposition
as well as   connective
at   adessive (case), essive (case), illative (case), inessive (case),
  preposition
at last   adverb of sequence
be   adverb of manner, auxiliary verb, cleft sentence, comparative
  clause, copula, copulative (conjunction), first person, future
  perfect progressive (aspect), future progressive (aspect), locative
  adverb, number concord, passive auxiliary, passive perfect
  infinitive, passive progressive perfect infinitive, past perfect
  progressive (aspect), past progressive (aspect), past subjunctive
  (mood), periphrastic future tense, personal verb, present perfect
  progressive (aspect), present progressive (aspect), progressive
  (aspect), progressive auxiliary, stative verb, third person, verbal
  auxiliary
because   causal clause, subordinating conjunction
because of   complex preposition
become   copulative (conjunction)
been   verbal auxiliary
before   preposition, relative adverb, subordinating conjunction

behind   inessive (case), preposition

being   verbal auxiliary

below   preposition

beneath   preposition

beside   preposition

besides   conjunctive (adverb), copulative (conjunction), preposition

be that as it may   conjunct

between   dual number, preposition

beyond   preposition

both   collective pronoun, copulative (conjunction), dual number, indefinite adjective, indefinite pronoun, number concord, partitive phrase, predeterminer, pronominal adjective

both—and   correlative (conjunction)

but   concessive conjunction, coordinating conjunction, disjunctive (conjunction), preposition

by   agent, instructive (case), instrumental (case), logical subject, passive voice, preposition

by means of   complex preposition, instructive (case), instrumental (case)

can   defective verb, modal verb, permissive mood, verbal auxiliary

concerning   preposition

consequently   illative conjunction

conversely   conjunctive (adverb)

could   modal (auxiliary), verbal auxiliary

did   verbal auxiliary

do   auxiliary verb, comparative clause, emphatic auxiliary, emphatic mood, first person, number concord, personal verb, pro-verb, verbal auxiliary

does   verbal auxiliary

down   preposition

downwards   adverbial genitive

due to   complex preposition

during   preposition

each   definitive (adjective), indefinite adjective, indefinite pronoun, separative pronoun

each one   separative pronoun

each other   reciprocal pronoun

either   definitive (adjective), disjunctive (conjunction), indefinite
   adjective, indefinite pronoun, separative pronoun

either—or   correlative (conjunction)

enough   definitive (adjective)

even if   concessive conjunction, subordinating conjunction

even though   concessive conjunction

ever   adverb of frequency

every   definitive (adjective), separative pronoun

everybody   indefinite pronoun, separative pronoun

everyone   indefinite pronoun, separative pronoun

everything   indefinite pronoun, separative pronoun

except   disjunctive (conjunction), preposition

excepting   subordinating conjunction

feel   copulative (conjunction)

few   collective pronoun, indefinite pronoun, (indefinite) quantifier

few of   (indefinite) quantifier

finally   conjunct, connective

first   adverb of sequence

for   benefactive case, coordinating conjunction, preposition,
   subordinating conjunction

frequently   adverb of frequency

from   ablative (case), preposition

from among   complex preposition

further   conjunctive (adverb)

furthermore   conjunctive (adverb)

given   subordinating conjunction

given (that)   conditional conjunction

going to   periphrastic future tense

had   verbal auxiliary

had to   modal (auxiliary)

half   partitive, partitive phrase, predeterminer

hardly   adverb of frequency

hardly ever   adverb of frequency, negative pronoun

has   personal ending, verbal auxiliary

have   auxiliary verb, comparative clause, first person, future
   perfect progressive (aspect), future perfect (tense), passive
   perfect infinitive, passive progressive perfect infinitive, past
   participle, past perfect progressive (aspect), past perfect (tense),

perfect auxiliary, perfect infinitive, personal ending, personal verb, present perfect progressive (aspect), present perfect (tense), progressive perfect infinitive, stative verb, third person, verbal auxiliary

have to modal (auxiliary), necessitative mood

he arbitrary gender, common gender, (grammatical) gender, (grammatical) person, masculine (gender), subjective pronoun, third person

hence conjunctive (adverb), illative conjunction

her definitive (adjective), descriptive adverb, determinative possessive pronoun, feminine (gender), (grammatical) gender, (grammatical) person, joint possession, object(ive) case, objective pronoun, possessive pronoun, third person

hers feminine (gender), (grammatical) gender, (grammatical) person, independent possessive (pronoun), joint possession, possessive pronoun

herself intensive (personal) pronoun, reflexive pronoun

him arbitrary gender, common gender, (grammatical) gender, (grammatical) person, masculine (gender), object(ive) case, objective pronoun, third person

himself intensive (personal) pronoun, reflexive pronoun

his arbitrary gender, common gender, definitive (adjective), descriptive adverb, determinative possessive pronoun, (grammatical) gender, (grammatical) person, independent possessive (pronoun), joint possession, masculine (gender), possessive pronoun, third person

how interrogative (adverb), subordinating conjunction, *wh*-clause, *wh*-question, *wh*-word

however conjunctive (adverb), connective

I first person, (grammatical) person, proper noun, subjective pronoun

if conditional clause, conditional conjunction, subjunctive (mood), subordinating conjunction

if—then correlative (conjunction)

in adessive (case), essive (case), inessive (case), preposition

in accordance with complex preposition

in addition conjunctive (adverb)

inasmuch as causal clause, subordinating conjunction

in back of   complex preposition, inessive (case)

in case   conditional conjunction, subordinating conjunction

in conclusion   conjunct

in front of   complex preposition

in order that   clause of purpose, subordinating conjunction

in order to   clause of purpose

in other words   conjunct

in respect to   complex preposition

inside of   complex preposition

in spite of   complex preposition

in spite of that   conjunct

instead of   complex preposition

in that   subordinating conjunction

into   illative (case), preposition

is   personal ending, verbal auxiliary

it   anticipatory subject, cleft sentence, expletive, (grammatical) gender, (grammatical) person, impersonal verb, neuter (gender), postponed subject, subjective pronoun, third person

its   definitive (adjective), determinative possessive pronoun, (grammatical) gender, (grammatical) person, independent possessive (pronoun), joint possession, neuter (gender), possessive pronoun, *s*-genitive, third person

itself   intensive (personal) pronoun, reflexive pronoun

least   comparative (degree), periphrastic comparison

less   periphrastic comparison

lest   disjunctive (conjunction), subordinating conjunction

like   clause of manner, preposition

likewise   copulative (conjunction)

long ways   adverbial genitive

many   collective pronoun, indefinite pronoun, (indefinite) quantifier, nonspecific determiner, number concord, partitive phrase

may   defective verb, modal (auxiliary), modal verb, permissive mood, verbal auxiliary

me   (grammatical) person, object(ive) case, objective pronoun

might   defective verb, modal (auxiliary), modal verb, permissive mood, verbal auxiliary

mine (grammatical) person, independent possessive (pronoun), joint possession, possessive pronoun

more collective pronoun, comparative (degree), double comparative, indefinite pronoun

moreover copulative (conjunction)

more than comparative clause

most collective pronoun, double superlative, indefinite pronoun, partitive, partitive phrase, superlative (degree)

much indefinite pronoun, (indefinite) quantifier, partitive, partitive phrase

must defective verb, modal (auxiliary), modal verb, necessitative mood, verbal auxiliary

must be apodictive mood

my definitive (adjective), descriptive adverb, determinative possessive pronoun, (grammatical) person, joint possession, possessive pronoun

myself intensive (personal) pronoun, reflexive pronoun

near preposition

neither definitive (adjective), disjunctive (conjunction), indefinite adjective, indefinite pronoun, negative pronoun, separative pronoun

neither—nor correlative (conjunction)

never adverb of frequency, negative pronoun

nevertheless conjunct, conjunctive (adverb)

next adverb of sequence

no definitive (adjective), determiner, negative, negative particle

nobody indefinite pronoun, negative pronoun

none indefinite pronoun, negative, negative pronoun

nonetheless conjunct, conjunctive (adverb)

no one indefinite pronoun, negative pronoun

nor coordinating conjunction, disjunctive (conjunction)

not negative particle

nothing indefinite pronoun, negative pronoun, negator

not only—but also correlative (conjunction)

notwithstanding disjunctive (conjunction)

now adverb of sequence

occasionally adverb of frequency

of   double genitive, genitive (case), *of*-genitive, periphrastic genitive, preposition

off   preposition

often   adverb of frequency

on   essive (case), inessive (case), preposition

once   adverb of recurrence

one   determiner, indefinite pronoun

one another   reciprocal pronoun

on the condition (that)   conditional conjunction

on the contrary   connective

or   coordinating conjunction, disjunctive (conjunction), subdisjunctive (conjunction)

other   collective pronoun, indefinite pronoun

others   indefinite pronoun

ought   defective verb, modal (auxiliary), modal verb

our   common gender, definitive (adjective), descriptive adverb, determinative possessive pronoun, (grammatical) person, joint possession, possessive pronoun

ours   common gender, independent possessive (pronoun), (grammatical) person, joint possession, possessive pronoun

ourselves   intensive (personal) pronoun, reflexive pronoun

out   preposition

out of   ablative (case), complex preposition

over   preposition

past   preposition

provided   disjunctive (conjunction), subordinating conjunction

provided (that)   conditional conjunction

rarely   adverb of frequency

save   disjunctive (conjunction)

scarcely ever   adverb of frequency

second   adverb of sequence

seem   copulative (conjunction)

seldom   adverb of frequency, negative pronoun

seldom if ever   adverb of frequency

several   collective pronoun, indefinite pronoun, (indefinite) quantifier, separative pronoun

shall   defective verb, future perfect (tense), modal verb, periphrastic future tense, simple futurity, verbal auxiliary

she feminine (gender), (grammatical) gender, (grammatical) person, subjective pronoun, third person

should modal (auxiliary), obligative mood, verbal auxiliary

since causal clause, preposition, relative adverb, subordinating conjunction

since—therefore correlative (conjunction)

slow flat adverb

so adverb substitute, clause of result

some collective pronoun, definitive (adjective), indefinite adjective, indefinite pronoun, nonspecific determiner, partitive, partitive phrase, pronominal adjective

somebody indefinite pronoun

someone indefinite pronoun

something indefinite pronoun

sometimes adverb of frequency

soon adverb of sequence

so that clause of purpose, clause of result, subordinating conjunction

such definitive (adjective)

such that subordinating conjunction

supposing (that) conditional conjunction

than clause of degree, comparative clause, comparison of adverbs, disjunctive (conjunction), subordinating conjunction

that clause of purpose, clause of result, conjunctive pronoun, connective, definitive (adjective), demonstrative (pronoun), determiner, restrictive (relative) clause, subordinating conjunction

that way adverb substitute

the article, definite article, definitive (adjective), determiner

their arbitrary gender, common gender, definitive (adjective), descriptive adverb, determinative possessive pronoun, (grammatical) gender, (grammatical) person, joint possession, possessive pronoun, third person

theirs arbitrary gender, common gender, (grammatical) gender, (grammatical) person, independent possessive (pronoun), joint possession, possessive pronoun

them arbitrary gender, common gender, (grammatical) gender, (grammatical) person, object(ive) case, objective pronoun, third person

themselves intensive (personal) pronoun, reflexive pronoun

then adverb of sequence, adverb substitute, conjunctive (adverb), copulative (conjunction), illative conjunction, subordinating conjunction

there adverb substitute

therefore conjunct, conjunctive (adverb), connective, illative conjunction

these definitive (adjective), demonstrative (pronoun)

they anticipatory subject, arbitrary gender, common gender, (grammatical) gender, (grammatical) person, subjective pronoun, third person

third adverb of sequence

this definitive (adjective), demonstrative (pronoun), determiner

this way adverb substitute

those definitive (adjective), demonstrative (pronoun)

though concessive conjunction, conditional conjunction, disjunctive (conjunction), subordinating conjunction

though—still correlative (conjunction)

though—yet correlative (conjunction)

through preposition

throughout preposition

thus adverb substitute, conjunctive (adverb)

to allative (case), bare infinitive, complementizer, illative (case), infinitive, infinitive marker, infinitive phrase, passive perfect infinitive, passive progressive perfect infinitive, perfect infinitive, preposition, progressive perfect infinitive, simple verb, stem, supine, *to*-infinitive

toward allative (case), illative (case), preposition

towards preposition

twice adverb of recurrence, predeterminer

under inessive (case), preposition

underneath preposition

unless conditional conjunction, disjunctive (conjunction), subordinating conjunction

until preposition, subordinating conjunction

unto preposition

up preposition

upon   preposition

upwards   adverbial genitive

us   common gender, (grammatical) person, object(ive) case, objective pronoun

used to   habitual aspect

usually   adverb of frequency

via   instructive (case)

was   personal ending, subjunctive (mood), verbal auxiliary

we   common gender, exclusive pronoun, first person, (grammatical) person, subjective pronoun

were   past subjunctive (mood), personal ending, subjunctive (mood), verbal auxiliary

what   conjunctive pronoun, definitive (adjective), interrogative (adverb), subordinating conjunction, *wh*-question, *wh*-word

whatever   indefinite pronoun

when   clause of time, interrogative (adverb), subordinating conjunction, *wh*-question, *wh*-word

whenever   clause of time, subordinating conjunction

where   clause of place, interrogative (adverb), locative adverb, subordinating conjunction, *wh*-question, *wh*-word

whereas   disjunctive (conjunction), subordinating conjunction

wherefore   illative conjunction

wherever   clause of place

whether   disjunctive (conjunction)

whether—or   correlative (conjunction)

which   conjunctive pronoun, connective, definitive (adjective), interrogative (adverb), restrictive (relative) clause, *wh*-question, *wh*-word

while   clause of time, concessive conjunction, subordinating conjunction

who   conjunctive pronoun, interrogative (adverb), objective pronoun, relative pronoun, restrictive (relative) clause, subordinating conjunction, *wh*-question, *wh*-word

whoever   indefinite pronoun, subordinating conjunction

whom   interrogative (adverb), object(ive) case, objective pronoun, restrictive (relative) clause, subordinating conjunction, *wh*-question, *wh*-word

whomever   subordinating conjunction
whose   independent possessive (pronoun), interrogative (adverb), possessive pronoun, restrictive (relative) clause
why   interrogative (adverb), *wh*-question, *wh*-word
will   defective verb, future perfect (tense), modal verb, periphrastic future tense, simple futurity, verbal auxiliary
will have to   necessitative mood
with   comitative (case), instrumental (case), preposition
within   inessive (case), preposition
without   preposition
without a doubt   conjunct
would   modal (auxiliary), verbal auxiliary
yet   disjunctive (conjunction)
you   (grammatical) person, imperative sentence, impersonal pronoun, objective pronoun, subjective pronoun, understood
your   definitive (adjective), descriptive adverb, determinative possessive pronoun, ethical genitive, (grammatical) person, impersonal pronoun, joint possession, possessive pronoun
yours   (grammatical) person, independent possessive (pronoun), joint possession, possessive pronoun
yourself   intensive (personal) pronoun, reflexive pronoun
yourselves   intensive (personal) pronoun, reflexive pronoun

Bibliography

Allen, R. L. 1972. *English Grammars and English Grammar.* New York: Scribners.

Callihan, E. L. 1975. *Grammar for Journalists.* Radnor, PA: Chilton Book Co.

Cattell, N. R. 1969. *The New English Grammar.* Cambridge: The MIT Press.

Cook, Walter A. 1989. *Case Grammar Theory.* Washington, DC: Georgetown University Press.

Corbin, R. K., and P. G. Perrin. 1966. *Guide to Modern English.* Glenview, IL: Scott, Foresman & Co.

Crystal, David. 1987. *The Cambridge Encyclopedia of Language.* Cambridge: Cambridge University Press.

Curme, G. O. 1925. *College English Grammar.* Richmond, VA: Johnson Books.

Evans, Bergen, and C. Evans. 1957. *A Dictionary of Contemporary American Usage.* New York: Random House.

Fillmore, Charles J. 1987. *Fillmore's Case Grammar: A Reader.* Edited by Rene Dirven and Gunter Radden. Heidelberg: J. Groos.

Fowler, H. W. (1926) 1958. *A Dictionary of Modern English Usage.* London: Oxford University Press.

Francis, W. Nelson. 1958. *The Structure of American English.* New York: Ronald Press.

Friend, Jewel A. 1976. *Traditional Grammar: A Short Summary.* Carbondale, IL: Southern Illinois University Press.

Friend, Joseph. 1967. *An Introduction to English Linguistics.* Cleveland: World.

Fries, Charles C. 1952. *The Structure of English.* New York: Harcourt Brace Jovanovich.

Hall, Eugene J. 1986. *Grammar for Use*. Lincolnwood, IL: National Textbook Company.

Hodges, John C., and Mary E. Whitten. 1986. *Harbrace College Handbook*. 10th ed. San Diego: Harcourt Brace Jovanovich.

Huddleston, Rodney. 1988. *English Grammar: An Outline*. Cambridge: Cambridge University Press.

Kittredge, G. L., and F. E. Farley. 1913. *An Advanced English Grammar*. Boston: Atheneum Publishers.

Lyons, John. 1968. *Introduction to Theoretical Linguistics*. London: Cambridge University Press.

Newby, Michael. 1987. *The Structure of English*. Cambridge: Cambridge University Press.

Pratt, Lorraine Nichols. 1979. *Grammar Step-by-Step*. 2 vols. Lincolnwood, IL: National Textbook Company.

Quirk, R., S. Greenbaum, G. Leech, and J. Svartik. 1985. *A Comprehensive Grammar of the English Language*. New York: Longman.

Richards, Jack, J. Platt, and H. Weber. 1985. *Longman Dictionary of Applied Linguistics*. Essex: Longman.

Roberts, P. 1954. *Understanding Grammar*. New York: Harper & Row, Publishers Inc.

Wardhaugh, Ronald. 1977. *Introduction to Linguistics*. 2nd ed. New York: McGraw-Hill.

Warriner, J. E., and F. Griffith. 1973. *English Grammar and Composition*. Chicago: Harcourt Brace Jovanovich.

Webster, Noah. 1828. *An American Dictionary of the English Language*. New York: S. Converse.

Weseen, Maurice H. 1928. *Crowell's Dictionary of English Grammar and Handbook of American Usage*. New York: Crowell.